The Iliad of Homer. Translated From the Greek, by Alexander Pope, Esq; In Four Volumes. ... of 4

THE

ILIAD

OF

HOMER.

TRANSLATED FROM THE GREEK,

BY

ALEXANDER POPE, Efq;

IN FOUR VOLUMES.

VOLUME THE FOURTH.

GLASGOW, Printed ·
LIVERPOOL; Sold by ROBERT WILLIAMSON,
at his *Circulating Library*, near the *Exchange*.

MDCCLV.

THE

I L I A D.

B O O K   XIX.

THE ARGUMENT.

The reconciliation of Achilles and Agamemnon.

THETIS brings to her son the armour made by Vulcan. She preserves the body of his friend from corruption, and commands him to assemble the army, to declare his resentment at an end. Agamemnon and Achilles are solemnly reconciled the speeches, presents, and ceremonies on that occasion Achilles is with great difficulty persuaded to refrain from the battle till the troops have refreshed themselves, by the advice of Ulysses The presents are conveyed to the tent of Achilles, where Briseis laments over the body of Patroclus. The hero obstinately refuses all repast, and gives himself up to lamentations for his friend Minerva descends to strengthen him, by the order of Jupiter He arms for the fight his appearance described. He addresses himself to his horses, and reproaches them with the death of Patroclus. One of them is miraculously endued with voice, and inspired to prophesy his fate, but the hero, not astonished by that prodigy, rushes with fury to the combate.
The thirtieth day. The scene is on the sea-shore.

SOON as Aurora heav'd her orient head
    Above the waves, that blush'd with early red,
(With new born day to gladden mortal sight,
And gild the courts of heav'n with sacred light,)

Th' immortal arms the Goddefs-mother bears   5
Swift to her fon: her fon fhe finds in tears
Stretch'd o'er Patroclus' corfe; while all the reft
Their fov'reign's forrows in their own expreft.
A ray divine her heav'nly prefence fhed,
And thus, his hand foft-touching, Thetis faid.   10

Supprefs (my fon) this rage of grief, and know
It was not man, but heav'n that gave the blow;
Behold what arms by Vulcan are beftow'd,
Arms worthy thee, or fit to grace a God.

Then drops the radiant burden on the ground;   15
Clang the ftrong arms, and ring the fhores around:
Back fhrink the Myrmidons with dread furprize,
And from the broad effulgence turn their eyes.
Unmov'd, the hero kindles at the fhow,
And feels with rage divine his bofom glow;   20
From his fierce eye-balls living flames expire,
And flafh inceffant like a ftream of fire·
He turns the radiant gift, and feeds his mind
On all th' immortal artift had defign'd.

⊻ 13. *Behold what arms*, etc] It is not poetry only
which has had this idea, of giving divine arms to a hero;
we have a very remarkable example of it in our holy
books. In the fecond of Maccabees, chap. 16. Judas
fees in a dream the prophet Jeremiah bringing to him a
fword as from God though this was only a dream, or
a vifion, yet ftill it is the fame idea.   This example is
likewife fo much the more worthy of obfervation, as it
is much later than the age of Homer, and as thereby it
is feen, that the fame way of thinking continued a long
time amongft the orientals.   Dacier.

Goddefs (he cry'd) thefe glorious arms that fhine 25
With matchlefs art, confefs the hand divine.
Now to the bloody battel let me bend:
But ah ! the relics of my flaughter'd friend !
In thofe wide wounds thro' which his fpirit fled,
Shall flies, and worms obfcene, pollute the dead ? 30

℣ 30. *Shall flies, and worms obfcene, pollute the dead ?*]
The care which Achilles takes in this place to drive a-
way the flies from the dead body of Patroclus, feems to
us a mean employment, and a care unworthy of a hero.
But that office was regarded by Homer, and by all the
Greeks of his time, as a pious duty confecrated by cuftom
and religion; which obliged the kindred and friends of
the deceafed to watch his corps, and prevent any corruption before the folemn day of his funerals. It is
plain this devoir was thought an indifpenfable one, fince
Achilles could not difcharge himfelf of it but by impof-
ing it upon his mother. It is alfo clear, that in thofe
times the prefervation of a dead body was accounted a
very important matter, fince the Goddeffes themfelves,
nay the moft delicate of the Goddeffes, made it the fubject of their utmoft attention. As Thetis preferves the
body of Patroclus, and chafes from it thofe infects that
breed in the wounds and caufe putrefaction, fo Venus
is employed day and night about that of Hector, in driving away the dogs to which Achilles had expofed it.
Apollo, on his part, covers it with a thick cloud, and
preferves its frefhnefs amidft the greateft heats of the
fun: and this care of the deities over the dead was
looked upon by men as a fruit of their piety.
There is an excellent remark upon this paffage in
Boffu's admirable treatife of the epic poem, lib 3. c. 10.
" To fpeak (fays this author) of the arts and fciences
" as a poet ought, we fhould veil them under names
" and actions of perfons, fictitious, and allegorical.

That unavailing care be laid afide,
(The azure Goddefs to her fon reply'd)
Whole years untouch'd, uninjur'd fhall remain
Frefh as in life, the carcâfe of the flain.
But go, Achilles, (as affairs require)   35
Before the Grecian peers renounce thine ire:
Then uncontroll'd in boundlefs war engage,
And heav'n with ftrength fupply the mighty rage!
    Then in the noftrils of the flain fhe pour'd
Nectareous drops, and rich ambrofia fhower'd   40
O'er all the corfe.   The flies forbid their prey,
Untouch'd it refts, and facred from decay.
Achilles to the ftrand obedient went:
The fhores refounded with the voice he fent.
The heroes heard, and all the naval train   45
That tend the fhips, or guide them o'er the main,

" Homer will not plainly fay that falt has the virtue to
" preferve dead bodies, and prevent the flies from en-
" gendering worms in them; he will not fay, that the
" fea prefented Achilles a remedy to preferve Patroclus
" from putrefaction; but he will make the fea a God-
" defs, and tell us, that Thetis to comfort Achilles,
" engaged to perfume the body with an ambrofia which
" fhould keep it a whole year from corruption. it is
" thus Homer teaches the poets to fpeak of arts and
" fciences.   This example fhews the nature of the
" things, that flies caufe putrefaction, that falt preferves
" bodies from it; but all this is told us poetically, the
" whole is reduced into action. the fea is made a per-
" fon who fpeaks and acts, and this profopopœia is ac-
" companied with paffion, tendernefs, and affection;
" in a word, there is nothing which is not (according
" to Ariftotle's précept) endued with manners."

Alarm'd, tranſported, at the well known ſound,
Frequent and full, the great aſſembly crown'd ;
Studious to ſee that terror of the plain,
Long loſt to battel, ſhine in arms again.   50
Tydides and Ulyſſes firſt appear,
Lame with their wounds, and leaning on the ſpear;
Theſe on the ſacred ſeats of council plac'd,
The king of men, Atrides came the laſt:
He too ſore wounded by Agenor's ſon,   55
Achilles (riſing in the midſt) begun.

O monarch ! better far had been the fate
Of thee, of me, of all the Grecian ſtate,
If (ere the day when by mad paſſion ſway'd,
Raſh we contended for, the black ey'd maid)   60.
Preventing Dian had diſpatch'd her dart,
And ſhot the ſhining miſchief to the heart !

℣. 61. *Preventing Dian had diſpatch'd her dart,*
          And ſhot the ſhining miſchief to the heart.]
Achilles wiſhes Briſeis had died before ſhe had occa-
ſioned ſo great calamities to his countrymen: I will not
ſay, to excuſe him, that his virtue here overpowers his
love, but that the wiſh is not ſo very barbarous as it
may ſeem by the phraſe to a modern reader.   It is not,
that Diana had actually killed her, as by a particular
ſtroke or judgment from heaven; it means no more
than a natural death, as appears from this paſſage in
Odyſſ. 15.

When age and ſickneſs have unnerv'd the ſtrong,
Apollo comes, and Cynthia comes along,
They bend the ſilver bows for ſudden ill,
And every ſhining arrow flies to kill.

Then many a hero had not prefs'd the fhore,
Nor Troy's glad fields been fatten'd with our gore:
Long, long fhall Greece the woes we caus'd, bewail, 65
And fad pofterity repeat the tale.
But this, no more the fubject of debate,
Is paft, forgotten, and refign'd to fate:
Why fhould (alas) a mortal man, as I,
Burn with a fury that can never die?   70
Here then my anger ends: let war fucceed,
And ev'n as Greece has bled, let Ilion bleed.
Now call the hofts, and try, if in our fight,
Troy yet fhall dare to camp a fecond might?
I deem, their mightieft, when this arm he knows,   75
Shall 'fcape with tranfport, and with joy repofe.

He faid: his finifh'd wrath with loud acclaim
The Greeks accept, and fhout Pelides' name.
When thus, not rifing from his lofty throne,
In ftate unmov'd, the king of men begun.   80

Hear me, ye fons of Greece! with filence hear!
And grant your monarch an impartial ear;
A while your loud, untimely joy fufpend,
And let your rafh, injurious clamours end.
Unruly murmurs, or ill tim'd applaufe,   85
Wrong the beft fpeaker, and the jufteft caufe.
Nor charge on me, ye Greeks, the dire debate:
Know, angry Jove, and all-compelling Fate,

And he does not wifh her death now, after fhe had
been his miftrefs, but only that fhe had died, before he
knew, or loved her.

With fell Erinnys, urg'd my wrath that day
When from Achilles' arms I forc'd the prey.   90
What then could I, againſt the will of heav'n?
Not by myſelf, but vengeful Ate driv'n;
She, Jove's dread daughter, fated to infeſt
The race of mortals, enter'd in my breaſt.

℣. 93. *She, Jove's dread daughter.*] This ſpeech of
Agamemnon, conſiſting of little elſe than the long ſtory
of Jupiter's caſting Diſcord out of heaven, ſeems odd
enough at firſt ſight; and does not indeed anſwer what
I believe every reader expects, at the conference of theſe
two princes.   Without excuſing it from the juſtneſs
and proper application of the allegory in the preſent
caſe, I think it a piece of artifice, very agreeable to the
character of Agamemnon, which is a mixture of haugh-
tineſs and cunning; he cannot prevail with himſelf any
way to leſſen the dignity of the royal character, of which
he every where appears jealous: ſomething he is obliged
to ſay in public, and not brooking directly to own himſelf in the wrong, he ſlurs it over with this tale.   With
what ſtatelineſs is it that he yields! " I was miſled,
" (ſays he) but I was miſled like Jupiter.   We inveſt you
" with our powers, take our troops and our treaſures: our
" royal promiſe ſhall be fulfilled, but be you pacified."
  ℣. 93. *She, Jove's dread daughter, fated to infeſt*
          The race of mortals———]
It appears from hence, that the ancients owned a Dæmon, created by God himſelf, and totally taken up in
doing miſchief.
  This fiction is very remarkable, in as much as it
proves that the Pagans knew that a dæmon of diſcord
and malediction was in heaven, and afterwards precipi-
tated to earth, which perfectly agrees with holy hiſtory.
St. Juſtin will have it, that Homer attained to the
knowlege thereof in Ægypt, and that he had even read

Not on the ground that haughty fury treads,　　95
But prints her lofty footfteps on the heads
Of mighty men; inflicting as fhe goes
Long feft'ring wounds, inextricable woes !
Of old, fhe ftalk'd amid the bright abodes;
And Jove himfelf, the fire of men and Gods,　　100
The world's great ruler, felt her venom'd dart;
Deceiv'd by Juno's wiles, and female art;
For when Alcmena's nine long months were run,
And Jove expected his immortal fon;
To gods and goddeffes th' unruly joy　　105
He fhow'd, and vaunted of his matchlefs boy:
From us (he faid) this day an infant fprings,
Fated to rule, and born a king of kings.
Saturnia afk'd an oath, to vouch the truth,
And fix dominion on the favour'd youth.　　110
The thund'rer unfufpicious of the fraud,
Pronounc'd thofe folemn words that bind a God.
The joyful Goddefs, from Olympus' height,
Swift to Achaian Argos bent her flight;

what Ifaiah writes, chap. 14　*How art thou fallen from
heaven, O Lucifer, fon of the morning, how art thou cut
down to the ground which didft weaken the nations ?*　But
our poet could not have feen the prophecy of Ifaiah, becaufe he lived 100, or 150 years before that prophet;
and this anteriority of time makes this paffage the more
obfervable　Homer therein bears authentic witnefs to
the truth of the ftory, of an angel thrown from heaven,
and gives this teftimony above 100 years before one of
the greateft prophets fpoke of it.　Dacier.

Scarce fev'n moons gone, lay Sthenelus his wife; 115
She puſh'd her ling'ring infant into life:
Her charms Alcmena's coming labours' ſtay,
And ſtop the babe, juſt iſſuing to the day.
Then bids Saturnius bear his oath in mind;
" A youth (ſaid ſhe) of Jove's immortal kind 120
" Is this day born: from Sthenelus he ſprings,
" And claims thy promiſe to be king of kings.
Grief ſeiz'd the thund'rer, by his oath engag'd;
Stung to the ſoul, he ſorrow'd, and he rag'd.
From his ambroſial head, where perch'd ſhe ſate, 125
He ſnatch'd the fury-Goddeſs of Debate,
The dread, th' irrevocable oath he ſwore,
Th' immortal ſeats ſhould ne'er behold her more;
And whirl'd her headlong down, for ever driv'n
From bright Olympus and the ſtarry heav'n: 130
Thence on the nether world the fury fell;
Ordain'd with man's contentious race to dwell.
Full oft' the God his ſon's hard toils bemoan'd,
Curs'd the dire fury, and in ſecret groan'd.
Ev'n thus, like Jove himſelf, was I miſled, 135
While raging Hector heap'd our camps with dead.
What can the errors of my rage atone?
My martial troops, my treaſures are thy own:
This inſtant from the navy ſhall be ſent
Whate'er Ulyſſes promis'd at thy tent: 140
But thou! appeas'd, propitious to our pray'r,
Reſume thy arms, and ſhine again in war.

O king of nations! whose superior sway
(Returns Achilles) all our hosts obey!
To keep or send the presents, be thy care;   145
To us, 'tis equal: all we ask is war.
While yet we talk, or but an instant shun
The fight, our glorious work remains undone.
Let ev'ry Greek, who sees my spear confound
The Trojan ranks, and deal destruction round,   150
With emulation, what I act, survey,
And learn from thence the business of the day,

  The son of Peleus thus: and thus replies
The great in councils, Ithacus the wise.
Tho' godlike thou art by no toils opprest,   155
At least our armies claim repast and rest:
Long and laborious must the combate be,
When by the Gods inspir'd, and led by thee.
Strength is deriv'd from spirits and from blood,
And those augment by gen'rous wine and food;   160

Ў. 145. *To keep or send the presents be thy care.*]
Achilles neither refuses nor demands Agamemnon's presents: the first would be too contemptuous, and the o-
ther would look too selfish. It would seem as if Achilles
fought only for pay like a mercenary, which would be
utterly unbecoming a hero, and dishonourable to that
character: Homer is wonderful as to the manners.
Spond. Dacier.

  Ў. 159. *Strength is deriv'd from spirits, etc.*] This
advice of Ulysses, that the troops should refresh themselves
with eating and drinking, was extremely necessary after a
battel of so long continuance as that of the day before:
and Achilles's desire that they should charge the enemy
immediately,

What boaftful fon of war, without that ftay,
Can laft a hero thro' a fingle day?
Courage may prompt; but, ebbing out his ftrength,
Mere unfupported man muft yield at length;
Shrunk with dry famine, and with toils declin'd, 165
The dropping body will defert the mind:
But built a-new with ftrength-conferring fare,
With limbs and foul untam'd, he tires a war.
Difmifs the people then, and give command,
With ftrong repaft to hearten 'ev'ry band; 170
But let the prefents to Achilles made,
In full affembly of all Greece be laid.
The king of men fhall rife in public fight,
And folemn fwear (obfervant of the rite)
That fpotlefs as fhe came, the maid removes, 175
Pure from his arms, and guiltlefs of his loves.
That done, a fumptuous banquet fhall be made,
And the full price of injur'd honour paid.

immediately, without any reflection on the neceffity of
that refrefhment, was alfo highly natural to his violent
character. This forces Ulyffes to repeat that advice,
and infift upon it fo much. which thofe critics did not
fee into, who through a falfe delicacy are fhocked at his
infifting fo warmly upon eating and drinking. Indeed
to a common reader who is more fond of heroic and
romantic, than of juft and natural images, this at firft
fight may have an air of ridicule; but I'll venture to
fay there is nothing ridiculous in the thing itfelf, nor
mean and low in Homer's manner of expreffing it: and
I believe the fame of this tranflation, though I have not
foftened or abated of the idea they are fo offended with.

Stretch not henceforth, O prince! thy fov'reign might,
Beyond the bounds of reafon and of right;   180
'Tis the chief praife that e'er to kings belong'd
To right with juftice whom with pow'r they wrong'd.
    To him the monarch.   Juft is thy decree,
Thy words give joy, and wifdom breathes in thee.
Each due atonement gladly I prepare;   185
And heav'n regard me as I juftly fwear!
Here then a while let Greece affembled ftay,
Nor great Achilles grudge this fhort delay;
'Till from the fleet our prefents be convey'd,
And, Jove attefting, the firm compact made.   190
A train of noble youth the charge fhall bear;
Thefe to felect, Ulyffes, be thy care:
In order rank'd let all our gifts appear,
And the fair train of captives clofe the rear:
Talthybius fhall the victim boar convey,   195
Sacred to Jove, and yon' bright orb of day,
    For this (the ftern Æacides replies)
Some lefs important feafon may fuffice,

℣ 197. *The ftern Æacides replies.*] The Greek verfe is,

Τον δ' απαμειβομενο, προσεφη ποδας ωκυς Αχιλλευς

Which is repeated very frequently throughout the Iliad.
It is a very juft remark of a French critic, that what
makes it fo much taken notice of, is the rumbling found
and length of the word απαμειβομενος this is fo true,
that if in a poem or romance of the fame length as the
Iliad, we fhould repeat *The hero anfwered*, full as often,
we fhould never be fenfible of that repetition.   And if
we are not fhocked at the like frequency of thofe ex-

When the ftern fury of the war is o'er,
And wrath extinguifh'd burns my breaft no more. 200

preffions in the *Æneid, fic ore refert, talia voce refert, talia dicta dabat, vix ea fatus erat,* etc. it is only becaufe the found of the Latin words does not fill the ear like that of the Greek ἀναμειβόμενος

The difcourfe of the fame critic upon thefe fort of repetitions in general, deferves to be tranfcribed. That ufelefs nicety (fays he) of avoiding every repetition, which the delicacy of later times has introduced, was not known to the firft ages of antiquity: the books of Mofes abound with them. Far from condemning their frequent ufe in the moft ancient of all the poets, we fhould look upon them as the certain character of the age in which he lived they fpoke fo in his time, and to have fpoken otherwife had been a fault And indeed nothing is in itfelf fo contrary to the true fublime, as that painful and frivolous exactnefs, with which we avoid to make ufe of a proper word becaufe it was ufed before. It is certain that the Romans were lefs fcrupulous as to this point: you have often in a fingle page of Tully, the fame word five or fix times over. If it were really a fault, it is not to be conceived how an author who fo little wanted variety of expreffions as Homer, could be fo very negligent herein. On the contrary, he feems to have affected to repeat the fame things in the fame words, on many occafions.

It was from two principles equally true, that among feveral people, and in feveral ages, two practices intirely different took their rife. Mofes, Homer, and the writers of the firft times, had found that repetitions of the fame words recalled the ideas of things, imprinted them much more ftrongly, and rendered the difcourfe more intelligible. Upon this principle, the cuftom of repeating words, phrafes, and even intire fpeeches, infenfibly eftablifhed itfelf both in profe and poetry, efpecially in narrations.

By Hector slain, their faces to the sky,
All grim with gaping wounds, our heroes lie:

The writers who succeeded them observed, even from
Homer himself, that the greatest beauty of style consisted
in variety. This they made their principle: they
therefore avoided repetitions of words, and still more
of whole sentences; they endeavoured to vary their
transitions; and found out new turns and manners of
expressing the same things.

Either of these practices is good, but the excess of
either vicious: we should neither on the one hand,
through a love of simplicity and clearness, continually
repeat the same words, phrases, or discourses, nor on
the other, for the pleasure of variety, fall into a childish
affectation of expressing every thing twenty different
ways, though it be never so natural and common

Nothing so much cools the warmth of a piece, or
puts out the fire of poetry, as that perpetual care to vary
incessantly even in the smallest circumstances   In this;
as in many other points, Homer has despised the un-
grateful labour of too scrupulous a nicety.   He has
done like a great painter, who does not think himself
obliged to vary all his pieces to that degree, as not one
of them shall have the least resemblance to another.   if
the principal figures are intirely different, we easily excuse a resemblance in the landscapes, the skies, or the
draperies   Suppose a gallery full of pictures, each of
which represents a particular subject.   in one I see A-
chilles in fury, menacing Agamemnon; in another the
same hero with regret delivers up Briseis to the heralds;
in a third it is still Achilles, but Achilles overcome with
grief, and lamenting to his mother   If the air, the
gesture, the countenance, the character of Achilles, are
the same in each of these three pieces.   if the ground of
one of these be the same with that of the others in the
composition and general design, whether it be landscape
or architecture, then indeed one should have reason to

Those call to war! and might my voice incite,
Now, now, this instant shou'd commence the fight.
Then, when the day's complete, let gen'rous bowls, 205
And copious banquets, glad your weary souls.
Let not my palate know the taste of food,
'Till my insatiate rage be cloy'd with blood:
Pale lies my friend, with wounds disfigur'd o'er,
And his cold feet are pointed to the door. 210

blame the painter for the uniformity of his figures and
grounds. But if there be no sameness but in the folds
of a few draperies, in the structure of some part of a
building, or in the figure of some tree, mountain, or
cloud, it is what no one would regard as a fault. The
application is obvious: Homer repeats, but they are
not the great strokes which he repeats, not those which
strike and fix our attention: they are only the little
parts, the transitions, the general circumstances, or familiar images, which recur naturally, and upon which
the reader but casts his eye carelefly: such as the descriptions of sacrifices, repasts, or embarquements · such
in short, as are in their own nature much the same,
which it is sufficient just to shew, and which are in a
manner incapable of different ornaments.

℣ 209 *Pale lies my friend*, etc] It is in the Greek,
*l es extended in my tent with his face turning towards the
door*, ἀνὰ πρόθυρον τετραμμένος, that is to say, as the scho-
liast has explained it, *having his feet turned towards the
door* For it was thus the Greeks placed their dead in
the porches of their houses, as likewise in Italy.

In portam rigidos calces extendit. Persius.

———*Recepitque ad limina gressum
Corpus ubi exanimi positum Pallantis Acœtes
Servabat senior*———

Revenge is all my foul! no meaner care,
Int'reft, or thought, has room to harbour there;
Deftruction be my feaft, and mortal wounds,
And fcenes of blood, and agonizing founds.

O firft of Greeks (Ulyffes thus rejoin'd)   215
The beft and braveft of the warrior-kind!
Thy praife it is in dreadful camps to fhine,
But old experience and calm wifdom, mine.
Then hear my counfel, and to reafon yield,
The braveft foon are fatiate of the field;   220
Tho' vaft the heaps that ftrow the crimfon plain,
The bloody harveft brings but little gain:
The fcale of conqueft ever wav'ring lies,
Great Jove but turns it, and the victor dies!
The great, the bold, by thoufands daily fall,   225
And endlefs were the grief, to weep for all.
Eternal forrows what avails to fhed?
Greece honours not with folemn fafts the dead:
Enough, when death demands the brave, to pay
The tribute of a melancholy day.   230

Thus we are told by Suetonius, of the body of Auguftus
——Eq efter or lo fufcepit, urbique intulit, atque in ve-
ftibulo domus collocavit.

℣. 221 *Tho' vaft the heaps,* etc] Ulyffes's expreffion
in the original is very remarkable, he calls καλάμην,
ftraw or chaff, fuch as are killed in the battel, and he
calls ἄμητον, the *crop,* fuch as make their efcape.   This
is very conformable to the language of holy fcripture,
wherein thofe who perifh are called *chaff,* and thofe who
are faved are called *corn.*   Dacier.

One chief with patience to the grave refign'd,
Our care devolves on others left behind.
Let gen'rous food fupplies of ftrength produce,
Let rifing fpirits flow from fprightly juice,
Let their warm heads with fcenes of battel glow, 235
And pour new furies on the feebler foe.
Yet a fhort interval, and none fhall dare
Expect a fecond fummons to the war;
Who waits for that, the dire effect fhall find,
If trembling in the fhips he lags behind. 240
Embodied, to the battel let us bend,
And all at once on haughty Troy defcend.

  And now the delegates Ulyffes fent,
To bear the prefents from the royal tent.
The fons of Neftor, Phyleus' valiant heir, 245
Thias and Merion, thunderbolts of war,
With Lycomedes of Creiontian ftrain,
And Melanippus, form'd the chofen train.
Swift as the word was giv'n, the youths obey'd;
Twice ten bright vafes in the midft they laid; 250

℣ 237. ———— *None fhall dare*
          Expect a fecond fummons to the war.]
This is very artful: Ulyffes, to prevail upon Achilles to
let the troops take repaft, and yet in fome fort to fecond
his impatience, gives with the fame breath orders for
battel, by commanding the troops to march, and expect
no farther orders.   Thus though the troops go to take
repaft, it looks as if they do not lofe a moment's time,
but are going to put themfelves in array of battel.
Dacier.

A row of fix fair tripods then fucceeds;
And twice the number of high-bounding fteeds;
Sev'n captives next a lovely line compofe;
The eighth Brifeis, like the blooming rofe,
Clos'd the bright band: great Ithacus, before,   255
Firft of the train, the golden talents bore;
The reft in public view the chiefs difpofe,
A fplendid fcene¹ then Agamemnon rofe:
The boar Talthybius held: the Grecian lord
Drew the broad cutlace fheath'd befide his fword: 160
The ftubborn briftles from the victim's brow
He crops, and off'ring meditates his vow.
His hands uplifted to th' attefting fkies,
On heav'n's broad marble roof were fix'd his eyes,
The folemn words, a deep attention draw,   265
And Greece around fate thrill'd with facred awe.

   Witnefs thou firft! thou greateft pow'r above!
All-good, all-wife, and all-furveying Jove!
And mother-earth, and heav'n's revolving light,
And ye, fell furies of the realms of night,   270
Who rule the dead, and horrid woes prepare
For perjur'd kings, and all who falfely fwear!
The black-ey'd maid inviolate removes,
Pure and unconfcious of my manly loves.
If this be faife, heav'n all its vengeance fhed,   275
And levell'd thunder ftrike my guilty head!

   With that, his weapon deep inflicts the wound;
The bleeding favage tumbles to the ground,

The facred herald rolls the victim flain
(A feaft for fifh) into the foming main.   ´ 280

Then thus Achilles.   Hear, ye Greeks ' and know
Whate'er we feel, 'tis Jove inflicts the woe:
Not elfe Atrides could our rage inflame,
Nor from my arms, unwilling, force the dame.
'Twas Jove's high will alone, o'er-ruling all,   285
That doom'd our ftrife, and doom'd the Greeks to fall.
Go then, ye chiefs! indulge the genial rite;
Achilles waits ye, and expects the fight.

The fpeedy council at his word adjourn'd :
To their black veffels all the Greeks return'd.   290
Achilles fought his tent.   His train before
March'd onward, bending with the gifts they bore.
Thofe in the tents the fquires induftrious fpread :
The foaming courfers to the ftalls they led.
To their new feats the female captives move;   295
Brifeis, radiant as the queen of love,
Slow as fhe paft, beheld with fad furvey
Where gafh'd with cruel wounds, Patroclus lay.

$\dot{y}$. 280. *Rolls the victim into the main.*] For it was
not lawful to eat the flefh of the victims facrificed in
confirmation of oaths; fuch were victims of malediction.
Euftathius.

$\dot{y}$. 281. *Hear, ye Greeks,* etc.] Achilles, to let them
fee that he is intirely appeafed, juftifies Agamemnon himfelf, and enters into the reafons with which that prince
had coloured his fault.   But in that juftification he
perfectly well preferves his character, and illuftrates the
advantage he has over that king who offended him.
Dacier.

Prone on the body fell the heav'nly fair,

Beat her sad breast, and tore her golden hair;   300

All beautiful in grief, her humid eyes

Shining with tears, she lifts, and thus she cries.

Ah youth for ever dear, for ever kind,

Once tender friend of my distracted mind!

I left thee fresh in life, in beauty gay;   305

Now find thee cold, inanimated clay!

What woes my wretched race of life attend?

Sorrows on sorrows, never doom'd to end!

The first lov'd confort of my virgin bed

Before these eyes in fatal battel bled: 310

My three brave brothers in one mournful day

All trod the dark, irremeable way:

Thy friendly hand uprear'd me from the plain,

And dry'd my forrows for a husband slain;

Achilles' care you promis'd I should prove,   315

The first, the deareft partner of his love,

℣ 303 etc The lamentation of Briseis over Patroclus] This speech (says Dionysius of Halicarnaffus) is
not without its artifice: while Briseis seems only to be
deploring Patroclus, she reprefents to Achilles who
stands by, the breach of the promifes he had made her,
and upbraids him with the neglect he had been guilty of
in refigning her up to Agamemnon.   He adds, that
Achilles hereupon acknowleges the justice of her complaint, and makes anfwer that his promifes should be
performed: it was a flip in that great critic's memory,
for the verfe he cites is not in this part of the author,
[περι ισχηματισμενων, Part 2.]

℣. 315. Achilles' care you promis'd, etc.] In thefe
days when our manners are fo different from thofe of

That rites divine should ratify the band,
And make me emprefs in his native land.
Accept thefe grateful tears! for thee they flow,
For thee, that ever felt another's woe!   320

Her fifter captives echo'd groan for groan,
Nor mourn'd Patroclus' fortunes, but their own.
The leaders prefs'd the chief on every fide;
Unmov'd, he heard them, and with fighs deny'd.

If yet Achilles have a friend, whofe care   325
Is bent to pleafe him, this requeft forbear:
Till yonder fun defcend, ah let me pay
To grief and anguifh one abftemious day.

the ancients, and we fee none of thofe difmal cataftro-
phes which laid whole kingdoms wafte, and fubjeéted
princeffes and queens to the power of the conqueror;
it will perhaps feem aftonifhing, that a princefs of Brifeis's birth, the very day that her father, brothers, and
hufband were killed by Achilles, fhould fuffer herfelf to
be comforted, and even flattered with the hopes of be-
coming the fpoufe of the murderer. But fuch were the
manners of thofe times, as ancient hiftory teftifies: and
a poet reprefents them as they were; but if there was a
neceffity for juftifying them, it might be faid that flavery
was at that time fo terrible, that in truth a princefs like
Brifeis was pardonable, to chufe rather to become A-
chilles's wife than his flave. Dacier.

Ŷ. 322. *Nor mourn'd Patroclus' fortunes, but their
own*] Homer adds this touch to heighten the charaéter
of Brifeis, and to fhew the difference there was between
her and the other captives. Brifeis, as a well-born
princefs, really bewailed Patroclus out of gratitude; but
the others, by pretending to bewail him, wept only out
of intereft. Dacier.

He fpoke, and from the warriors turn'd his face:
Yet ftill the brother-kings of Atreus' race,   330
Neftor, Idomeneus, Ulyffes fage,
And Phœnix, ftrive to calm his grief and rage:
His rage they calm not, nor his grief controul;
He groans, he raves, he forrows from his foul.

Thou too, Patroclus! (thus his heart he vents) 335
Once fpread th' inviting banquet in our tents:
Thy fweet fociety, thy winning care,
Once ftay'd Achilles, rufhing to the war.
But now alas! to death's cold arms refign'd,
What banquet but revenge can glad my mind?   340
What greater forrow could afflict my breaft,
What more, if hoary Peleus were deceas'd?
Who now, perhaps, in Phthia dreads to hear
His fon's fad fate, and drops a tender tear.
What more, fhould Neoptolemus the brave   345
(My only offspring) fink into the grave?
If yet that offspring lives, (I diftant far,
Of all neglectful, wage a hateful war)
I cou'd not this, this cruel ftroke attend;
Fate claim'd Achilles, but might fpare his friend. 350

℣. 335 Thou too, Patroclus! etc] This lamentation
is finely introduced while the generals are perfuading
him to take fome refrefhment, it naturally awakens in
his mind the remembrance of Patroclus, who had fo often
brought him food every morning before they went to
battel: this is very natural, and admirably well conceals
the art of drawing the fubject of his difcourfe from the
things that prefent themfelves.   Spondanus.

I hop'd

I hop'd Patroclus might survive, to rear
My tender orphan with a parent's care,
From Scyros isle conduct him o'er the main,
And glad his eyes with his paternal reign,
The lofty palace, and the large domain.   355
For Peleus breathes no more the vital air;
Or drags a wretched life of age and care,
But till the news of my sad fate invades
His hastening soul, and sinks him to the shades.

   Sighing he said · his grief the heroes join'd,   360
Each stole a tear for what he left behind.
Their mingled grief the sire of heav'n survey'd,
And thus, with pity, to his blue-ey'd maid.

   Is then Achilles now no more thy care,
And dost thou thus desert the great in war?   365
Lo, where yon' sails their canvas wings extend,
All comfortless he sits, and wails his friend:
Ere thirst and want his forces have opprest,
Haste and infuse ambrosia in his breast.

   He spoke, and sudden as the word of Jove,   370
Shot the descending goddess from above.

   ⊻. 351 *I hop'd Patroclus might survive,* etc] Patroclus was young, and Achilles who had but a short time to live, hoped that after his death his dear friend would be as a father to his son, and put him into the possession of his kingdom: Neoptolemus would in Patroclus find Peleus and Achilles; whereas when Patroclus was dead, he must be an orphan indeed. Homer is particularly admirable for the sentiments, and always follows nature. Dacier.

So fwift thro' æther the fhrill Harpye fprings,

The wide air floating to her ample wings,

To great Achilles fhe her flight addreft,

And pour'd divine ambrofia in his breaft,   ╌   375

With nectar fweet, (refection of the Gods ')

Then, fwift afcending, fought the bright abodes.

Now iffued from the fhips the warrior train,

And like a deluge pour'd upon the plain.

As when the piercing blafts of Boreas blow,   380

And fcatter o'er the fields the driving fnow;

From dufky clouds the fleecy winter flies,

Whofe dazling luftre whitens all the fkies:

So helms fucceeding helms, fo fhields from fhields

Catch the quick beams, and brighten all the fields; 385

Broad glitt'ring breaft-plates, fpears with pointed rays

Mix in one ftream, reflecting blaze on blaze:

Thick beats the center as the courfers bound,

With fplendour flame the fkies, and laugh the fields around.

Ɣ . 384. *So helms fucceeding helms, fo fhields from fhields*
         Catch the quick beams, and brighten all the
         fields]

It is probable the reader may think the words, *fhining,*
fplendid, and others derived from the luftre of arms, too
frequent in thefe books.   My author is to anfwer for
it; but it may be alleged in his excufe, that when it
was the cuftom for every foldier to ferve in armour,
and when thofe arms were of brafs before the ufe of iron
became common, thefe images of luftre were lefs avoid-
able, and more neceffarily frequent in defcriptions of
this nature.

Full in the midſt, high tow'ring o'er the reſt, 390
His limbs in arms divine Achilles dreſt;
Arms which the father of the fire beſtow'd,
Forg'd on th' eternal anvils of the God.
Grief and revenge his furious heart inſpire,
His glowing eye-balls roll with living fire; 395
He grinds his teeth, and furious with delay
O'erlooks th' embattled hoſt, and hopes the bloody day.

The ſilver cuiſhes firſt his thigh infold·
Then o'er his breaſt was brac'd the hollow gold:
The brazen ſword a various baldric ty'd, 400
That, ſtarr'd with gems, hung glitt'ring at his ſide;
And like the moon, the broad refulgent ſhield
Blaz'd with long rays, and gleam'd athwart the field.

So to night wand'ring ſailors, pale with fears,
Wide o'er the wat'ry waſte, a light appears, 405
Which on the far-ſeen mountain blazing high,
Streams from ſome lonely watch-tow'r to the ſky:
With mournful eyes they gaze, and gaze again;
Loud howls the ſtorm, and drives them o'er the main.

℣. 390. *Achilles arming himſelf*, etc.] There is a
wonderful pomp in this deſcription of Achilles's arming
himſelf, every reader without being pointed to it, will
ſee the extreme grandeur of all theſe images; but what
is particular, is, in what a noble ſcale they riſe one a-
bove another, and how the hero is ſet ſtill in a ſtronger
point of light than before; till he is at laſt in a manner
covered over with glories: he is at firſt likened to the
moon-light, then to the flames of a beacon, then to a
comet, and laſtly to the ſun itſelf.

Next, his high head the helmet grac'd; behind   410
The sweepy crest hung floating in the wind:
Like the red star, that from his flaming hair
Shakes down difeafes, pestilence and war;
So stream'd the golden honours from his head,
Trembled the sparkling plumes, and the loose glories shed.

The chief beholds himself with wond'ring eyes;   416
His arms he poises, and his motions tries;
Buoy'd by some inward force, he seems to swim,
And feels a pinion lifting ev'ry limb.

And now he shakes his great paternal spear,   420
Pond'rous and huge! which not a Greek could rear.
From Pelion's cloudy top an ash entire
Old Chiron fell'd, and shap'd it for his fire;
A spear which stern Achilles only wields,
The death of heroes, and the dread of fields: 425
    Automedon and Alcimus prepare
Th' immortal coursers, and the radiant car,
(The filver traces sweeping at their side)
Their fiery mouths refplendent bridles ty'd,
The iv'ry-studded reins, return'd behind,   430
Wav'd o'er their backs, and to the chariot join'd.
The charioteer then whirl'd the lash around,
And swift ascended at one active bound.
All bright in heav'nly arms, above his squire
Achilles mounts, and sets the field on fire;   435
Not brighter Phœbus in th' ethereal way,
Flames from his chariot, and restores the day.

High o'er the host, all terrible he stands,
And thunders to his steeds these dread commands.

Xanthus and Balius! of Podarges' strain,   440
(Unless ye boast that heav'nly race in vain)
Be swift, be mindful of the load ye bear,
And learn to make your master more your care:
Thro' falling squadrons bear my slaught'ring sword,
Nor, as ye left Patroclus, leave your lord.   445

The gen'rous Xanthus, as the words he said,
Seem'd sensible of woe, and droop'd his head,
Trembling he stood before the golden wain,
And bow'd to dust the honours of his mane,
When, strange to tell! (so Juno will'd) he broke   450
Eternal silence, and portentous spoke.

℣. 450. *When strange to tell! (so Juno will'd) he broke*
Eternal silence, and portentous spoke.]
It is remarked, in excuse of this extravagant fiction of a
horse speaking, that Homer was authorized herein by
fable, tradition, and history.   Livy makes mention of
two oxen that spoke on different occasions, and recites
the speech of one, which was, *Roma cave tibi*.   Pliny
tells us, these animals were particularly gifted this way,
l 8. c. 45. *Est frequens in prodigiis priscorum, bovem lo-*
cutum.   Besides Homer had prepared us for expecting
something miraculous from these horses of Achilles, by
representing them to be immortal.   We have seen them
already sensible, and weeping at the death of Patroclus:
and we must add to all this, that a goddess is concerned
in working this wonder: it is Juno that does it.   Op-
pian alludes to this in a beautiful passage of his first
book: not having the original by me, I shall quote
(what I believe is no less beautiful) Mr. Fenton's trans-
lation of it.

C 3

Achilles! yes! this day at leaft we bear
Thy rage in fafety thro' the files of war:
But come it will, the fatal time muft come,
Nor ours the fault, but God decrees thy doom.   455
Not thro' our crime, or flownefs in the courfe,
Fell thy Patroclus, but by heav'nly force;
The bright far-fhooting God who gilds the day,
(Confeft we faw him) tore his arms away.
No—could our fwiftnefs o'er the winds prevail,   460
Or beat the pinions of the weftern gale,

Of all the prone creation, none difplay
A friendlier fenfe of man's fuperior fway:
Some in the filent pomp of grief complain,
For the brave chief, by doom of battel flain:
And when young Peleus in his rapid car
Rufh'd on, to rouze the thunder of the war,
With human voice infpir'd, his fteed deplor'd
The fate impending dreadful o'er his Lord.

                              Cyneg. lib. 1.

Spondanus and Dacier fail not to bring up Balaam's
afs on this occafion. But methinks the commentators
are at too much pains to difcharge the poet from the
imputation of extravagant fiction, by accounting for
wonders of this kind: I am afraid, that next to the ex-
travagance of inventing them, is that of endeavouring
to reconcile fuch fictions to probability. Would not
one general anfwer do better, to fay once for all, that
the above-cited authors lived in the *age of wonders:* The
tafte of the world has been generally turned to the
miraculous; wonders were what the people would have,
and what not only the poets, but the priefts, gave them.

All were in vain—the fates thy death demand,
Due to a mortal and immortal hand.

 Then ceas'd for ever, by the Furies ty'd,
His fate-ful voice. Th' intrepid chief reply'd 465
With unabated rage——So let it be [1]
Portents and prodigies are loft on me.
I know my fates: to die, to fee no more
My much-lov'd parents, and my native fhore——
Enough—when heav'n ordains, I fink in night ; 470
Now perifh Troy! he faid, and rufh'd to fight.

 ⅰ. 464. *Then ceas'd for ever, by the furies ty'd,*
   His fate-ful voice——
The poet had offended againft probability if he had
made Juno take away the voice; for Juno (which fignifies the air) is the caufe of the voice. Befides, the
poet was willing to intimate that the privation of the
voice is a thing fo difmal and melancholy, that none
but the Furies can take upon them fo cruel an employment. Euftathius.

THE

ILIAD.

BOOK XX.

THE ARGUMENT.

The battel of the Gods, and the acts of Achilles.

JUPITER upon Achilles's return to the battel, calls a council of the Gods, and permits them to assist either party. The terrors of the combate described, when the deities are engaged. Apollo encourages Æneas to meet Achilles. After a long conversation, these two heroes encounter; but Æneas is preserved by the assistance of Neptune. Achilles falls upon the rest of the Trojans, and is upon the point of killing Hector, but Apollo conveys him away in a cloud. Achilles pursues the Trojans with a great slaughter.

The same day continues. The scene is in the field before Troy.

THUS round Pelides breathing war and blood,
 Greece sheath'd in arms, beside her vessels stood;
While near impending from a neighb'ring height,
Troy's black battalions wait the shock of fight.
Then Jove to Themis gives command, to call 5
The Gods to council in the starry hall:

℣. 5. *Then Jove to Themis gives command, etc.*] The poet is now to bring his hero again into action, and he

Swift o'er Olympus' hundred hills she flies,
And summons all the senate of the skies.
These shining on, in long procession come
To Jove's eternal adamantine dome.   10
Not one was absent, not a rural pow'r,
That haunts the verdant gloom, or rosy bow'r,
Each fair-hair'd dryad of the shady wood,
Each azure sister of the silver flood;
All but old Ocean, hoary sire [1] who keeps   15
His ancient seat beneath the sacred deeps.

other reason he draws from the allegory of Oceanus,
introduces him with the utmost pomp and grandeur: the
gods are assembled only upon this account, and Jupiter
permits several deities to join with the Trojans, and
hinder Achilles from over ruling destiny itself.

The circumstance of sending Themis to assemble the
gods is very beautiful; she is the goddess of justice; the
Trojans by the rape of Helen, and by repeated per-
juries having broken her laws, she is the properest messenger to summon a synod to bring them to punish-
ment. Eustathius.

Proclus has given a farther explanation of this. Themis or Justice (says he) is made to assemble the gods
round Jupiter, because it is from him that all the powers
of nature take their virtue, and receive their orders;
and Jupiter sends them to the relief of both parties, to
shew that nothing falls out but by his permission, and
that neither angels, nor men, nor the elements, act but
according to the power which is given them.

𝖸. 15. *All but old Ocean.*] Eustathius gives two rea-
sons why Oceanus was absent from this assembly. the
one is because he is fabled to be the original of all the
gods, and it would have been a piece of indecency for
him to see the deities, who were all his descendants, war
upon one another by joining adverse parties: the other

On marble thrones with lucid columns crown'd,
(The work of Vulcan) fate the pow'rs around.
Ev'n * he whofe trident fways the wat'ry reign,
Heard the loud fummons, and forfook the main, 20
Affum'd his throne amid the bright abodes,
And queftion'd thus the fire of men and Gods.

What moves the God who heav'n and earth commands,
And grafps the thunder in his awful hands,
Thus to convene the whole æthereal ftate? 25
Is Greece and Troy the fubject in debate?
Already met, the low'ring hofts appear,
And death ftands ardent on the edge of war.

'Tis true (the cloud-compelling Pow'r replies)
This day, we call the council of the fkies 30
In care of human race; ev'n Jove's own eye
Sees with regret unhappy mortals die.
Far on Olympus' top in fecret ftate
Ourfelf will fit, and fee the hand of fate
Work out our will. Celeftial pow'rs! defcend, 35
And as your minds direct, your fuccour lend

* Neptune.

which fignifies the element of water, and confequently
the whole element could not afcend into the Æther;
but whereas Neptune, the rivers, and the fountains are
faid to have been prefent, this is no way impoffible, if
we confider it in an allegorical fenfe, which implies,
that the rivers, feas, and fountains fupply the air with
vapours, and by that means afcend into the Æther.

℣. 35. ——*Celeftial pow'rs! defcend,*
   And as your minds direct, your fuccour lend
   To either hoft——]
Euftathius informs us, that the ancients were very much

To either hoft.   Troy foon muft lie o'erthrown,
If uncontroll'd Achilles fights alone:
Their troops but lately durft not meet his eyes;
What can they now, if in his rage he rife?   40
Affift them, Gods! or Ilion's facred wall
May fall this day, tho' fate forbids the fall.

divided upon this paffage of Homer   Some have criticiz-
ed it, and others have anfwered their criticifm; but he
reports nothing more than the objection, without tran-
fmitting the anfwer to us.   Thofe who condemned
Homer, faid Jupiter was for the Trojans; he faw the
Greeks were the ftrongeft, fo permitted the gods to
declare themfelves, and go to the battel.   But therein
that God is deceived, and does not gain his point; for
the gods who favour the Greeks being ftronger than
thofe who favour the Trojans, the Greeks will ftill have
the fame advantage   I do not know what anfwer the
partifans of Homer made, but for my part, I think this
objection is more ingenious than folid.   Jupiter does
not pretend that the Trojans fhould be ftronger than
the Greeks, he has only a mind that the decree of Deftiny
fhould be executed   Deftiny had refufed to Achilles
the glory of taking Troy, but if Achilles fights fingly
againft the Trojans, he is capable of forcing Deftiny, (as
Homer has already elfewhere faid, that there had been
brave men who had done fo)   Whereas if the gods
took part, though thofe who followed the Grecians were
ftronger than thofe who were for the Trojans, the latter would however be ftrong enough to fupport deftiny,
and to hinder Achilles from making himfelf mafter of
Troy. this was Jupiter's fole view.   Thus is this paffage far from being blameable, it is on the contrary very
beautiful, and infinitely glorious for Achilles.   Dacier.

ỳ . 41 ——Or Ilion's facred wall
       May fall this day, tho' fate forbids the fall]
Monf de la Motte criticizes on this paffage, as thinking

He faid, and fir'd their heav'nly breafts with rage:
On adverfe parts the warring Gods engage.
Heav'n's awful queen, and he whofe azure round   45
Girds the vaft globe; the maid in arms renown'd;

it abfurd and contradictory to Homer's own fyftem, to
imagine, that what fate had ordained fhould not come
to pafs.   Jupiter here feems to fear that Troy will be
taken this very day in fpite of deftiny, ὑπὲρ μόρον   M.
Boivin anfwers, that the explication hereof depends
wholly upon the principles of the ancient Pagan theology, and their doctrine concerning fate   It is certain,
according to Homer and Virgil, that what deftiny had
decreed did not conftantly happen in the precife time
marked by deftiny; the fatal moment was not to be re-
tarded, but might be haftened. for example, that of the
death of Dido was advanced by the blow fhe gave herfelf, her hour was not then come

A.   ————Nec fato, merita nec morte peribat,
      Sed mifera arte dem————

Every violent death was accounted ὑπὲρ μόρον, that is,
before the fated time, or (which is the fame thing) a-
gainft the natural order, turbato mortalitatis ordine, as
the Romans expreffed it.   And the fame might be faid
of any misfortunes which men drew upon themfelves
by their own ill conduct   (See the note on ψ 560.
lib. 16)   In a word, it muft be allowed that it was
not eafy, in the Pagan religion, to form the jufteft ideas
upon a doctrine fo difficult to be cleared, and upon
which it is no great wonder if a poet fhould not always
be perfectly confiftent with himfelf, when it has puzzled
fuch a number of divines and philofophers

   ℣ 44 On adverfe parts the warring Gods engage.
         Heav'n's awful queen, etc.]
Euftathius has a very curious remark upon this divifion of the gods in Homer, which M. Dacier has en-

Hermes, of profitable arts the fire,
And Vulcan, the black fov'reign of the fire:
Thefe to the fleet repair with inftant flight;
The veffels tremble as the Gods alight.   50

In aid of Troy, Latona, Phœbus came,
Mars fiery-helm'd, the laughter-loving dame,

tirely borrowed (as indeed no commentator ever borrowed more, or acknowleged lefs, than fhe has every
where done from Euftathius)   This divifion, fays he,
is not made at random, but founded upon very folid
reafons, drawn from the nature of thofe two nations.
He places on the fide of the Greeks all the gods who
prefide over arts and fciences, to fignify how much in
that refpect the Greeks excelled all other nations. Juno,
Pallas, Neptune, Mercury and Vulcan are for the Greeks ;
Juno, not only as the goddefs who prefides over marriage, and who is concerned to revenge an injury done
to the nuptial bed, but likewife as the goddefs who reprefents monarchial government, which was better eftablifhed in Greece than any where elfe; Pallas, becaufe
being the goddefs of war and wifdom, fhe ought to affift
thofe who are wronged; befides the Greeks underftood
the art of war better than the Barbarians; Neptune, becaufe he was an enemy to the Trojans upon account
of Laomedon's perfidioufnefs, and becaufe moft of the
Greeks being come from iflands or peninfulas, they were
in fome fort his fubjects; Mercury, becaufe he is a God
who prefides over ftratagems of war, and becaufe Troy
was taken by that of the wooden horfe, and laftly Vulcan as the declared enemy of Mars and of all adulterers,
and as the father of arts.

V. 52. *Mars, fiery-helm'd, the laughter-loving dame.*]
The reafons why Mars and Venus engage for the Trojans, are very obvious; the point in hand was to favour
ravifhers and debauchees.   But the fame reafon, you

Xanthus whose streams in golden currents flow,
And the chaste huntress of the silver bow.
Ere yet the Gods their various aid employ, 55
Each Argive bosom swell'd with manly joy,
While great Achilles, (terror of the plain)
Long lost to battel, shone in arms again.
Dreadful he stood in front of all his host;
Pale Troy beheld, and seem'd already lost; 60
Her bravest heroes pant with inward fear,
And trembling see another God of war.

But when the pow'rs descending swell'd the fight,
Then tumult rose; fierce rage and pale affright
Vary'd each face; then Discord sounds alarms, 65
Earth echoes, and the nations rush to arms.
Now-thro' the trembling shores Minerva calls,
And now she thunders from the Grecian walls.
Mars hov'ring o'er his Troy, his terror shrouds
In gloomy tempests, and a night of clouds: 70
Now thro' each Trojan heart he fury pours
With voice divine from Ilion's topmost tow'rs,
Now shouts to Simois, from her beauteous hill;
The mountain shook, the rapid stream stood still.

will say, does not serve for Apollo, Diana and Latona.
It is urged that Apollo is for the Trojans, because of
the darts and arrows which were the principal strength
of the Barbarians; and Diana, because she presided over
dancing, and those Barbarians were great dancers: and
Latona, as influenced by her children.   Xanthus being
a Trojan river, is interested for his country.   Eustathius.

Above, the fire of Gods his thunder rolls,   75
And peals on peals redoubled rend the poles.
Beneath, ftern Neptune fhakes the folid ground;
The forefts wave, the mountains nod around ;
Thro' all their fummits tremble Ida's woods,
And from their fources boil her hundred floods.   80

℣ 75 *Above, the fire of Gods*, etc] " The images
" (favs Longinus) which Homer gives of the combat
" of the gods, have in them fomething prodigioufly great
" and magnificent   We fee in thefe verfes, the earth
" opened to its very center, hell ready to difclofe itfelf,
" the whole machine of the world upon the point to be
" deftroyed and overturned: to fhew that in fuch a
" confliĉt, heaven and hell, all things mortal and im-
' mortal, the whole creation in fhort was engaged in
" this battel, and all the extent of nature in danger."

Non fe- cc f qua pen tus vi terra dehifcens
In   s e ect fides et regna reeludat
P   , D   fite te urm ne barathrum
C   , tr p deutque ri ji lumine manes
                                              Virgil.

Madam Dacier rightly obferves that this copy is inferior to the original on this account, that Virgil has
made a comparifon of that which Homer made an action   This occafions an infinite difference, which is
eafy to be perceived
One may compare with this noble paffage of Homer,
the battel of the gods and giants in Hefiod's Theogony,
which s one of the fublimeft parts of that author, and
Milton's battel of the Angels in the fixth book : the e-
levation and enthufiafm of our great countryman feems
owing to this original.

Troy's turrets totter on the rocking plain;

And the tofs'd navies beat the heaving main.

Deep in the difmal regions of the dead,

Th' infernal monarch rear'd his horrid head,

Leap'd from his throne, left Neptune's arm fhould lay 85

His dark dominions open to the day,

And pour in light on Pluto's drear abodes,

Abhorr'd by men, and dreadful ev'n to Gods.

Such war th' immortals wage: fuch horrors rend

The world's vaft concave, when the Gods contend. 90

Firft filver-fhafted Phœbus took the plain

Againft blue Neptune, monarch of the main:

The God of arms his giant bulk difplay'd,

Oppos'd to Pallas, war's triumphant maid.

Againft Latona march'd the fon of May;   95

The quiver'd Dian, fifter of the day,

(Her golden arrows founding at her fide)

Saturnia, majefty of heav'n, defy'd.

℣ 91 *Firft filver-fhafted Phœbus took the plain,* etc]
With what art does the poet engage the gods in this
conflict ! Neptune oppofes Apollo, which implies that
things moift and dry are in continual difcord: Pallas
fights with Mars, which fignifies that rafhnefs and wifdom always difagree· Juno is againft Diana, that is,
nothing more differs from a marriage ftate, than celibacy:
Vulcan engages Xanthus, that is, fire and water are in
perpetual variance.   Thus we have a fine allegory concealed under the veil of excellent poetry, and the reader
receives a double fatisfaction at the fame time from
beautiful verfes, and an inftructive moral.   Euftathius.

D 3

With fiery Vulcan laft in battel ftands
The facred flood that rolls on golden fands;   100
Xanthus his name with thofe of heav'nly birth,
But call'd Scamander by the fons of earth.

While thus the Gods in various league engage,
Achilles glow'd with more than mortal rage:
Hector he fought; in fearch of Hector turn'd   105
His eyes around, for Hector only burn'd;
And burft like light'ning thro' the ranks, and vow'd
To glut the God of battels with his blood.

Æneas was the firft who dar'd to ftay;
Apollo wedg'd him in the warrior's way,   110
But fwell'd his bofom with undaunted might,
Half-forc'd, and half-perfuaded to the fight.
Like young Lycaon, of the royal line,
In voice and afpect feem'd the power divine;
And bade the chief reflect, how late with fcorn   115
In diftant threats he brav'd the Goddefs-born.

Then thus the hero of Anchifes' ftrain.
To meet Pelides you perfuade in vain ·
Already have I met, nor void of fear
Obferv'd the fury of his flying fpear;   120

V. 119. *Already have I met*, etc.] Euftathius remarks
that the poet lets no opportunity pafs of inferting into
his poem the actions that preceded the tenth year of the
war, efpecially the actions of Achilles the hero of it. In
this place he brings in Æneas extolling the bravery of
his enemy, and confeffing himfelf to have formerly been
vanquifhed by him at the fame time he preferves a
piece of ancient hiftory, by inferting into the poem the
hero's conqueft of Pedafus and Lyrneffus.

From Ida's woods he chas'd us to the field,
Our force he scatter'd, and our herds he kill'd:
Lyrnessus, Pedasus in ashes lay;
But (Jove assisting) I surviv'd the day.
Else had I sunk opprest in fatal fight, 125
By fierce Achilles and Minerva's might.
Where'er he mov'd the goddess shone before,
And bath'd his brazen lance in hostile gore.
What mortal man Achilles can sustain?
Th' immortals guard him thro' the dreadful plain, 130
And suffer not his dart to fall in vain.
Were God my aid, this arm should check his pow'r,
Tho' strong in battel as a brazen tow'r

To whom the son of Jove   That God implore,
And be, what great Achilles was before. 135
From heav'nly Venus thou deriv'st thy strain,
And he, but from a sister of the main;
An aged sea God, father of his line,
But Jove himself the sacred source of thine.

℣. 121. *From Ida's woods he chas'd us——*
But Jove assisting I surviv'd]
It is remarkable that Æneas owed his safety to his flight
from Achilles, but it may seem strange that Achilles,
who was so famed for his swiftness should not be able
to overtake him, even with Minerva for his guide. Eustathius answers, that this might proceed from the better knowlege Æneas might have of the ways and
defiles: Achilles being a stranger, and Æneas having
long kept his father's flocks in those parts.

He farther observes, that the word φάος discovers that
it was in the night that Achilles pursued Æneas.

Then lift thy weapon for a noble blow,   140
Nor fear the vaunting of a mortal foe.

   This said, and spirit breath'd into his breast,
Thro' the thick troops th' embolden'd hero prest:
His vent'rous act the white-arm'd queen survey'd,
And thus, assembling all the pow'rs, she said   145

   Behold an action, Gods! that claims your care,
Lo great Æneas rushing to the war;
Against Pelides he directs his course,
Phœbus impels, and Phœbus gives him force.
Restrain his bold career; at least, t'attend   150
Our favour'd hero, let some pow'r descend.
To guard his life, and add to his renown,
We, the great armament of heav'n, came down.
Hereafter let him fall, as fates design,
That spun so short his life's illustrious line: 155
But left some adverse God now cross his way,
Give him to know, what pow'rs assist this day:
For how shall mortal stand the dire alarms,
When heav'n's refulgent host appear in arms?

   Thus she, and thus the God whose force can make 160
The solid globe's eternal basis shake.
Against the might of man, so feeble known,
Why should celestial pow'rs exert their own?
Suffice, from yonder mount to view the scene;
And leave to war the fates of mortal men.   165
But if th' armipotent, or God of light,
Obstruct Achilles, or commence the fight,

Thence on the Gods of Troy we fwift defcend:
Full foon, I doubt not, fhall the conflict end,
And thefe, in ruin and confufion hurl'd,   170
Yield to our conqu'ring arms the lower world.

Thus having faid, the tyrant of the fea,
Cærulean Neptune, rofe, and led the way.
Advanc'd upon the field there ftood a mound
Of earth congefted, wall'd, and trench'd around;   175
In elder times to guard Alcides made,
(The work of Trojans, with Minerva's aid)
What time, a vengeful monfter of the main
Swept the wide fhore, and drove him to the plain.

℣. 174. *Advanc'd upon the field there ftood a mound,*
etc] It may not be unneceffary to explain this paffage
to make it underftood by the reader   the poet is very
fhort in the defcription, as fuppofing the fact already
known, and haftens to the combate between Achilles
and Æneas   This is very judicious in Homer, not to
dwell on a piece of hiftory that had no relation to his
action, when he has raifed the reader's expectation by
fo pompous an introduction, and made the Gods themfelves his fpectators
The ftory is as follows · Laomedon having defrauded
Neptune of the reward he promifed him for the building
the walls of Troy, Neptune fent a monftrous whale, to
which Laomedon expofed his daughter Hefione: but
Hercules having undertaken to deftroy the monfter, the
Trojans raifed an intrenchment to defend Hercules from
his purfuit : this being a remarkable piece of conduct
in the Trojans, it gave occafion to the poet to adorn a
plain narration with fiction, by afcribing the work to
Pallas the goddefs of wifdom.   Euftathius.

Here Neptune, and the Gods of Greece repair, 180
With clouds encompafs'd, and a veil of air:
The adverfe pow'rs, around Apollo laid,
Crown the fair hills that filver Simois fhade.
In circle clofe each heav'nly party fate,
Intent to form the future fcheme of fate;   185
But mix not yet in fight, tho' Jove on high
Gives the loud fignal, and the heav'ns reply.

Meanwhile the rufhing armies hide the ground;
The trampled centre yields a hollow found ·
Steeds cas'd in mail, and chiefs in armour bright,   190
The gleamy champain glows with brazen light.
Amid both hofts (a dreadful fpace) appear
There, great Achilles; bold Æneas here.
With tow'ring ftrides Æneas firft advanc'd;
The nodding plumage on his helmet danc'd,   195

ỿ. 180. *Here Neptune and the Gods*, etc.] I wonder
why Euftathius and all other commentators fhould be
filent upon this recefs of the gods: it feems ftrange at
the firft view, that fo many deities, after having entered
the fcene of action, fhould perform fo fhort a part, and
immediately become themfelves fpectators? I conceive
the reafon of this conduct in the poet to be, that A-
chilles has been inactive during the greateft part of the
poem; and as he is the hero of it, ought to be the
chief character in it: the poet therefore withdraws the
gods from the field, that Achilles may have the whole
honour of the day, and not act in fubordination to the
deities: befides the poem now draws to a conclufion,
and it is neceffary for Homer to enlarge upon the exploits of Achilles, that he may leave a noble idea of his
valour upon the mind of the reader.

Spread o'er his breaft the fencing fhield he bore,
And, as he mov'd, his jav'lin flam'd before.
Not fo Pelides; furious to engage,
He rufh'd impetuous.   Such the lion's rage,
Who viewing firft his foes with fcornful eyes,   200
Tho' all in arms the peopled city rife,
Stalks carelefs on, with unregarding pride;
'Till at the length, by fome brave youth defy'd,
To his bold fpear the favage turns alone,
He murmurs fury with an hollow groan;   205
He grins, he foams, he rolls his eyes around;
Lafh'd by his tail his heaving fides refound;
He calls up all his rage; he grinds his teeth,
Refolv'd on vengeance, or refolv'd on death.
So fierce Achilles on Æneas flies;   210
So ftands Æneas, and his force defies.
Ere yet the ftern encounter join'd, begun
The feed of Thetis thus to Venus' fon

Why comes Æneas thro' the ranks fo far?
Seeks he to meet Achilles' arm in war,   215

ỳ. 214, etc The converfation of Achilles and Æneas.]
I fhall lay before the reader the words of Euftathius in
defence of this paffage, which I confefs feems to me to
be faulty in the poet.   The reader (fays he) would naturally expect fome great and terrible atchievements
fhould enfue from Achilles on his firft enterance upon action   The poet feems to prepare us for it, by his
magnificent introduction of him into the field: but in-
ftead of a ftorm, we have a calm; he follows the fame
method in this book as he did in the third, where when
both armies were ready to engage in a general conflict,

In hope the realms of Priam to enjoy,

And prove his merits to the throne of Troy?

Grant that beneath thy lance Achilles dies,

The partial monarch may refuse the prize;

Sons he has many; those thy pride may quell;   426

And 'tis his fault to love those sons too well.

Or, in reward of thy victorious hand,

Has Troy propos'd some spacious tract of land?

An ample forest, or a fair domain,

Of hills for vines, and arable for grain?   235

Ev'n this, perhaps will hardly prove thy lot.

But can Achilles be so soon forgot?

he ends the day in a single combat between two heroes:
thus he always agreeably surprizes his readers. Besides
the admirers of Homer reap a farther advantage from
this conversation of the heroes: there is a chain of ancient history as well as a series of poetical beauties.

Madam Dacier's excuse is very little better. and to
shew that this is really a fault in the poet, I believe I
may appeal to the taste of every reader who certainly
finds himself disappointed our expectation is raised to
see gods and heroes engage, when suddenly it all sinks
into such a combat, in which neither party receives a
wound. and (what is more extraordinary) the gods are
made the spectators of so small an action! what occasion
was there for thunder, earthquakes, and descending
deities, to introduce a matter of so little importance?
neither is it any excuse to say he has given us a piece
of ancient history; we expected to read a poet, not an
historian.   In short, after the greatest preparation for
action imaginable, he suspends the whole narration, and
from the heat of a poet, cools at once into the simplicity of an historian.

Once

Once (as I think) you faw this brandifh'd fpear,
And then the great Æneas feem'd to fear.
With hearty hafte from Ida's mount he fled,   230
Nor, 'till he reach'd Lyrneffus, turn'd his head.
Her lofty walls not long our progrefs ftay'd;
Thofe, Pallas, Jove, and we, in ruins laid:
In Grecian chains her captive race were caft;
'Tis true, the great Æneas fled too faft,   235
Defrauded of my conqueft once before,
What then I loft, the Gods this day reftore.
Go; while thou may'ft, avoid the threaten'd fate;
Fools ftay to feel it, and are wife too late.

    To this Anchifes' fon. Such words employ   240
To one that fears thee, fome unwarlike boy;
Such we difdain; the beft may be defy'd
With mean reproaches, and unmanly pride:
Unworthy the high race from which we came,
Proclaim'd fo loudly by the voice of fame;   245
Each from illuftrious fathers draws his line;
Each goddefs-born; half human, half divine.
Thetis' this day, or Venus' offspring dies,
And tears fhall trickle from celeftial eyes:
For when two heroes, thus deriv'd, contend,   250
'Tis not in words the glorious ftrife can end.
If yet thou farther feek to learn my birth
(A tale refounded thro' the fpacious earth)
Hear how the glorious origin we prove
From ancient Dardanus, the firft from Jove: 255
    VOL. IV.   E

Dardania's walls he rais'd; for Ilion, then,
(The city since of many-languag'd men)
Was not.   The natives were content to till
The shady foot of Ida's fount-full hill.
From Dardanus, great Erichthonius springs,   260
The richest, once, of Asia's wealthy kings;
Three thousand mares his spacious pastures bred,
Three thousand foals beside their mothers fed.
Boreas, enamour'd of the sprightly train,
Conceal'd his godhead in a flowing mane,   265

> ỳ 258. *The natives were content to till*
> *The shady foot of Ida's fount-ful hill.*
>
> Κτίσσε δὲ Δαρδανίην, ἐπεὶ ὄπω Ἴλιος ἰρὴ
> Ἐν πεδίῳ πεπόλιστο πόλις μερόπων Ἀνθρώπων
> Ἀλλ' ἔθ' ὑπωρείας ᾤκεον πολυπιδάκυ Ἴδης

Plato and Strabo understand this passage as favouring
the opinion that the mountainous parts of the world
were first inhabited, after the universal deluge; and that
mankind by degrees descended to dwell in the lower
parts of the hills (which they would have the word
ὑπωρεια signify) and only in greater process of time
ventured into the valleys: Virgil however seems to have
taken this word in a sense something different where he
alludes to this passage. Æn. 3. 109.

> ————— ——*Nondum Ilium et arces*
> *Pergameæ steterant, habitabant vallibus imis.*

ỳ 262. *Three thousand mares,* etc.] The number of
the horses and mares of Erichthonius may seem incredible, were we not assured by Herodotus that there were
in the stud of Cyrus at one time (besides those for the
service of war) eight hundred horses and six thousand
six hundred mares.   Eustathius.

y. 264. *Boreas enamour'd,* etc.] Homer has the hap-

With voice diffembled to his loves he neigh'd,
And cours'd the dappled beauties o'er the mead:
Hence fprung twelve others of unrival'd kind,
Swift as their mother mares, and father wind.
Thefe lightly fkimming, when they fwept the plain, 270
Nor ply'd the grafs, nor bent the tender grain;

pinefs of making the leaft circumftance confiderable; the
fubject grows under his hands, and the plaineft matter
fhines in his drefs of poetry; another poet would have
faid thefe horfes were as fwift as the wind, but Homer
tells you that they fprung from Boreas the god of the
wind, and thence drew their fwiftnefs.

ỹ 270 *Thefe lightly fkimming, as they fwept the
plain*] The poet illuftrates the fwiftnefs of thefe horfes
by defcribing them as running over the ftanding corn,
and furface of waters, without making any impreffion.
Virgil has imitated thefe lines, and adapts what Homer
fays of thefe horfes to the fwiftnefs of Camilla. Æn.
7 809.

*Illa vel intactae fegetis per fumma volaret
Gramina, nec teneras curfu laefiffet ariftas ·
Vel mare per medium, fluctu fufpenfa tumenti
Ferret iter, celeres nec tingeret æquore plantas.*

The reader will eafily perceive that Virgil's is almoft a
literal tranflation: he has imitated the very run of the
verfes, which flow nimbly away in dactyls, and as fwift
as the wind they defcribe.

I cannot but obferve one thing in favour of Homer,
that there can no greater commendation be given to
him, than by confidering the conduct of Virgil: who,
though undoubtedly the greateft poet after him, feldom
ventures to vary much from his original in the paffages
he takes from him, as in a defpair of improving, and
contented if he can but equal them.

And when along the level feas they flew,
Scarce on the furface curl'd the briny dew.
Such Erichthonius was: from him there came
The facred Tros, of whom the Trojan name.   275
Three fons renown'd adorn'd his nuptiul bed,
Ilus, Affaracus, and Ganymed:
The matchlefs Ganymed, divinely fair,
Whom heav'n enamour'd fnatch'd to upper air,
To bear the cup of Jove (æthereal gueft)   28e
The grace and glory of th' ambrofial feaft.
The two remaining fons the line divide:
Firft rofe Laomedon from Ilus' fide;
From him Tithonus, now in cares grown old,
And Priam, (bleft with Hector, brave and bold:)   284
Clytius and Lampus, ever-honour'd pair;
And Hicetaon, thunderbolt of war.
From great Affaracus fprung Capys, He
Begat Anchifes, and Anchifes me.

♈ 280. *To bear the cup of Jove.*] To be a cupbearer
has in all ages and nations been reckoned an honourable
employment. Sappho mentions it in honour of her
brother Labichus, that he was cup-bearer to the nobles
of Mit'ere: the fon of Menelaus executed the fame office; Hebe and Mercury ferved the gods in the fame
ftation.

It was the cuftom in the Pagan worfhip to employ
noble youths to pour the wine upon the facrifice. in this
office Ganymede might probably attend upon the altar
of Jupiter. and from thence was fabled to be his cup-
bearer. Eustathius.

Such is our race: 'tis fortune gives us birth,   290
But Jove alone endues the foul with worth:
He, fource of pow'r and might! with boundlefs fway,
All human courage gives, or takes away.
Long in the field of words we may contend,
Reproach is infinite, and knows no end,   295
Arm'd or with truth or falfhood, right or wrong,
So voluble a weapon is the tongue;
Wounded, we wound; and neither fide can fail,
For every man has equal ftrength to rail
Women alone, when in the ftreets they jar,   300
Perhaps excel us in this wordy war;
Like us they ftand, encompafs'd with the croud,
And vent their anger impotent and loud.
Ceafe then——Our bufinefs in the field of fight
Is not to queftion, but to prove our might.   305
To all thofe infults thou haft offer'd here,
Receive this anfwer: 'tis my flying fpear.

   He fpoke.   With all his force the jav'lin flung,
Fix'd deep, and loudly in the buckler rung.
Far on his out-ftretch'd arm, Pelides held   310
(To meet the thund'ring lance) his dreadful fhield,
That trembled as it ftuck, nor void of fear
Saw, ere it fell, th' immeafurable fpear.
His fears were vain, impenetrable charms
Secur'd the temper of th' æthereal arms.   315
Thro' two ftrong plates the point its paffage held,
But ftopp'd, and refted, by the third repell'd;

Five plates of various metal, various mold,
Compos'd the shield, of brass each outward fold,
Of tin each inward, and the middle gold :   320
There stuck the lance.   Then rising ere he threw,
The forceful spear of great Achilles flew,
And pierc'd the Dardan shield's extremest bound,
Where the shrill brass return'd a sharper sound:
Thro' the thin verge the Pelean weapon glides,   325
And the slight cov'ring of expanded hides.
Æneas his contracted body bends,
And o'er him high the riven targe extends,
Sees thro' its parting plates, the upper air,
And at his back perceives the quiv'ring spear: 330
A fate so near him, chills his soul with fright,
And swims before his eyes the many-colour'd light.
Achilles, rushing in with dreadful cries,
Draws his broad blade, and at Æneas flies :
Æneas rouzing as the foe came on,   335
(With force collected) heaves a mighty stone:
A mass enormous ! which in modern days
No two of earth's degen'rate sons could raise.
But Ocean's God, whose earthquakes rock the ground,
Saw the distress, and mov'd the pow'rs around.   340

ỷ. 329. *But Ocean's God*, etc.] The conduct of the
poet in making Æneas owe his safety to Neptune in this
place is remarkable : Neptune is an enemy to the Trojans, yet he dares not suffer so pious a man to fall, lest
Jupiter should be offended : this shews, says Eustathius,
that piety is always under the protection of God; and
that favours are sometimes conferred not out of kindness,

Lo ! on the brink of fate Æneas ftands,
An inftant victim to Achilles' hands:
By Phœbus urg'd; but Phœbus has beftow'd
His aid in vain: the man o'erpow'rs the God.
And can ye fee this righteous chief alone   345
With guiltlefs blood, for vices not his own?
To all the Gods his conftant vows were paid:
Sure, tho' he wars for Troy, he claims our aid.
Fate wills not this; nor thus can Jove refign
The future father of the Dardan line: 350
The firft great anceftor obtain'd his grace,
And ftill his love defcends on all the race.
For Priam now, and Priam's faithlefs kind,
At length are odious to th' all-feeing mind;

but to prevent a greater detriment: thus Neptune preferves Æneas, left Jupiter fhould revenge his death upon the Grecians.

℣. 345. *And can ye fee this righteous chief*, etc]
Though Æneas is reprefented a man of great courage,
yet his piety is his moft fhining character: this is the
reafon why he is always the care of the gods, and they
favour him conftantly through the whole poem with
their immediate protection.

It is in this light that Virgil has prefented him to the
view of the reader: his valour bears but the fecond
place in the Æneis.   In the Ilias indeed he is drawn in
miniature, and in the Æneis at full length; but there
are the fame features in the copy, which are in the original, and he is the fame Æneas in Rome as he was in
Troy.

On great Æneas shall devolve the reign, 355
And sons succeeding sons the lasting line sustain.

ỵ. 355. On great Æneas shall devolve the reign,
   And sons succeeding sons the lasting line sustain]
The story of Æneas s founding the Roman empire, gave
Virgil the finest occasion imaginable of paying a complement to Augustus, and his countrymen, who were
fond of being thought the descendants of Troy He
has translated these two lines literally, and put them in
the nature of a prophecy; as the favourers of the opinion of Æneas's sailing into Italy, imagine Homer's
to be

—— ——— ——— Αἰνε'αν ὅ'η Τρώεσσιν ἀνάξει
Κα   παῖδες παίδ..ι τοιτι μετόπισθε γενωνται.

Hic demus Æreæ cunctis dominabitur oris,
Et nati natorum et qui nascentur ab illis.

There has been a very ancient alteration made (as
Strabo observes) in these two lines, by substituting πάν-
τεσσι, in the room of -, ' σοι   It is not improbable but
Virgil might give occasion for it, by his *cunctis domina-*
bitur oris.

Eustathius does not intirely discountenance this story:
if it be understood, says he, as a prophecy, the poet
might take it from the Sibylline oracles. He farther
remarks, that the poet artfully interweaves into his
poem not only the things which happened before the
commencement, and in the prosecution of the Trojan
war, but other matters of importance which happened
even after that war was brought to a conclusion. Thus
for instance, we have here a piece of history not extant
in any other author, by which we are informed that the
house of Æneas succeeded to the crown of Troas, and
to the kingdom of Priam   Eustathius.

This passage is very considerable, for it ruins the famous chimæra of the Roman empire, and of the family

The great earth-fhaker thus: to whom replies
Th' imperial Goddefs with the radiant eyes.

of the Cæfars, who both pretended to deduce their original from Venus by Æneas, alleging that after the taking of Troy, Æneas came into Italy: and this preten-
fion is hereby actually deftroyed.   This teftimony of
Homer ought to be looked upon as an authentic act, the
fidelity and verity thereof cannot be queftioned.   Neptune, as much an enemy as he is to the Trojans, declares that Æneas, and after him his pofterity, fhall reign
over the Trojans.   Would Homer have put this prophecy in Neptune's mouth, if he had not known that
Æneas did not leave Troy, but that he reigned there,
and if he had not feen in his time the defcendants of
that prince reign there likewife ? That poet wrote two
hundred and fixty years, or thereabouts, after the taking
of Troy ; and what is very remarkable, he wrote in fome
of the towns of Ionia, that is to fay, in the neighbour-
hood of Phrygia, fo that the time and place give fuch a
weight to his depofition, that nothing can invalidate it.
All that the hiftorians have written concerning Æneas's
voyage into Italy, ought to be confidered as a romance,
made on purpofe to deftroy all hiftorical truth , for the
moft ancient is pofterior to Homer by fome ages   Before Dionyfius of Halicarnaffus, fome writers being fenfible of the ftrength of this paffage of Homer, undertook
to explain it fo as to reconcile it with this fable, and
they faid that Æneas, after having been in Italy, returned to Troy, and left his fon Afcanius there   Dionyfius of Halicarnaffus, little fatisfied with this folution,
which did not feem to him to be probable has taken
another method he would have it, that by thefe words,
" He fhall reign over the Trojans," Homer meant,
He fhall reign over the Trojans whom he fhall carry
with him into Italy   " For is it not poffible, fays he,
" that Æneas fhould reign over the Trojans, whom he
" had taken with him, though fettled elfewhere ?"

Good as he is, to immolate or fpare

The Dardan prince, O Neptune, be thy care;   360

Pallas and I, by all that Gods can bind,

Have fworn deftruction to the Trojan kind;

Not ev'n an inftant to protract their fate,

Or fave one member of the finking ftate,

Till her laft flame be quench'd with her laft gore, 365

And ev'n her crumbling ruins are no more,

The king of Ocean to the fight defcends,

Thro' all the whiftling darts his courfe he bends,

Swift interpos'd between the warriors flies,

And cafts thick darknefs o'er Achilles' eyes.   370

That hiftorian, who wrote in Rome itfelf, and in the
very reign of Auguftus, was willing to make his court
to that prince, by explaining this paffage of Homer, fo
as to favour the chimæra he was poffeffed with   And
this is a reproach that may with fome juftice be caft on
him ; for poets may by their fictions flatter princes, and
welcome. it is their trade.   But for hiftorians to cor-
rupt the gravity and feverity of hiftory, to fubftitute
fable in the place of truth, is what ought not to be par-
doned   Strabo was much more fcrupulous, for though
he wrote his books of geography towards the beginning
of Tiberius's reign, yet he had the courage to give a
right explication to this paffage of Homer, and to aver,
that this poet faid, and meant, that Æneas remained at
Troy, that he reigned therein, Priam's whole race being
extinguifhed, and that he left the kingdom to his children after him, lib 13. You may fee this whole matter
difcuffed in a letter from M. Bochart to M. de Sagrais,
who has prefixed it to his remarks upon the tranflation
of Virgil.

From great Æneas' fhield the fpear he drew,
And at its mafter's feet the weapon threw.
That done, with force divine he fnatch'd on high
The Dardan prince, and bore him thro' the fky,
Smooth gliding without ftep, above the heads   375
Of warring heroes, and of bounding fteeds.
Till at the battel's utmoft verge they light,
Where the flow Caucans clofe the rear of fight:

 378 *Where the flow Caucans clofe the rear.*] The Caucones (fays Euftathius) were of Paphlagonian extract · and this perhaps was the reafon why they are not diftinctly mentioned in the catalogue, they being included under the general name of Paphlagonians: though two lines are quoted which are faid to have been left out by fome tranfcriber, and immediately followed this,

Κρῶμιαν τ' Αἰγιαλόντε καὶ ὑψηλὰς Ἐρυθίνυς.

Which verfes are thefe,

Καύκανας αὐτ' ἦγε πολυκλίος υἱὸς Ἀμύμων.

Or as others read it, Ἀμεῖβος

Οἱ περὶ παρθένιον ποταμὸν κλυτὰ δώματ' ἔναιον.

Or according to others,

Κατὰ δώματ' ἔναιον,

Yet I believe thefe are not Homer's lines but rather the addition of fome tranfcriber; and it is evident by confulting the paffage from which they are faid to have been curtailed, that they would be abfurd in that place; for the fecond line is actually there already; and as thefe Caucons are faid to live upon the banks of the Parthenius, fo are the Paphlagonians in the above-mentioned paffage. It is therefore more probable that the Caucons are included in the Paphlagonians.

The Godhead there (his heav'nly form confefs'd)
With words like thefe the panting chief addrefs'd. 380
   What pow'r, O prince, with force inferior far
Urg'd thee to meet Achilles' arm in war!
Henceforth beware, nor antedate thy doom,
Defrauding fate of all thy fame to come.
But when the day decreed (for come it muft)   385
Shall lay this dreadful hero in the duft,
Let then the furies of that arm be known,
Secure, no Grecian force tranfcends thy own.
   With that, he left him wond'ring as he lay,
Then from Achilles chas'd the mift away: 390
Sudden, returning with the ftream of light,
The fcene of war came rufhing on his fight.
Then thus, amaz'd: what wonders ftrike my mind!
My fpear, that parted on the wings of wind,
Laid here before me! and the Dardan lord   395
That fell this inftant, vanifh'd from my fword!
I thought alone with mortals to contend,
But pow'rs celeftial fure this foe defend.
Great as he is, our arm he fcarce will try,
Content for once, with all his Gods, to fly.   400
Now then let others bleed——This faid, aloud
He vents his fury, and inflames the croud,
O Greeks (he cries, and ev'ry rank alarms)
Join battel, man to man, and arms to arms!
'Tis not in me, tho' favour'd by the fky,   405
To mow whole troops, and make whole armies fly:

No

No God can fingly fuch a hoft engage,
Not Mars himfelf, nor great Minerva's rage.
But whatfoe'er Achilles can infpire,
Whate'er of active force, or acting fire,   410
Whate'er this heart can prompt, or hand obey;
All, all Achilles, Greeks ' is yours to-day.
Thro' yon' wide hoft this arm fhall fcatter fear,
And thin the fquadrons with my fingle fpear.

 He faid: nor lefs elate with martial joy,   415
The god-like Hector warm'd the troops of Troy.
Trojans, to war! think Hector leads you on;
Nor dread the vaunts of Peleus' haughty fon.
Deeds muft decide our fate. Ev'n thofe with words
Infult the brave, who tremble at their fwords   420
The weakeft atheift-wretch all heav'n defies,
But fhrinks and fhudders, when the thunder flies.
Nor from yon' boafter fhall your chief retire,
Not tho' his heart were fteel, his hands were fire;
That fire, that fteel, your Hector fhould withftand, 425
And brave that vengeful heart, that dreadful hand

 Thus (breathing rage thro' all) the hero faid;
A wood of lances rifes round his head,
Clamours on clamours tempeft all the air,
They join, they throng, they thicken to the war. 430
But Phœbus warns him from high heav'n to fhun
The fingle fight with Thetis' god like fon;
More fafe to combate in the mingled band,
Nor tempt too near the terrors of his hand.

He hears, obedient to the God of light,   435
And plung'd within the ranks, awaits the fight.

  Then fierce Achilles, shouting to the skies,
On Troy's whole force with boundless fury flies.
First falls Iphytion, at his army's head;
Brave was the chief, and brave the host he led,   440
From great Otrynteus he deriv'd his blood,
His mother was a Nais of the flood;
Beneath the shades of Tmolus, crown'd with snow,
From Hyde's walls he rul'd the lands below,
Fierce as he springs, the sword his head divides;   445
The parted visage falls on equal sides:
With loud-resounding arms he strikes the plain;
While thus Achilles glories o'er the slain.

  Lie there, Otryntides¹ the Trojan earth
Receives thee dead, tho' Gygæ boast thy birth;   450
Those beauteous fields where Hyllus' waves are roll'd,
And plenteous Hermus swells with tides of gold,
Are thine no more——Th' insulting hero said,
And left him sleeping in eternal shade.
The rolling wheels of Greece the body tore,   455
And dash'd their axles with no vulgar gore.

  Demoleon next, Antenor's offspring, laid
Breathless in dust, the price of rashness paid.
Th' impatient steel with full descending sway
Forc'd thro' his brazen helm its furious way,   460
Resistless drove the batter'd skull before,
And dash'd and mingled all the brains with gore.

This sees Hippodamas, and seiz'd with fright,
Deserts his chariot for a swifter flight:
The lance arrests him: an ignoble wound   465
The panting Trojan rivets to the ground.
He groans away his soul: not louder rores
At Neptune's shrine on Helice's high shores
The victim bull; the rocks rebellow round,
And Ocean listens to the grateful sound.   470

   Then fell on Polydore his vengeful rage,
The youngest hope of Priam's stooping age:

 ỳ. 467.——Not louder rores
    At Neptune's shrine on Helice's high shores, etc]
In Helice, a town of Achaia, three quarters of a league
from the gulph of Corinth, Neptune had a magnificent
temple, where the Ionians offered every year to him a
sacrifice of a bull; and it was with these people an au-
spicious sign, and a certain mark, that the sacrifice would
be accepted, if the bull bellowed as he was led to the
altar After the Ionic migration, which happened a-
bout 140 years after the taking of Troy, the Ionians of
Asia assembled in the fields of Priene to celebrate the
same festival in honour of Heliconian Neptune; and as
those of Priene valued themselves upon being originally
of Helice, they chose for the king of the sacrifice a
young Prienian. It is needless to dispute from whence
the poet has taken his comparison, for as he lived 100,
or 121 years after the Ionic migration, it cannot be
doubted but he took it in the Asian Ionia, and at Priene
itself, where he had probably often assisted at that sacrifice, and been witness of the ceremonies therein observed This poet always appears strongly addicted to
the customs of the Ionians, which makes some conjecture that he was an Ionian himself. Eustathius. Dacier.
  ỳ. 571. Then fell on Polydore his vengeful rage.]

(Whofe feet for fwiftnefs in the race furpaft)
Of all his fons, the deareft, and the laft.
To the forbidden field he takes his flight   475
In the firft folly of a youthful knight,
To vaunt his fwiftnefs wheels around the plain,
But vaunts not long, with all his fwiftnefs flain.
Struck where the croffing belts unite behind,
And golden rings the double back-plate join'd :   480
Forth thro' the navel burft the thrilling fteel ;
And on his knees with piercing fhrieks he fell ;
The rufhing entrails pour'd upon the ground
His hands collect ; and darknefs wraps him round.
When Hector view'd, all ghaftly in his gore   485
Thus fadly flain, th' unhappy Polydore ;
A cloud of forrow overcaft his fight,
His foul no longer brook'd the diftant fight,
Full in Achilles' dreadful front he came,
And fhook his jav'lin like a waving flame.   490

Euripides in his Hecuba has followed another tradition,
when he makes Polydorus the fon of Priam and of Hecuba, and flain by Polymneftor king of Thrace, after
the taking of Troy, for according to Homer, he is not
the fon of Hecuba, but of Laothoe, as he fays in the
following book, and is flain by Achilles. Virgil too
has rather chofen to follow Euripides than Homer.

ŷ 489 *Full in Achil'es' dreadful front he came.*] The
great judgment of the poet in keeping the character of
his hero, is in this place very evident   when Achilles
was to engage Æneas, he holds a long conference with
him, and with patience bears the reply of Æneas: had
he purfued the fame method with Hector, he had departed from his character.   Anger is the prevailing paf-

The fon of Peleus fees, with joy poffeft,
His heart high-bounding in his rifing breaft:
And, lo! the man, on whom black fates attend;
The man, that flew Achilles, in his friend!
No more fhall Hector's and Pelides' fpear   495
Turn from each other in the walks of war——
Then with revengeful eyes he fcan'd him o'er:
Come, and receive thy fate! he fpake no more.

 Hector, undaunted, thus. Such words employ
To one that dreads thee, fome unwarlike boy: 500
Such we could give, defying and defy'd,
Mean intercourfe of obloquy and pride!
I know thy force to mine fuperior far;
But heav'n alone confers fuccefs in war:
Mean as I am, the Gods may guide my dart,   505
And give it entrance in a braver heart.

 Then parts the lance but Pallas' heav'nly breath
Far from Achilles wafts the winged death·
The bidden dart again to Hector flies,
And at the feet of its great mafter lies.   510
Achilles clofes with his hated foe,
His heart and eyes with flaming fury glow:

fion in Achilles· he left the field in a rage againft Agamemnon, and entered it again to be revenged of Hector the poet therefore judicioufly makes him take fire
at the fight of his enemy: he defcribes him as impatient
to kill him, he gives him a haughty challenge, and that
challenge is comprehended in a fingle line: his impatience to be revenged, would not fuffer him to delay it
by a length of words.

    F 3

But prefent to his aid, Apollo fhrouds
The favour'd hero in a veil of clouds.
Thrice ftruck Pelides with indignant heart,   515
Thrice in impaffive air he plung'd the dart:
The fpear a fourth time bury'd in the cloud,
He foams with fury, and exclaims aloud.

Wretch ! thou haft fcap'd again, once more thy flight
Has fav'd thee, and the partial God of light.   520
But long thou fhalt not thy juft fate withftand,
If any power affift Achilles' hand.
Fly then inglorious ! but thy flight this day
Whole hecatombs of Trojan ghofts fhall pay.

With that, he gluts his rage on numbers flain: 525
Then Dryops tumbled to th' enfanguin'd plain,
Pierc'd thro' the neck : he left him panting there,
And ftopp'd Demuchus, great Philetor's heir,

y. 513. *But prefent to his aid, Apollo.*] It is a common obfervation, that a God fhould never be introduced
into a poem but where his prefence is neceffary.   And
it may be afked why the life of Hector is of fuch importance that Apollo fhould refcue him from the hand
of Achilles here, and yet fuffer him to fall fo foon after?
Euftathius anfwers, that the poet had not yet fufficiently
exalted the valour of Achilles, he takes time to enlarge
upon his atchievements, and rifes by degrees in his character, till he completes both his courage and refentment
at one blow in the death of Hector.   And the poet,
adds he, pays a great compliment to his favourite countryman, by fhewing that nothing but the intervention
of a God could have faved Æneas and Hector from the
hand of Achilles.

Gigantic chief¹ deep gafh'd th' enormous blade,

And for the foul an ample paffage made.　　　　530

Laogonus and Dardanus expire,

The valiant fons of an unhappy fire;

Both in one inftant from the chariot hurl'd,

Sunk in one inftant to the nether world;

This diff'rence only their fad fates afford,　　　535

That one the fpear deftroy'd, and one the fword.

　　Nor lefs unpity'd, young Alaftor bleeds;

In vain his youth, in vain his beauty pleads:

In vain he begs thee with a fuppliant's moan,

To fpare a form, an age fo like thy own!　　　540

Unhappy boy! no pray'r, no moving art,

E'er bent that fierce, inexorable heart!

While yet he trembled at his knees, and cry'd,

The ruthlefs falchion ope'd his tender fide;

℣. 541. ——*No pray'r, no moving art*
　　　　E'er bent that fierce, inexorable heart!]

I confefs it is a fatisfaction to me, to obferve with what
art the poet purfues his fubject: the opening of the
poem profeffes to treat of the anger of Achilles; that
anger draws on all the great events of the ftory: and
Homer at every opportunity awakens the reader to an
attention to it, by mentioning the effects of it: fo that
when we fee in this place the hero deaf to youth and
compaffion, it is what we expect· mercy in him would
offend, becaufe it is contrary to his character.　Homer
propofes him not as a pattern for imitation; but the
moral of the poem which he defigned the reader fhould
draw from it, is, that we fhould avoid anger, fince it is
ever pernicious in the event.

The painting liver pours a flood of gore   545
That drowns his bosom till he pants no more.

Thro' Mulius' head then drove th' impetuous spear,
The warrior falls, transfix'd from ear to ear.
Thy life, Echeclus! next the sword bereaves,
Deep thro' the front the pond'rous faulchion cleaves;   550
Warm'd in the brain the smoaking weapon lies,
The purple death comes floating o'er his eyes.
Then brave Deucalion dy'd · the dart was flung
Where the knit nerves the pliant elbow strung;
He dropt his arm, an unassisting weight,   555
And stood all impotent, expecting fate:
Full on his neck the falling faulchion sped,
From his broad shoulders hew'd his crested head:
Forth from the bone the spinal marrow flies,
And sunk in dust, the corps extended lies   560
Rhigmus, whose race from fruitful Thracia came,
(The son of Pireus, an illustrious name,)
Succeeds to fate: the spear his belly rends;
Prone from his car the thund'ring chief descends:
The squire, who saw expiring on the ground   565
His prostrate master, rein'd the steeds around:
His back scarce turn'd the Pelian jav'lin gor'd;
And stretch'd the servant o'er his dying lord.
As when a flame the winding valley fills,
And runs on crackling shrubs between the hills;   570
Then o'er the stubble up the mountain flies,
Fires the high woods, and blazes to the skies,

This way and that, the spreading torrent rores;
So sweeps the hero thro' the wasted shores ;
Around him wide, immense destruction pours,   575
And earth is delug'd with the sanguine show'rs.

As with autumnal harvests cover'd o'er,

And thick bestrown, lies Ceres' sacred floor,

When round and round, with never-weary'd pain,

The trampling steers beat out th' un-number'd grain. 580

℣. 580. *The trampling steers beat out th' un number'd grain*] In Greece, instead of threshing the corn as we do, they caused it to be trod out by oxen; this was likewise practised in Judæa, as is seen by the law of God, who forbad the Jews to muzzle the ox who trod out the corn. *Non ligabis os bovis terentis in area fruges tuas.* Deut. xxv. Dacier.
The same practice is still preserved among the Turks and modern Greeks.

The similes at the end.] It is usual with our author to heap his similes very thick together at the conclusion of a book. He has done the same in the seventeenth ; it is the natural discharge of a vast imagination, heated in its progress, and giving itself vent in this croud of images.

I cannot close the notes upon this book, without observing the dreadful idea of Achilles, which the poet leaves upon the mind of the reader. He drives his chariot over shields, and mangled heaps of slain: the wheels, the axle tree, and the horses are stained with blood, the hero's eyes burn with fury, and his hands are red with slaughter. A painter might form from this passage the picture of Mars in the fullness of his terrors, as well as Phidias is said to have drawn from another, that of Jupiter in all his majesty.

So the fierce courfers, as the chariot rolls,
Tread down whole ranks, and crufh out heroes fouls.
Dafh'd from their hoofs while o'er the dead they fly,
Black, bloody drops the fmoaking chariot dye:
The fpiky wheels thro' heaps of carnage tore;   585
And thick the groaning axles dropp'd with gore.
High o'er the fcene of death Achilles ftood,
All grim with duft, all horrible in blood:
Yet ftill infatuate, ftill with rage on flame;
Such is the luft of never dying fame!   590

THE
ILIAD.

BOOK XXI.

THE ARGUMENT.

The battel in the river Scamander.

THE Trojans fly before Achilles, some towards the town, others to the river Scamander: he falls upon the latter with great slaughter, takes twelve captives alive, to sacrifice to the shade of Patroclus; and kills Lycaon and Asteropæus. Scamander attacks him with all his waves; Neptune and Pallas assist the hero; Simois joins Scamander; at length Vulcan, by the instigation of Juno, almost dries up the river. This combate ended, the other Gods engage each other. Meanwhile Achilles continues the slaughter, drives the rest into Troy: Agenor only makes a stand, and is conveyed away in a cloud by Apollo, who (to delude Achilles) takes upon him Agenor's shape, and while he pursues him in that disguise, gives the Trojans an opportunity of retiring into their city.

The same day continues. The scene is on the banks and in the stream of Scamander.

A ND now to Xanthus' gliding stream they drove,
 Xanthus, immortal progeny of Jove,
The river here divides the flying train.
Part to the town fly diverse o'er the plain,

This book is intirely different from all the foregoing: though it be a battel, it is intirely of a new and

Where late their troops triumphant bore the fight, 5
Now chas'd, and trembling in ignoble flight:
(These with a gather'd mist Saturnia shrouds,
And rolls behind the rout a heap of clouds)
Part plunge into the stream: old Xanthus rores,
The flashing billows beat the whiten'd shores: 10
With cries promiscuous all the banks resound,
And here, and there, in eddies whirling round,
The flouncing steeds and shrieking warriors drown'd. ⎬

surprizing kind, diversified with a vast variety of ima-
gery and description. The scene is totally changed:
he paints the combate of his hero with the rivers, and
describes a battel amidst an inundation It is observable, that though the whole war of the Iliad was upon the
banks of these rivers, Homer has artfully left out the
machinery of river-gods in all the other battels, to ag-
grandize this of his hero. There is no book of the
poem that has more force of imagination, or in which
the great and inexhausted invention of our author is
more powerfully exerted. After this description of an
inundation, there follows a very beautiful contrast in
that of the drought: the part of Achilles is admirably
sustained, and the new strokes which Homer gives to his
picture are such, as are derived from the very source of
his character, and finish the intire draught of this hero.

How far all that appears wonderful or extravagant
in this episode, may be reconciled to probability, truth
and natural reason, will be considered in a distinct note
on that head: the reader may find it on ẏ. 447.

ẏ. 2 *Xanthus, immortal progeny of Jove.*] The river
is here said to be the son of Jupiter, on account of its
being supplied with waters that fall from Jupiter, that
is, from heaven. Eustathius.

As

As the ſcorch'd locuſts from their fields retire,
While faſt behind them runs the blaze of fire;   15
Driv'n from the land before the ſmoaky cloud,
The cluſt'ring legions ruſh into the flood:
So plung'd in Xanthus by Achilles' force,
Roars the reſounding ſurge with men and horſe.

v. 14. *As the ſcorch'd locuſts*, etc.] Euſtathius obſerves that ſeveral countries have been much infeſted
with armies of locuſts; and that, to prevent their de-
ſtroying the fruits of the earth, the countrymen by
kindling large fires drove them from their fields; the locuſts to avoid the intenſe heat were forced to caſt themſelves into the water.   From this obſervation the poet
draws his alluſion, which is very much to the honour of
Achilles, ſince it repreſents the Trojans with reſpect to
him as no more than ſo many inſects.

The ſame commentator takes notice, that becauſe
the iſland of Cyprus in particular was uſed to practiſe
this method with the locuſts, ſome authors have conjectured that Homer was of that country.   But if this
were a ſufficient reaſon for ſuch a ſuppoſition, he might
be ſaid to be born in almoſt all the countries of the world,
ſince he draws his obſervations from the cuſtoms of
them all.

We may hence account for the innumerable armies
of theſe locuſts, mentioned among the plagues of Ægypt,
without having recourſe to an immediate creation, as
ſome good men have imagined, whereas the miracle indeed conſiſts in the wonderful manner of bringing them
upon the Ægyptians.   I have often obſerved with pleaſure the ſimilitude which many of Homer's expreſſions
bear with the holy ſcriptures, and that the moſt ancient
heathen writer in the world, often ſpeaks in the idiom
of Moſes: thus as the locuſts in Exodus are ſaid to be driven
into the ſea, ſo in Homer they are forced into a river.

His bloody lance the hero cafts afide,   20
(Which fpreading tam'rifks on the margin hide)
Then, like a God, the rapid billows braves,
Arm'd with his fword, high-brandifh'd o'er the waves:
Now down he plunges; now he whirls it round,
Deep groan'd the waters with the dying found;   25
Repeated wounds the red'ning river dy'd,
And the warm purple circled on the tide.
Swift thro' the foamy flood the Trojans fly,
And clofe in rocks or winding caverns lie.
So the huge dolphin tempefting the main,   30
In fhoals before him fly the fcaly train.
Confus'dly heap'd they feek their inmoft caves,
Or pant and heave beneath the floating waves.
Now tir'd with flaughter, from the Trojan band
Twelve chofen youths he drags alive to land;   35

℣. 30. *So the huge Dolphin*, etc] It is obfervable
with what juftnefs the author diverfifies his comparifons
according to the different fcenes and elements he is engaged in: Achilles has been hitherto on the land, and
compared to land-animals, a lion, etc.   Now he is in
the water, the poet derives his images from thence, and
likens him to a dolphin.   Euftathius.

℣. 34 *Now tir'd with flaughter.*] This is admirably
well fuited to the character of Achilles, his rage bears
him headlong on the enemy, he kills all that oppofe
him, and ftops not, until nature itfelf could not keep
pace with his anger; he had determined to referve
twelve noble youths to facrifice them to the Manes of
Patroclus, but his refentment gives him no time to think
of them, until the hurry of his paffion abates, and he is
tired with flaughter. without this circumftance, I think

With their rich belts their captive arms conftrains,
(Late their proud ornaments, but now their chains.)
Thefe his attendants to the fhips convey'd,
Sad victims! deftin'd to Patroclus' fhade.

an objection might naturally be raifed, that in the time
of a purfuit Achilles gave the enemy too much leifure to
efcape, while he bufied himfelf with tying thefe pri-
foners: though it is not abfolutely neceffary to fuppofe
he tyed them with his own hands.

ẏ. 35. *Twelve chofen youths.*] This piece of cruelty
in Achilles has appeared fhocking to many, and indeed
is what I think can only be excufed by confidering the
ferocious and vindictive fpirit of this hero   It is however certain that the cruelties exercifed on enemies in
war were authorifed by the military laws of thofe times;
nay, religion itfelf became a fanction to them.   It is
not only the fierce Achilles, but the pious and religious
Æneas, whofe very character is virtue and compaffion,
that referves feveral young unfortunate captives taken
in battel, to facrifice them to the Manes of his favourite
hero, Æn. 10. ẏ. 517.

——————Sulmone creatos
Quatuor hic juvenes, totidem quos educat Ufens
Viventes rapit, inferias quos immolet umbris,
Captivoque rogi perfundat fanguine flammas.

And Æn. 11. ẏ. 81.

Vinxerat et poft terga manus, quos mitteret umbris,
Inferias, cæfo fparfuros fanguine flammam.

And (what is very particular) the Latin poet expreffes
no difapprobation of the action, which the Grecian does
in plain terms, fpeaking of this in Iliad 23. ẏ. 176.

------------Κακὰ δὲ φρεσὶ μήδετο ἔργα.

Then, as once more he plung'd amid the flood,   40
The young Lycaon in his paffage ftood;
The fon of Priam, whom the hero's hand
But late made captive in his father's land,
(As from a fycamore, his founding fteel
Lopp'd the green arms to fpoke a chariot-wheel)   45
To Lemnos ifle he fold the royal flave,
Where Jafon's fon the price demanded gave;
But kind Eetion touching on the fhore,
The ranfom'd prince to fair Arifbe bore.
Ten days were paft, fince in his father's reign   50
He felt the fweets of liberty again;

ỳ 41. *The young Lycaon*, etc.] Homer has a wonderful art and judgment in contriving fuch incidents as
fet the characteriftic qualities of his heroes in the higheft
point of light.   There is hardly any in the whole Iliad
more proper to move pity than this circumftance of
Lycaon, or to raife terror, than this view of Achilles.
It is alfo the fineft picture of them both imaginable: we
fee the different attitude of their perfons, and the different paffions which appeared in their countenances:
at firft Achilles ftands erect, with furprize in his looks
at the fight of one whom he thought it impoffible to
find there, while Lycaon is in the pofture of a fuppliant,
with looks that plead for compaffion; with one hand
holding the hero's lance, and his knee with the other:
afterwards, when at his death he lets go the fpear, and
places himfelf on his knees with his arms extended, to
receive the mortal wound, how lively and how ftrongly
is this painted! I believe every one perceives the beauty
of this paffage, and allows that poetry (at leaft in Homer) is truly a fpeaking picture.

The next, that God whom men in vain withstand,
Gives the same youth to the same conqu'ring hand;
Now never to return! and doom'd to go
A sadder journey to the shades below.   55
His well known face when great Achilles ey'd,
(The helm and visor he had cast aside
With wild affright, and drop'd upon the field
His useless lance and unavailing shield.)
As trembling, panting, from the stream he fled,   60
And knock'd his fault'ring knees, the hero said.

   Ye mighty Gods! what wonders strike my view!
Is it in vain our conqu'ring arms subdue?
Sure I shall see yon' heaps of Trojans kill'd,
Rise from the shades, and brave me on the field: 65
As now the captive, whom so late I bound,
And sold to Lemnos, stalks on Trojan ground!
Not him the sea's unmeasur'd deeps detain,
That barr such numbers from their native plain:
Lo! he returns.   Try then, my flying spear!   70
Try, if the grave can hold the wanderer;
If earth at length this active prince can seize,
Earth, whose strong grasp has held down Hercules.

   Thus while he spake, the Trojan, pale with fears,
Approach'd, and sought his knees with suppliant tears; 75
Loth as he was to yield his youthful breath,
And his soul shiv'ring at th' approach of death.
Achilles rais'd the spear, prepar'd to wound;
He kiss'd his feet, extended on the ground:

And while above the spear suspended stood,   80
Longing to dip its thirsty point in blood,
One hand embrac'd them close, one stopt the dart;
While thus these melting words attempt his heart.

Thy well-known captive, great Achilles! see,
Once more Lycaon trembles at thy knee.   85
Some pity to a supplicant's name afford,
Who shar'd the gifts of Ceres at thy board;
Whom late thy conqu'ring arm to Lemnos bore,
Far from his father, friends, and native shore;

℣. 84. *The speeches of Lycaon and Achilles.*] It is impossible for any thing to be better imagined than these
two speeches: that of Lycaon is moving and compassionate; that of Achilles haughty and dreadful; the one
pleads with the utmost tenderness, the other denies with
the utmost sternness: one would think it impossible to
amass so many moving arguments in so few words as
those of Lycaon: he forgets no circumstance to soften
his enemy's anger, he flatters the memory of Patroclus,
is afraid of being thought too nearly related to Hector,
and would willingly put himself upon him as a supplicant,
and consequently as an inviolable person: but Achilles
is immoveable, his resentment makes him deaf to intreaties, and it must be remembered that anger, not
mercy, is his character.

I must confess I could have wished Achilles had spar-
ed him: there are so many circumstances that speak in
his favour, that he deserved his life, had he not asked it
in terms a little too abject.

There is an air of greatness in the conclusion of the
speech of Achilles, which strikes me very much: he
speaks very unconcernedly of his own death, and upbraids his enemy for asking life so earnestly, a life that
was of so much less importance than his own.

A hundred oxen were his price that day,   90
Now fums immenfe thy mercy fhall repay.
Scarce refpited from woes I yet appear,
And fcarce twelve morning funs have feen me here;
Lo! Jove again fubmits me to thy hands,
Again, her victim cruel fate demands!   95
I fprung from Priam, and Laothoe fair,
(Old Alte's daughter, and Lelegia's heir;
Who held in Pedafus his fam'd abode,
And rul'd the fields where filver Satnio flow'd)
Two fons (alas! unhappy fons) fhe bore;   100
For ah! one fpear fhall drink each brother's gore,
And I fucceed to flaughter'd Polydore.
How from that arm of terror fhall I fly?
Some dæmon urges! 'tis my doom to die!
If ever yet foft pity touch'd thy mind,   105
Ah! think not me too much of Hector's kind!
Not the fame mother gave thy fuppliant breath,
With his, who wrought thy lov'd Patroclus' death.

   Thefe words, attended with a fhow'r of tears,
The youth addreft to unrelenting ears: 110
Talk not of life, or ranfom, (he replies)
Patroclus dead, whoever meets me, dies:
In vain a fingle Trojan fues for grace;
But leaft, the fons of Priam's hateful race.
Die then, my friend! what boots it to deplore?   115
The great, the good Patroclus is no more!
He, far thy better, was foredoom'd to die,
" And thou, doft thou, bewail mortality?

See'ft thou not me, whom nature's gifts adorn,
Sprung from a hero, from a Goddefs born;   120
The day fhall come (which nothing can avert)
When by the fpear, the arrow, or the dart,
By night, or day, by force or by defign,
Impending death and certain fate are mine.
Die then——he faid ; and as the word he fpoke,   125
The fainting ftripling funk, before the ftroke:
His hand forgot its grafp, and left the fpear ;
While all his trembling frame confeft his fear.
Sudden, Achilles his broad fword difplay'd,
And buried in his neck the reeking blade.   130
Prone fell the youth ; and panting on the land,
The gufhing purple dy'd the thirfty fand :
The victor to the ftream the carcafs gave,
And thus infults him, floating on the wave.

   Lie there, Lycaon ! let the fifh furround   135
Thy bloated corfe, and fuck thy goary wound ·
There no fad mother fhall thy fun'rals weep,
But fwift Scamander roll thee to the deep,
Who'e ev'ry wave fome wat'ry monfter brings,
To feaft unpunifh'd on the fat of kings.   140

Ỳ. 121. *The day fha'll come——*
    When by the fpear, the arrow, or the dart
This is not fpoken at random, but with an air of fuperiority ; when Achilles fays he fhall fall by an arrow,
a dart or a fpear, he infinuates that no man will have
the coarage to approach him in a clofe fight, or engage
him hand to hand.   Euftathius.

So perish Troy, and all the Trojan line!
Such ruin theirs, and such compaffion mine.
What boots ye now Scamander's worfhip'd ftream,
His earthly honours, and immortal name!
In vain your immolated bulls are flain,   145
Your living courfers glut his gulphs in vain:
Thus he rewards you, with this bitter fate;
Thus, till the Grecian vengeance is compleat;
Thus is aton'd Patroclus' honour'd fhade,
And the fhort abfence of Achilles paid.   150

    Thefe boaftful words provoke the raging God;
With fury fwells the violated flood.

    x. 146. Your living courfers glut his gulphs in vain]
It was an ancient cuftom to caft living horfes into the
fea, and into rivers, to honour, as it were, by thefe
victims, the rapidity of their ftreams. This practice continued a long time, and hiftory fupplies us with examples of it · Aurelius Victor fays of Pompey the younger,
*Cum mari feliciter uteretur, Neptuni fe filium confeffus eft,
eumque bobus auratis et equo placavit.* He offered oxen
in facrifice, and threw a living horfe into the fea, as appears from Dion, which is perfectly conformable to this
of Homer. Euftathius. Dacier.

    x. 152. With fury fwells the violated flood] The
poet has been preparing us for the epifode of the river
Xanthus ever fince the beginning of the laft book; and
here he gives us an account why the river wars upon
Achilles. it is not only becaufe he is a river of Troas,
but, as Euftathius remarks, becaufe it is in defence of a
man that was defcended from a brother river-God: he
was angry too with Achilles on another account, becaufe
he had choaked up his current with the bodies of his
countrymen, the Trojans.

What means divine may yet the pow'r employ,
To check Achilles, and to rescue Troy?
Meanwhile the hero springs in arms, to dare   155
The great Asteropeus to mortal war;
The son of Pelagon, whose lofty line
Flows from the source of Axius, stream divine!
(Fair Peribæa's love the God had crown'd,
With all his refluent waters circled round)   160
On him Achilles rush'd: he fearless stood,
And shook two spears, advancing from the flood;
The flood impell'd him, on Pelides' head
T' avenge his waters choak'd with heaps of dead,
Near as they drew, Achilles thus began.   165

What art thou, boldest of the race of man?
Who, or from whence? Unhappy is the fire,
Whose son encounters our resistless ire.

O son of Peleus! what avails to trace
(Reply'd the warrior) our illustrious race?   170
From rich Pæonia's valleys I command
Arms with protended spears, my native band;

℣. 171 *From rich Pæonia's——*etc.] In the catalogue Pyræchmes is said to be commander of the Pæonians, where they are described as bow-men; but here
they are said to be armed with spears, and to have Asteropæus for their general. Eustathius tells us, some critics asserted that this line in the Cat. ℣. 355.

Πηλεγόνος θ' υἱὸς περιδέξιος Ἀστεροπαῖος,
followed
Αὐτὰρ Πυραίχμης ἄγε Παίονας ἀγκυλοτόξυς.

But I see no reason for such an assertion. Homer has

Now fhines the tenth bright morning fince I came
In aid of Ilion to the fields of fame :
Axius, who fwells with all the neighb'ring rills,   175
And wide around the floated region fills,
Begot my fire, whofe fpear fuch glory won :
Now lift thy arm, and try that hero's fon!

　　Threat'ning he faid : the hoftile chiefs advance :
At once Afteropeus difcharg'd each lance,   180
(For both his dext'rous hands the lance cou'd wield)
One ftruck, but pierc'd not the Vulcanian fhield ;
One raz'd Achilles' hand ; the fpouting blood
Spun forth, in earth the faften'd weapon ftood.
Like lightning next the Pelian jav'lin flies :   185
Its erring fury hifs'd along the fkies :
Deep in the fwelling bank was driv'n the fpear,
Ev'n to the middle earth'd ; and quiver'd there.

exprefly told us in this fpeech that it was but ten days
fince he came to the aid of Troy ; he might be made
general of the Pæonians upon the death of Pyræchmes,
who was killed in the fixteenth book.   Why alfo might
not the Pœonians, as well as Teucer, excel in the management both of the bow and the fpear?
　　ỳ. 187. *Deep in the fwelling bank was driv'n the fpear*
　　　　　Ev'n to the middle earth'd,———]
It was impoffible for the poet to give us a greater idea
of the ftrength of Achilles than he has by this circumftance : his fpear pierc'd fo deep into the ground, that
another hero of great ftrength could not difengage it by
repeated efforts, but immediately after, Achilles draws
it with the utmoft eafe· how prodigious was the force
of that arm that could drive at one throw a fpear half
way into the earth, and then with a touch releafe it?

Then from his fide the fword Pelides drew,
And on his foe with doubled fury flew.   190
The foe thrice tugg'd, and fhook the rooted wood;
Repulfive of his might the weapon ftood:
The fourth, he tries to break the fpear in vain;
Bent as he ftands, he tumbles to the plain;
His belly open'd with a ghaftly wound,   195
The reeking entrails pour upon the ground.
Beneath the hero's feet he panting lies,
And his eye darkens, and his fpirit flies:
While the proud victor thus triumphing faid,
His radiant armour tearing from the dead: 200
    So ends thy glory! fuch the fate they prove
Who ftrive prefumptuous with the fons of Jove.
Sprung from a river didft thou boaft thy line,
But great Saturnius is the fource of mine.
How durft thou vaunt thy wat'ry progeny?   205
Of Peleus, Æacus, and Jove, am I;
The race of thefe fuperior far to thofe,
As he that thunders to the ftream that flows.
What rivers can, Scamander might have fhown;
But Jove he dreads, nor wars againft his fon.   210
Ev'n Achelous might contend in vain,
And all the roaring billows of the main.
Th' eternal Ocean, from whofe fountains flow
The feas, the rivers, and the fprings below,
The thund'ring voice of Jove abhors to hear,   215
And in his deep abyffes fhakes with fear.

                                                    He

He said; then from the bank his jav'lin tore,
And left the breathless warrior in his gore.
The floating tides the bloody carcass lave,
And beat against it, wave succeeding wave;   220
Till roll'd between the banks, it lies the food
Of curling eels, and fishes of the flood.
All scatter'd round the stream (their mightiest slain)
Th' amaz'd Pæonians scour along the plain:
He vents his fury on the flying crew,   225
Thrasius, Astypylus, and Mnesus slew;
Mydon, Thersilochus, with Ænius fell;
And numbers more his lance had plung'd to hell;
But from the bottom of his gulphs profound,
Scamander spoke, the shores return'd the sound.   230

   O first of mortals! (for the Gods are thine)
In valour matchless, and in force divine!
If Jove have giv'n thee ev'ry Trojan head,
'Tis not on me thy rage should heap the dead.
See! my choak'd streams no more their course can keep,
Nor roll their wonted tribute to the deep.   236
Turn then, impetuous! from our injur'd flood:
Content, thy slaughters could amaze a God.

   In human form confess'd before his eyes
The river thus; and thus the chief replies.   240
O sacred stream! thy word we shall obey;
But not till Troy the destin'd vengeance pay,
Not till within her tow'rs the perjur'd train
Shall pant, and tremble at our arms again;

Not till proud Hector, guardian of her wall,   245
Or stain this lance, or see Achilles fall.

He said; and drove with fury on the foe.
Then to the Godhead of the silver bow
The yellow flood began : O son of Jove !
Was not the mandate of the sire above   250
Full and exprefs' that Phœbus fhould employ
His facred arrows in defence of Troy,
And make her conquer, till Hyperion's fall
In awful darknefs hide the face of all ?

He fpoke in vain——the chief without difmay   255
Ploughs thro' the boiling furge his defp'rate way.
Then rifing in his rage above the fhores,
From all his deep the bellowing river rores,
Huge heaps of flain difgorges on the coaft,
And round the banks the ghaftly dead are toft.   260
While all before, the billows rang'd on high
(A wat'ry bulwark) fkreen the bands who fly.
Now burfting on his head with thund'ring found,
The falling deluge whelms the hero round :

$\mathcal{Y}$. 263 *Now burft ng on his head*, etc.] There is a great beauty in the verfification of this whole paffage in Homer · fome of the verfes run hoarfe, full and fonorous, like the torrent they defcribe; others by their broken cadences, and fudden ftops, image the difficulty, labour and interruption of the hero's march againft it.   The fall of the elm, the tearing up of the bank, the rufhing of the branches in the water, are all put into fuch words, that almoft every letter correfponds in its found, and echoes to the fenfe, of each particular.

His loaded shield bends to the rushing tide;   265
His feet, upborn, scarce the strong flood divide,
Slidd'ring, and stagg'ring.   On the border stood
A spreading elm, that overhung the flood;
He seiz'd a bending bough, his steps to stay;
The plant uprooted to his weight gave way,   270
Heaving the bank, and undermining all;
Loud flash the waters to the rushing fall
Of the thick foliage.   The large trunk display'd
Bridg'd the rough flood across: the hero stay'd
On this his weight, and rais'd upon his hand,   275
Leap'd from the chanel, and regain'd the land.

℣. 274 *Bridg'd the rough flood across———*] If we
had no other account of the river Xanthus but this, it
were alone sufficient to shew that the current could not
be very wide; for the poet here says that the elm stretched from bank to bank, and as it were made a bridge o-
ver it · the suddenness of this inundation perfectly well
agrees with a narrow river.

℣. 276. *Leap'd from the chanel.*] Eustathius recites
a criticism on this verse; in the original the word Λίμνη
signifies Stagnum, Palus, a *standing water*, now this is
certainly contrary to the idea of a river, which always
implies a *current*: to solve this, says that author, some
have supposed that the tree which lay across the river
stopped the flow of the waters, and forced them to
spread as it were into a pool.   Others, dissatisfied with
this solution, think that a mistake is crept into the text,
and that instead of ἐκ Λίμνης, should be inserted ἐκ Δίνης.
But I do not see the necessity of having recourse to either of these solutions; for why may not the word Λίμνη
signify here the *chanel* of the river, as it evidently does
in the 317th verse?   And nothing being more common

Then blacken'd the wild waves; the murmur rofe;
The God purfues, a huger billow throws,
And burfts the bank, ambitious to deftroy
The man whofe fury is the fate of Troy.　　　　　　28$
He, like the warlike eagle fpeeds his pace,
(Swifteft and ftrongeft of th' aerial race)
Far as a fpear can fly, Achilles fprings
At ev'ry bound; his clanging armour rings:
Now here, now there, he turns on ev'ry fide,　　　　28$
And winds his courfe before the following tide;
The waves flow after, wherefoe'er he wheels,
And gather faft, and murmur at his heels.
So when a peafant to his garden brings
Soft rills of water from the bubbling fprings,　　　　290,

than to fubftitute a part for the whole, why may not the
chanel be fuppofed to imply the whole river?

ẏ. 289　So when a peafant to his garden brings, etc]
This changing of the character is very beautiful. no
poet ever knew, like Homer, to pafs from the vehement
and the nervous, to the gentle and agreeable; fuch tran-
fitions, when properly made, give a fingular pleafure,
as when in mufic a mafter paffes from the rough to the
tender.　Demetrius Phalereus, who only praifes this
comparifon for its clearnefs, has not fufficiently recommended its beauty and value　Virgil has transferred it
into his firft book of the Georgics, ẏ. 106.

Deinde fatis fluvium inducit, rivofque fequentes.
Et cum exuftus ager morientibus æftuat herbis,
Ecce fupercilio clivofi tramitis undam
Elicit. Illa cadens raucum per levia murmur
Saxa ciet, fcatebrifque arentia temperat arva.
　　　　　　　　　　　　　　　　　　Dacier.

And calls the floods from high, to bless his bow'rs,
And feed with pregnant streams the plants and flow'rs;
Soon as he clears whate'er their passage staid,
And marks the future current with his spade,
Swift o'er the rolling pebbles, down the hills   295
Louder and louder purl the falling rills,
Before him scatt'ring, they prevent his pains,
And shine in mazy wand'rings o'er the plains.

 Still flies Achilles, but before his eyes
Still swift Scamander rolls where-e'er he flies: 300
Not all his speed escapes the rapid floods;
The first of men, but not a match for Gods.
Oft' as he t rn'd the torrent to oppose,
And bravely try if all the pow'rs were foes;
So oft' the surge, in wat'ry mountains spread,   305
Beat on his back, or bursts upon his head.
Yet dauntless still the adverse flood he braves,
And still indignant bounds above the waves.
Tir'd by the tides, his knees relax with toil;
Wash'd from beneath him slides the slimy soil;   310
When thus (his eyes on heav'n's expansion thrown)
Forth bursts the hero with an angry groan.

 Is there no God Achilles to befriend,
No pow'r t'avert his miserable end?
Prevent, oh Jove! this ignominious date,   315
And make my future life the sport of fate.
Of all heav'n's oracles believ'd in vain,
But most of Thetis, must her son complain;

By Phœbus' darts she prophesy'd my fall,
In glorious arms before the Trojan wall.   320
Oh! had I dy'd in fields of battel warm,
Stretch'd like a hero, by a hero's arm!

℣. 321. *Oh had I dy'd in fields of battel warm!* etc]
Nothing is more agreeable than this wish to the heroic
character of Achilles· glory is his prevailing passion;
he grieves not that he must die, but that he should die
unlike a man of honour.   Virgil has made use of the
same thought in the same circumstance, where Æneas is
in danger of being drowned, Æn. 1 ℣. 98.

———— O terque quaterque beati,
Queis ante ora patrum Trojæ sub mœnibus altis
Contigit oppetere! O Danaum fortissime gentis
Tydide, mene Iliacis occumbere campis
Non potuisse? tuaque animam hanc effundere dextra?

Lucan in the fifth book of his Pharsalia, representing
Cæsar in the same circumstance, has (I think) carried
yet farther the character of ambition, and a boundless
thirst of glory, in his hero; when, after he has repined
in the same manner with Achilles, he acquiesces at last
in the reflection of the glory he had already acquired;

———————Licet ingentes abruperit actus
Festinata dies fat·s, sat magna peregi.
Arctoas domui gentes. Inimica subegi
Arma manu. Vidit Magnum mihi Roma secundum.

And only wishes that his obscure fate might be concealed, in the view that all the world might still fear and expect him.

———— ————Lacerum retinete cadaver
Fluctibus in mediis, desit mihi busta, rogusque,
Dum metuar semper terraque expecter ab omni.

Might Hector's spear this dauntless bosom rend,
And my swift soul o'ertake my slaughter'd friend!
Ah no! Achilles meets a shameful fate,   325
Oh how unworthy of the brave and great!
Like some vile swain, whom on a rainy day,
Crossing a ford, the torrent sweeps away,
An unregarded carcase to the sea.

  Neptune and Pallas haste to his relief,   330
And thus in human form address the chief:
The pow'r of Ocean first.   Forbear thy fear,
Oh son of Peleus! Lo thy Gods appear!
Behold! from Jove descending to thy aid,
Propitious Neptune, and the blue-ey'd maid.   335
Stay, and the furious flood shall cease to rave:
'Tis not thy fate to glut his angry wave.
But thou, the counsel heav'n suggests, attend!
Nor breathe from combate, nor thy sword suspend,
'Till Troy receive her flying sons, 'till all   340
Her routed squadrons pant behind their wall:
Hector alone shall stand his fatal chance,
And Hector's blood shall smoke upon thy lance.
Thine is the glory doom'd.   Thus spake the Gods:
Then swift ascended to the bright abodes.   345

  Stung with new ardour, thus by heav'n impell'd,
He springs impetuous, and invades the field:
O'er all th' expanded plain the waters spread;
Heav'd on the bounding billows danc'd the dead,
Floating 'midst scatter'd arms; while casques of gold   350
And turn'd-up bucklers glitter'd as they roll'd.

High o'er the furging tide, by leaps and bounds,
He wades, and mounts; the parted wave refounds.
Not a whole river ftops the hero's courfe,
While Pallas fills him with immortal force.   355
With equal rage, indignant Xanthus rores,
And lifts his billows, and o'erwhelms his fhores.

   Then thus to Simois: hafte, my brother flood!
And check this mortal that controuls a God:
Our braveft heroes elfe fhall quit the fight,   360
And Ilion tumble from her tow'ry height.
Call then thy fubject ftreams, and bid them rore,
From all thy fountains fwell thy wat'ry ftore,
With broken rocks, and with a load of dead
Charge the black furge, and pour it on his head.   365
Mark how refiftlefs thro' the floods he goes,
And boldly bids the warring Gods be foes !
But nor that force, nor form divine to fight
Shall ought avail him, if our rage unite:
Whelm'd under our dark gulphs thofe arms fhall lie, 370
That blaze fo dreadful in each Trojan eye;
And deep beneath a fandy mountain hurl'd,
Immers'd remain this terror of the world
Such pond'rous ruin fhall confound the place,
No Greek fhall e'er his perifh'd relicks grace,   375
No hand his bones fhall gather, or inhume;
Thefe his cold rites, and this his wat'ry tomb.

   He faid; and on the chief defcends amain,
Increas'd with gore, and fwelling with the flain.

Then murm'ring from his beds, he boils, he raves, 380
And a foam whitens on the purple waves:
At ev'ry step, before Achilles stood
The crimson surge, and delug'd him with blood.
Fear touch'd the queen of heav'n: she saw dismay'd,
She call'd aloud, and summon'd Vulcan's aid.   385

   Rise to the war! th' insulting flood requires
Thy wasteful arm: assemble all thy fires!
While to their aid, by our command enjoin'd,
Rush the swift eastern and the western wind:
These from old Ocean at my word shall blow,   390
Pour the red torrent on the wat'ry foe,
Corses and arms to one bright ruin turn,
And hissing rivers to their bottoms burn.
Go, mighty in thy rage! display thy pow'r,
Drink the whole flood, the crackling trees devour, 395
Scorch all the banks! and ('till our voice reclaim)
Exert th' unweary'd furies of the flame!

   The pow'r ignipotent her word obeys:
Wide o'er the plain he pours the boundless blaze;
At once consumes the dead, and dries the soil;   400
And the shrunk waters in their chanel boil:
As when autumnal Boreas sweeps the sky,
And instant blows the water'd gardens dry:
So look'd the field, so whiten'd was the ground,
While Vulcan breath'd the fiery blast around.   405

℣ 405 *While Vulcan breath'd the fiery blast around.*]
It is in the original, ℣. 355.

Πνοιῇ τειρόμενοι πολυμήτιος Ἡφαίσιο.

Swift on the sedgy reeds the ruin preys;
Along the margin winds the running blaze:
The trees in flaming rows to ashes turn,
The flow'ry Lotos, and the tam'risk burn,
Broad elm, and cypress rising in a spire;   410
The wat'ry willows hiss before the fire.
Now glow the waves, the fishes pant for breath,
The eels lie twisting in the pangs of death:
Now flounce aloft, now dive the scaly fry,
Or gasping, turn their bellies to the sky.   415
At length the river rear'd his languid head,
And thus, short-panting, to the God he said.

Oh Vulcan! oh! what pow'r resists thy might?
I faint, I sink, unequal to the fight——
I yield——Let Ilion fall; if fate decree——   420
Ah——bend no more thy fiery arms on me!

He ceas'd; wide conflagration blazing round;
The bubling waters yield a hissing sound.

The epithet given to Vulcan in this verse (as well as in
the 367th) Ἡφαίστοιο πολύφρονος, has no sort of allusion to
the action described: for what has his *wisdom* or *knowlege* to do with burning up the river Xanthus? This is
usual in our author, and much exclaimed against by his
modern antagonists, whom Mr. Boileau very well answers   " It is not so strange in Homer to give these
" epithets to persons upon occasions which can have
" no reference to them, the same is frequent in modern
" languages, in which we call a man by the name of
" Saint, when we speak of any action of his that has
" not the least regard to his *sanctity*   as when we say,
" for example, that St. Paul held the garments of those
" who stoned St. Stephen."

As when the flames beneath a caldron rise,
To melt the fat of some rich sacrifice,   425
Amid the fierce embrace of circling fires
The waters foam, the heavy smoak aspires:
So boils th' imprison'd flood, forbid to flow,
And choak'd with vapours, feels his bottom glow.
To Juno then, imperial queen of air,   430
The burning river sends his earnest pray'r.

Ah why, Saturnia! must thy son engage
Me, only me, with all his wasteful rage?
On other Gods his dreadful arm employ,
For mightier Gods assert the cause of Troy.   435
Submissive I desist, if thou command,
But ah! withdraw this all-destroying hand.
Hear then my solemn oath, to yield to fate
Unaided Ilion, and her destin'd state,
'Till Greece shall gird her with destructive flame,   440
And in one ruin sink the Trojan name.

𝒱. 424. *As when the flames beneath a caldron rise.*]
It is impossible to render literally such passages with any
tolerable beauty. These ideas can never be made to
shine in English, some particularities cannot be preserved, but the Greek language gives them lustre, the words
are noble and musical.

Ὡς δὲ λέβης ζῖ ἔνδοι ἐπειγόμενος περὶ πολλῷ,
Κνίσσῃ μελδόμενος ἀπαλοτρεφέος σιάλοιο,
Πάντοθεν ἀμβολάδην, ὑπὸ δὲ ξύλα κάγκανα κεῖται.

All therefore that can be expected from a translator is
to preserve the meaning of the simile, and embellish it
with some words of affinity that carry nothing low in
the sense or sound.

His warm intreaty touch'd Saturnia's ear:
She bade th' ignipotent his rage forbear,
Recall the flame, nor in a mortal cause
Infeſt a God: th' obedient flame withdraws: 445
Again, the branching ſtreams begin to ſpread,
And ſoft re-murmur in their wonted bed.

ẏ 447. *And ſoft re-murmur in their wonted bed.*]
Here ends the *epiſode* of the *river-fight*, and I muſt here
lay before the reader my thoughts upon the whole of it;
which appears to be in part an allegory, and in part a
true hiſtory. Nothing can give a better idea of Homer's
manner of enlivening his inanimate machines, and of
making the plaineſt and ſimpleſt incidents noble and
poetical, than to conſider the whole paſſage in the common hiſtorical ſenſe, which I ſuppoſe to be no more
than this.   There happened a great overflow of the
river Xanthus during the ſiege, which very much incom-
moded the aſſailants: this gave occaſion for the fiction
of an engagement between Achilles and the river-god:
Xanthus calling Simois to aſſiſt him, implies that theſe
two neighbouring rivers joined in the inundation Pallas and Neptune relieve Achilles, that is, Pallas, or the
wiſdom of Achilles, found ſome means to divert the
waters, and turn them into the *ſea*, wherefore Neptune,
the God of it, is feigned to aſſiſt him. Jupiter and Juno
(by which are underſtood the aerial regions) conſent to
aid Achilles; that may ſignify, that after this great flood
there happened a warm, dry, windy ſeaſon, which aſ-
ſuaged the waters, and dried the ground · and what
makes this in a manner plain, is, that Juno (which
ſignifies the *air*) promiſes to ſend the *north* and *weſt*
wind, to diſtreſs the river   Xanthus being conſumed
by Vulcan, that is, dried up with heat, prays to Juno
to relieve him . what is this, but that the drought having drunk up his ſtreams, he has recourſe to the *air* for
rains

While thefe by Juno's will the ftrife refign,
The warring Gods in fierce contention join:
Re-kindling rage each heav'nly breaft alarms;   450
With horrid clangor fhock'd th' æthereal arms ·
Heav'n in loud thunder bids the trumpet found;
And wide beneath them groans the rending ground.
Jove, as his fport, the dreadful fcene defcries,
And views contending Gods with carelefs eyes.   455

rains to re-fupply his current? Or, perhaps the whole may fignify no more, than that Achilles being on the farther fide of the river, plunged himfelf in to purfue the enemy; that in this adventure he run the rifk of being drowned; that to fave himfelf he laid hold on a fallen tree, which ferved to keep him a-float; that he was ftill carried down the ftream to the place where was the confluence of the two rivers (which is expreffed by the one calling the other to his aid) and that when he came nearer the fea [Neptune] he found means by his prudence [Pallas] to fave himfelf from his danger.

If the reader ftill fhould think, the fiction of rivers fpeaking and fighting is too bold, the objection will vanifh by confidering how much the heathen mythology authorizes the reprefentation of rivers as perfons: nay, even in old hiftorians nothing is more common than ftories of rapes committed by river-gods; and the fiction was no way unprecedented, after one of the fame nature fo well known, as the engagement between Hercules and the river Achelous.

℣. 454 *Jove, as his fport, the dreadful fcene defcries,*
And views contending Gods with carelefs eyes.]
I was at a lofs for the reafon why Jupiter is faid to fmile at the difcord of the gods, till I found it in Euftathius; Jupiter, fays he, who is the lord of nature, is well pleafed with the war of the gods, that is, of earth, fea, and air, etc. becaufe the harmony of all beings arifes

The pow'r of battels lifts his brazen spear,
And first assaults the radiant queen of war.

What mov'd thy madness, thus to dif-unite
Æthereal minds, and mix all heav'n in fight?
What wonder this, when in thy frantic mood   460
Thou drov'st a mortal to insult a God;
Thy impious hand Tydides' jav'lin bore,
And madly bath'd it in celestial gore.

He spoke, and smote the loud refounding shield,
Which bears Jove's thunder on its dreadful field;   465
The adamantine Ægis of her fire,
That turns the glancing bolt, and forked fire.

from that difcord · thus earth is oppofite to water, air
to earth, and water to them all; and yet from this oppofition arifes that difcordant concord by which all nature fubfifts.   Thus heat and cold, moift and dry, are
in a continual war, yet upon this depends the fertility of
the earth, and the beauty of the creation.   So that Jupiter, who according to the Greeks is the foul of all,
may well be faid to fmile at this contention.

ỳ. 456 *The power of battels*, etc] The combate of
Mars and Pallas is plainly allegorical juftice and wifdom
demanded that an end fhould be put to this terrible war:
the god of war oppofes this, but is worfted.   Euftathius
fays that this holds forth the oppofition of rage and
wifdom; and no fooner has our reafon fubdued one
temptation, but another fucceeds to reinforce it, as
Venus fuccours Mars.   The poet feems farther to in-
finuate, that reafon when it refifts a temptation vigoroaf-
ly, eafily overcomes it: fo it is with the utmoft facility,
that Pallas conquers both Mars and Venus   He adds,
that Pallas retreated from Mars in order to conquer him.
this fhews us, that the beft way to fubdue a temptation
is to retreat from it.

Then heav'd the Goddess in her mighty hand
A stone, the limit of the neighb'ring land,
There fix'd from eldest times; black, craggy, vast · 470
This, at the heav'nly homicide she cast.

𝒯. 468. *Then heav'd the Goddess in her mighty hand*
A stone, etc]

The poet has described many of his heroes in former parts
of his poem, as throwing stones of enormous bulk and
weight, but here he rises in his image he is describing
a goddess, and has found a way to make that action
excel all human strength, and be equal to a deity.

Virgil has imitated this passage in his twelfth book,
and applied it to Turnus, but I cannot help thinking
that the action in a mortal is somewhat extravagantly
imagined what principally renders it so, is an addition
of two lines to this simile which he borrows from another part of Homer, only with this difference, that whereas Homer says no two men could raise such a stone,
Virgil extends it to twelve.

———*Saxum circumspicit ingens,*
Saxum, antiquum, ingens, campo quod forte jacebat,
Limes agro positus, litam ut discernet et arvis.

(There is a beauty in the repetition of *saxum ingens*, in
the second line; it makes us dwell upon the image, and
gives us leisure to consider the vastness of the stone.)
the other two lines are as follow,

Vix illud, lecti bis sex cervice subirent,
Qualia nunc hominum producit corpora tellus.

May I be allowed to think too, they are not so well introduced in Virgil? For it is just after Turnus is described as weakened and oppressed with fears and ill
omens; it exceeds probability; and Turnus, methinks,
looks more like a knight-errant in a romance, than a
hero in an epic poem.

Thund'ring he falls; a mass of monstrous size,
And sev'n broad acres covers as he lies.
The stunning stroke his stubborn nerves unbound;
Loud o'er the fields his ringing arms resound·   475
The scornful dame her conquest views with smiles,
And glorying thus, the prostrate God reviles.

Hast thou not yet, insatiate fury! known
How far Minerva's force transcends thy own?
Juno, whom thou rebellious dar'st withstand,   480
Corrects thy folly thus by Pallas' hand;
Thus meets thy broken faith with just disgrace,
And partial aid to Troy's perfidious race.

The Goddess spoke, and turn'd her eyes away,
That beaming round, diffus'd celestial day.   485
Jove's Cyprian daughter, stooping on the land,
Lent to the wounded God her tender hand:
Slowly he rises, scarcely breathes with pain,
And propt on her fair arm, forsakes the plain.
This the bright empress of the heav'ns survey'd,   490
And scoffing, thus, to war's victorious maid.

Lo! what an aid on Mars's side is seen!
The Smiles and Loves unconquerable queen!
Mark with what insolence, in open view,
She moves. let Pallas, if she dares, pursue.   495

Minerva smiling heard, the pair o'ertook,
And slightly on her breast the wanton strook:
She, unresisting, fell; (her spirits fled)
On earth together lay the lovers spread.

And like thefe heroes, be the fate of all   500
(Minerva cries) who guard the Trojan wall!
To Grecian Gods fuch let the Phrygian be,
So dread, fo fierce, as Venus is to me;
Then from the loweft ftone fhall Troy be mov'd—
Thus fhe, and Juno with a fmile approv'd.   505

Meantime, to mix in more than mortal fight,
The God of Ocean dares the God of light.

℣. 507. *The God of Ocean dares the God of light*]
The interview between Neptune and Apollo is very judicioufly in this place enlarged upon by our author The
poem now draws to a conclufion; the Trojans are to be
punifhed for their perjury and violence. Homer accordingly with a poetical juftice fums up the evidence againft
them, and reprefents the very founder of Troy as an ir-
jurious perfon.   There have been feveral references to
this ftory fince the beginning of the poem, but he for-
bore to give it at large till near the end of it; that it
might be frefh upon the memory, and fhew, the Trojans
deferve the punifhment they are going to fuffer.

Euftathius gives the reafon why Apollo affifts the
Trojans, though he had been equally with Neptune af-
fronted by Laomedon this proceeded from the honours which Apollo received from the pofterity of Laomedon, Troy paid him no lefs worfhip than Cilla, or
Tenedos, and by thefe means won him over to a for-
givenefs. but Neptune ftill was flighted, and confequently continued an enemy to the whole race.

The fame author gives us various opinions why Neptune is faid to have built the Trojan wall, and to have
been defrauded of his wages Some fay that Laomedon
facrilegioufly took away the treafures out of the temples
of Apollo and Neptune, to carry on the fortifications;
from whence it was fabled that Neptune and Apollo built
the walls.   Others will have it, that two of the work-

L 3

What floth has feiz'd us, when the fields around [found?

Ring with conflicting pow'rs, and heav'n returns the

Shall ignominious we with fhame retire,   510

No deed perform'd, to our Olympian fire?

Come, prove thy arm ! for firft the war to wage,

Suits not my greatnefs, or fuperior age.

Rafh as thou art to prop the Trojan throne,

(Forgetful of my wrongs, and of thy own)   515

And guard the race of proud Laomedon !

men dedicated their wages to Apollo and Neptune; and
that Laomedon detained them · fo that he might in fome
fenfe be faid to defraud the deities themfelves, by with-
holding what was dedicated to their temples.

The reafon why Apollo is faid to have kept the herds
of Laomedon, is not fo clear. Euftathius obferves that
all plagues firft feife upon the four-footed creation, and
are fuppofed to arife from this deity: thus Apollo in the
firft book fends the plague into the Grecian army, the
ancients therefore made him to prefide over cattel, that
by preferving them from the plague, mankind might
be fafe from infectious difeafes. Others tell us, that
this employment is afcribed to Apollo, becaufe he figni-
fics the fun now the fun clothes the paftures with grafs
and herbs, fo that Apollo may be faid himfelf to feed
the cattel, by fupplying them with food   Upon either
of thefe accounts Laomedon may be faid to be ungrate-
ful to that deity, for raifing no temple to his honour.

It is obfervable that Homer, in this ftory, afcribes the
building of the wall to Neptune only : I fhould conjecture the reafon might be, that Troy being a fea-port
town, the chief ftrength of it depended upon its fituation, fo that the fea was in a manner a wall to it : upon
this account Neptune may not improbably be faid to
have built the wall.

Haft thou forgot, how at the monarch's pray'r,
We fhar'd the lengthen'd labours of a year!
Troy walls I rais'd (for fuch were Jove's commands)
And yon' proud bulwarks grew beneath my hands: 520
Thy tafk it was to feed the bellowing droves
Along fair Ida's vales, and pendent groves.
But when the circling feafons in their train
Brought back the grateful day that crown'd our pain;
With menace ftern the fraudful king defy'd   525
Our latent Godhead, and the prize deny'd:
Mad as he was, he threaten'd fervile bands,
And doom'd us exiles far in barb'rous lands.
Incens'd, we heav'nward fled with fwifteft wing,
And deftin'd vengeance on the perjur'd king.   530
Doft thou, for this, afford proud Ilion grace,
And not like us, infeft the faithlefs race?
Like us, their prefent, future fons deftroy,
And from its deep foundations heave their Troy?

    Apollo thus: To combate for mankind   535
Ill fuits the wifdom of celeftial mind:
For what is man? calamitous by birth,
They owe their life and nourifhment to earth;

   †. 537. *For what is man?* etc.] The poet is very
happy in interfperfing his poem with moral fentences;
in this place he fteals away his reader from war and
horror, and gives him a beautiful admonition of his
own frailty " Shall I (fays Apollo) contend with thee
" for the fake of man? man, who is no more than a
" leaf of a tree, now green and flourifhing, but foon
" withered away and gone?" The fon of Sirach has an

Like yearly leaves, that now, with beauty crown'd,
Smile on the sun; now, wither on the ground: 540
To their own hands commit the frantic scene,
Nor mix immortals in a cause so mean.
Then turns his face, far-beaming heav'nly fires,
And from the senior pow'r, submiss retires;
Him, thus retreating, Artemis upbraids,   545
The quiver'd huntress of the Sylvan shades.

And is it thus the youthful Phœbus flies,
And yields to Ocean's hoary sire, the prize?
How vain that martial pomp, and dreadful show
Of pointed arrows, and the silver bow!   550
Now boast no more in yon' celestial bow'r,
Thy force can match the great earth-shaking pow'r.

Silent, he heard the queen of woods upbraid:
Not so Saturnia bore the vaunting maid;
But furious thus   What insolence has driv'n   555
Thy pride to face the majesty of heav'n?

expression which very much resembles this, Ecclus. xiv.
18 *As the green leaves upon a thick tree, some fall, and
some grow, so is the generation of flesh and blood, one cometh
to an end, and one is born.*

 ỳ 544. *And from the senior pow'r, submiss retires*]
Two things hinder Homer from making Neptune and
Apollo fight. First, because having already described
the fight between Vulcan and Xanthus, he has nothing
farther to say here, for it is the same conflict between
humidity and dryness Secondly, Apollo being the
same with Destiny, and the ruin of the Trojans being
concluded upon and decided, that God can no longer
defer it. Dacier.

What tho' by Jove the female plague defign'd,
Fierce to the feeble race of woman-kind,
The wretched matron feels thy piercing dart;
Thy fex's tyrant, with a tyger's heart?   560
What tho' tremendous in the woodland chafe,
Thy certain arrows pierce the favage race?
How dares thy rafhnefs on the pow'rs divine
Employ thofe arms, or match thy force with mine?
Learn hence, no more unequal war to wage——— 565
She faid, and feiz'd her wrifts with eager rage;

⁂. 557. *The female plague———*
  Fierce to the feeble race of woman-kind etc.]
The words in the original are, *Though Jupiter has made
you a lion to women.* The meaning of this is, that Diana
was terrible to that fex, as being the fame with the
moon, and bringing on the pangs of child-birth: or elfe
that the ancients attributed all fudden deaths of women
to the darts of Diana, as of men to thofe of Apollo:
which opinion is frequently alluded to in Homer. Euftathius.

  ⁂. 566. *She faid, and feiz'd her wrifts,* etc.] I muft
confefs I am at a lofs how to juftify Homer in every
point of thefe combats with the gods: when Diana and
Juno are to fight, Juno calls her an *impudent bitch,* κυον
ἀδδεις. When they fight, fhe boxes her foundly, and
fends her crying and trembling to heaven: as foon as
fhe comes thither, Jupiter falls a laughing at her. indeed the reft of the deities feem to be in a merry vein
during all the action: Pallas beats Mars and laughs at
him, Jupiter fees them in the fame merry mood: Juno
when fhe had cuffed Diana is not more ferious: in
fhort, unlefs there be fome depths that I am not able to
fathom, Homer never better deferved than in this place
the cenfure paft upon him by the ancients, that as he

Thefe in her left hand lock'd, her right unty'd
The bow, the quiver, and its plumy pride.
About her temples flies the bufy bow;
Now here, now there, fhe winds her from the blow; 570
The fcatt'ring arrows rattling from the cafe,
Drop round, and idly mark the dufty place.
Swift from the field the baffled huntrefs flies,
And fcarce reftrains the torrent in her eyes:
So, when the falcon wings her way above,   575
To the cleft cavern fpeeds the gentle dove,
(Not fated yet to die) there fafe retreats,
Yet ftill her heart againft the marble beats.

   To her, Latona haftes with tender care;
Whom Hermes viewing, thus declines the war.   580

raifed the charaflers of his men up to gods, fo he funk
thofe of gods, down to men.

   Yet I think it but reafonable to conclude, from the
very abfurdity of all this, (fuppofing it had no hidden
meaning or allegory) that there muft therefore certainly
be fome.   Nor do I think it any inference to the contrary, that it is too obfcure for us to find out: the re-
motenefs of our times muft neceffarily darken yet more
and more fuch things as were myfteries at firft   Not
that it is at all impoffible, notwithftanding their prefent
darknefs, but they might then have been very obvious;
as it is certain, allegories ought to be difguifed, but not
obfcured· an allegory fhould be like a veil over a
beautiful face, fo fine and tranfparent, as to fhew the
very charms it covers.

   ỷ. 580 *Whom Hermes viewing, thus declines the war.*]
It is impoffible that Mercury fhould encounter Latona:
fuch a fiction would be unnatural, he being a planet, and

How fhall I face the dame, who gives delight
To him whofe thunders blacken heav'n with night?
Go, matchlefs Goddefs! triumph in the fkies,
And boaft my conqueft, while I yield the prize.

He fpoke; and paft: Latona, ftooping low,   585
Collects the fcatter'd fhafts, and fallen bow,
That glitt'ring on the duft, lay here and there;
Difhonour'd relicks of Diana's war.
Then fwift purfu'd her to her bleft abode,
Where, all confus'd, fhe fought the fov'reign God; 590
Weeping fhe grafp'd his knees: the ambrofial veft
Shook with her fighs, and panted on her breaft.

The fire, fuperior fmil'd; and bade her fhow
What heav'nly hand had caus'd his daughter's woe?
Abafh'd, fhe names his own imperial fpoufe; 595
And the pale crefcent fades upon her brows.

Thus they above   while fwiftly gliding down,
Apollo enters Ilion's facred town:
The guardian God now trembled for her wall,
And fear'd the Greeks, tho' fate forbad her fall. 600
Back to Olympus, from the war's alarms,
Return the fhining bands of Gods in arms;
Some proud in triumph, fome with rage on fire;
And take their thrones around th' æthereal fire:

Thro' blood, thro' death, Achilles ftill proceeds, 605
O'er flaughter'd heroes, and o'er rolling fteeds.

fhe reprefenting the night; for the planets owe all their
luftre to the fhades of the night, and then only become
vifible to the world.   Euftathius.

As when avenging flames with fury driv'n
On guilty towns exert the wrath of heav'n;
The pale inhabitants, some fall, some fly;
And the red vapours purple all the sky.   610
So rag'd Achilles: death and dire dismay,
And toils, and terrors, fill'd the dreadful day.

   High on a turret hoary Priam stands,
And marks the waste of his destructive hands;

   𝓌. 607. *As when avenging flames with fury driv'n,*
       On guilty towns exert the wrath of heav'n]
This passage may be explained two ways, each very remarkable. First, by taking this fire for a real fire, sent
from heaven to punish a criminal city, of which we have
example in holy writ.   Hence we find that Homer had
a notion of this great truth, that God sometimes exerts
his judgments on whole cities in this signal and terrible
manner.   Or if we take it in the other sense, simply as
a fire thrown into a town by the enemies who assault it,
and only expressed thus by the author in the same manner as Jeremy makes the city of Jerusalem say, when
the Chaldæans burnt the temple, *The Lord from above
hath sent fire into my bones,* Lament 1 13. Yet still thus
much will appear understood by Homer, that the fire
which is cast into a city comes not, properly speaking,
from men, but from God, who delivers it up to their
fury.   Dacier

   𝓌 613 *High on a turret hoary Priam,* etc.] The
poet still raises the idea of the courage and strength of
his hero, by making Priam in a terror that he should
enter the town after the routed troops for if he had
not surpassed all mortals, what could have been more
desirable for an enemy, than to have let him in, and
then destroyed him ?

   Here again there was need of another machine to
hinder him from entering the city, for Achilles being
                            vastly

Views, from his arm, the Trojans fcatter'd flight, 615
And the near hero rifing on his fight!
No ftop, no check, no aid! with feeble pace,
And fettled forrow on his aged face,
Faft as he could, he fighing quits the walls;
And thus, defcending on the guards he calls. 620

You to whofe care our city-gates belong,
Set wide your portals to the flying throng.
For lo! he comes, with unrefifted fway;
He comes, and defolation marks his way!
But when within the walls our troops take breath, 625
Lock faft the brazen bars, and fhut out death.
Thus charg'd the rev'rend monarch: wide were flung
The opening folds; the founding hinges rung.
Phœbus rufh'd forth, the flying bands to meet,
Strook flaughter back, and cover'd the retreat. 630

vaftly fpeedier than thofe he purfued, he muft neceffarily
overtake fome of them, and the narrow gates could not
let in a body of troops, without his mingling with the
hindmoft The ftory of Agenor is therefore admirably
contrived, and Apollo, (who was to take care that the
fatal decrees fhould be punctually executed) interpofes
both to fave Agenor and Troy, for Achilles might have
killed Agenor, and ftill entered with the troops if A-
pollo had not diverted him by the purfuit of that phantom. Agenor oppofed himfelf to Achilles only becaufe
he could not do better; for he fees himfelf reduced to a
dilemma, either inglorioufly to perifh among the fugi
tives, or hide himfelf in the foreft; both which were e-
qually unfafe: therefore he is purpofely infpired with a
generous refolution to try to fave his countrymen, and
as the reward of that fervice, is at laft faved himfelf.

On heaps the Trojans croud to gain the gate,
And gladſome ſee their laſt eſcape from fate:
Thither, all parch'd with thirſt, a heartleſs train,
Hoary with duſt, they beat the hollow plain:
And gaſping, panting, fainting, labour on   635
With heavier ſtrides, that lengthen tow'rd the town.
Enrag'd Achilles follows with his ſpear;
Wild with revenge, inſatiable of war.

  Then had the Greeks eternal praiſe acquir'd,
And Troy inglorious to her walls retir'd;   640
But * he, the God who darts æthereal flame,
Shot down to ſave her, and redeem her fame.
To young Agenor force divine he gave,
(Antenor's offspring, haughty, bold and brave)
In aid of him, beſide the beech he ſate,   645
And wrapt, in clouds, reſtrain'd the hand of fate.
When now the gen'rous youth Achilles ſpies,
Thick beats his heart, the troubled motions riſe,
(So, ere a ſtorm, the waters heave and roll)
He ſtops, and queſtions thus his mighty ſoul.   650
  What, ſhall I fly this terror of the plain?
Like others fly, and be like others ſlain?

* Apollo.

ẏ. 651 *What, ſhall I fly?* etc.] This is a very beautiful ſoliloquy of Agenor, ſuch a one as would naturally
ariſe in the ſoul of a brave man, going upon a deſperate
enterprize: he weighs every thing in the balance of
reaſon, he ſets before himſelf the baſeneſs of flight, and
the courage of his enemy, until at laſt the thirſt of glory
preponderates all other conſiderations.   From the con-

Vain hope! to fhun him by the felf-fame road
Yon' line of flaughter'd Trojans lately trod.
No: with the common heap I fcorn to fall—— 655
What if they pafs'd me to the Trojan wall,
While I decline to yonder path, that leads
To Ida's forefts and furrounding fhades?
So may I reach, conceal'd, the cooling flood,
From my tir'd body wafh the dirt and blood, 660
As foon as night her dufky veil extends,
Return in fafety to my Trojan friends,
What if?——But wherefore all this vain debate?
Stand I to doubt, within the reach of fate?
Ev'n now perhaps, ere yet I turn the wall, 665
The fierce Achilles fees me, and I fall:
Such is his fwiftnefs, 'tis in vain to fly,
And fuch his valour, that who ftands muft die.
Howe'er 'tis better, fighting for the ftate,
Here, and in public view, to meet my fate. 670
Yet fure he too is mortal; he may feel
(Like all the fons of earth) the force of fteel;
One only foul informs that dreadful frame;
And Jove's fole favour gives him all his fame.

    He faid, and ftood, collected in his might; 675
And all his beating bofom claim'd the fight.

clufion of this fpeech it is evident, that the ftory of
Achilles's being invulnerable except in the heel, is an
invention of latter ages; for had he been fo, there had
been nothing wonderful in his character. Euftathius.

So from some deep grown wood the panther starts,
Rous'd from his thicket by a storm of darts:
Untaught to fear or fly, he hears the sounds,
Of shouting hunters, and of clam'rous hounds;   680
Tho' struck, tho' wounded, scarce perceives the pain,
And the barb'd jav'lin stings his breast in vain:
On their whole war, untam'd the savage flies;
And tears his hunter, or beneath him dies.
Not less resolv'd, Antenor's valiant heir   685
Confronts Achilles, and awaits the war,
Disdainful of retreat: high-held before,
His shield (a broad circumference) he bore;
Then graceful as he stood, in act to throw
The lifted jav'lin, thus bespoke the foe.   690

   How proud Achilles glories in his fame!
And hopes this day to sink the Trojan name
Beneath her ruins! know, that hope is vain;
A thousand woes, a thousand toils remain.
Parents and children our just arms employ,   695
And strong, and many, are the sons of Troy.
Great as thou art, ev'n thou may'st stain with gore
These Phrygian fields, and press a foreign shore.

   He said · with matchless force the jav'lin flung
Smote on his knee; the hollow cuishes rung   700
Beneath the pointed steel, but safe from harms
He stands impassive in th' æthereal arms.
Then fiercely rushing on the daring foe,
His lifted arm prepares the fatal blow.

But jealous of his fame Apollo shrouds   705
The God-like Trojan in a veil of clouds:
Safe from pursuit, and shut from mortal view,
Dismiss'd with fame, the favour'd youth withdrew.
Meanwhile the God, to cover their escape,
Assumes Agenor's habit, voice, and shape,   710
Flies from the furious chief in this disguise,
The furious chief still follows where he flies:
Now o'er the fields they stretch with lengthen'd strides,
Now urge the course where swift Scamander glides:
The God now distant scarce a stride before,   715
Tempts his pursuit, and wheels about the shore:

ỷ. 709. *Meanwhile the God, to cover their escape*, etc]
The poet makes a double use of this fiction of Apollo's
deceiving Achilles in the shape of Agenor; by these
means he draws him from the pursuit, and gives the
Trojans time to enter the city, and at the same time
brings Agenor handsomely off from the combate. The
moral of this fable is, that destiny would not yet suffer
Troy to fall.

Eustathius fancies that the occasion of the fiction
might be this: Agenor fled from Achilles to the banks
of Xanthus, and might there conceal himself from the
pursuer behind some covert that grew on the shores;
this perhaps might be the whole of the story. So plain
a narration would have passed in the mouth of an historian, but the poet dresses it in fiction, and tells us that
Apollo (or Destiny) concealed him in a cloud from the
sight of his enemy.

The same author farther observes, that Achilles by
an unseasonable piece of vain-glory, in pursuing a single
enemy, gives time to a whole army to escape: he neither kills Agenor, nor overtakes the Trojans.

K 3

While all the flying troops their fpeed employ,
And pour on heaps into the walls of Troy.
No ftop, no ftay ; no thought to afk, or tell,
Who 'fcap'd by flight, or who by battel fell.   720
'Twas tumult all, and violence of flight;
And fudden joy confus'd, and mix'd affright :
Pale Troy againft Achilles fhuts her gate ;
And nations breathe, deliver'd from their fate.

THE

I L I A D.

B O O K XXII.

THE ARGUMENT.

The Death of Hector.

*THE Trojans being safe within the walls, Hector only
stays to oppose Achilles. Priam is struck at his approach,
and tries to persuade his son to re-enter the town. Hecuba joins her intreaties, but in vain. Hector consults
within himself what measures to take · but at the advance of Achilles, his resolution fails him, and he flies,
Achilles pursues him thrice round the walls of Troy
The Gods debate concerning the fate of Hector; at length
Minerva descends to the aid of Achilles She deludes
Hector in the shape of Deiphobus, he stands the combate, and is slain. Achilles drags the dead body at his
chariot, in the sight of Priam and Hecuba. Their lamentations, tears and despair. Their cries reach the ears of
Andromache, who, ignorant of this, was retired into the
inner part of the palace she mounts up to the walls, and
beholds her dead husband. She swoons at the spectacle.
Her excess of grief and lamentation.
The thirtieth day still continues. The scene lies under the
walls, and on the battlements of Troy.*

T HUS to their bulwarks, smit with panic fear,
   The herded Ilians rush like driven deer;

It is impossible but the whole attention of the reader
must be awakened in this book: the heroes of the two

There safe, they wipe the briny drops away,
And drown in bowls the labours of the day.
Clofe to the walls advancing o'er the fields,⠀⠀⠀⠀5
Beneath one roof of well compacted fhields,
March, bending on, the Greeks embody'd pow'rs,
Far-ftretching in the fhade of Trojan tow'rs.
Great Hector fingly ftay'd; chain'd down by fate,
There fixt he ftood before the Scæan gate;⠀⠀⠀10
Still his bold arms determin'd to employ,
The guardian ftill of long-defended Troy.

⠀⠀Apollo now to tir'd Achilles turns;
(The pow'r confeft in all his glory burns)
And what (he cries) has Peleus' fon in view,⠀⠀15
With mortal fpeed a Godhead to purfue?
For not to thee to know the Gods is giv'n,
Unfkill'd to trace the latent marks of heav'n.
What boots thee now, that Troy forfook the plain?
Vain thy paft labour, and thy prefent vain:⠀⠀20

armies are now to encounter; all the foregoing battels
have been but fo many preludes and under-actions, in
order to this great event, wherein the whole fate of
Greece and Troy is to be decided by the fword of A-
chilles and Hector

⠀⠀This is the book, which of the whole Iliad appears
to me the moft charming It affembles in it all that
can be imagined of great and important on the one hand,
and of tender and melancholy on the other: Terror and
Pity are here wrought up in perfection, and if the reader
is not fenfible of both in a high degree, either he is utterly void of all tafte, or the tranflator of all fkill, in
poetry.

Safe in their walls are now her troops beftow'd,
While here thy frantic rage attacks a God.

   The chief incens'd——Too partial God of day!
To check my conquefts in the middle way:
How few in Ilion elfe had refuge found ?   25
What gafping numbers now had bit the ground?
Thou robb'ft me of a glory juftly mine,
Pow'rful of Godhead, and of fraud divine:
Mean fame, alas! for one of heav'nly ftrain,
To cheat a mortal who repines in vain.   30

   Then to the city terrible and ftrong,
With high and haughty fteps he towr'd along.
So the proud courfer, victor of the prize,
To the near goal with double ardour flies.
Him, as he blazing fhot acrofs the field,   35
The careful eyes of Priam firft beheld.
Not half fo dreadful rifes to the fight
Thro' the thick gloom of fome tempeftuous night

   ℣. 37. *Not half fo dreadful rifes,* etc.] With how
much dreadful pomp is Achilles here introduced! how
noble, and in what bold colours hath he drawn the blazing of his arms, the rapidity of his advance, the terror
of his appearance, the defolation round him, but above
all, the certain death attending all his motions and his
very looks; what a croud of terrible ideas in this one
fimile!
   But immediately after this, follows the moving image
of the two aged parents, trembling, weeping, and imploring their fon. that is fucceeded again by the dreadful gloomy picture of Hector, all on fire, obftinately bent
on death, and expecting Achilles; admirably painted in
the fimile of the fnake rolled up in his den, and collect-

Orion's dog (the year when Autumn weighs)
And o'er the feebler ftars exerts his rays; 40
Terrific glory ' for his burning breath
Taints the red air with fevers, plagues, and death.
So flam'd his fiery mail. Then wept the fage;
He ftrikes his rev'rend head now white with age:
He lifts his wither'd arms; obtefts the fkies; 45
He calls his much-lov'd fon with feeble cries;
The fon, refolv'd Achilles' force to dare,
Full at the Scæan gates expefts the war:
While the fad father on the rampart ftands,
And thus adjures him with extended hands. 50

　　Ah ftay not, ftay not! guardlefs and alone;
Hector ! my lov'd, my deareft braveft fon!

ing his poifons and indeed, through the whole book,
this wonderful contraft, and oppofition of the *moving*
and of the *terrible*, is perpetually kept up, each heighten-
ing the other: I cannot find words to exprefs how fo
great beauties affect me.

　　✣. 51. *The fpeech of Priam to Hector.*] The poet has
entertained us all along with various fcenes of flaughter
and horror: he now changes to the pathetic, and fills
the mind of the reader with tender forrows. Euftathius
obferves that Priam preludes to his words by actions
expreffive of mifery: the unhappy orator introduces his
fpeech to Hector with groans and tears, and rending his
hoary hair The father and the king plead with Hector
to preferve his life and his country. He reprefents his
own age, and the lofs of many of his children; and adds,
that if Hector falls, he fhould then be inconfolable, and
the empire of Troy at an end.

　　It is a piece of great judgment in Homer, to make
the fall of Troy to depend upon the death of Hector:

Methinks already I behold thee flain,
And ftretch'd beneath that fury of the plain.
Implacable Achilles! might'ft thou be   55
To all the Gods no dearer than to me!
Thee, vultures wild fhould fcatter round the fhore,
And bloody dogs grow fiercer from thy gore.
How many valiant fons I late enjoy'd,
Valiant in vain! by thy curft arm deftroy'd: 60
Or, worfe than flaughter'd, fold in diftant ifles
To fhameful bondage and unworthy toils.
Two, while I fpeak, my eyes in vain explore,
Two from one mother fprung, my Polydore,
And lov'd Lycaon; now perhaps no more!   65
Oh! if in yonder hoftile camp they live,
What heaps of gold, what treafures would I give?
(Their grandfire's wealth, by right of birth their own,
Confign'd his daughter with Lelegia's throne)
But if (which heav'n forbid) already loft,   70
All pale they wander on the Stygian coaft;
What forrows then muft their fad mother know,
What anguifh I? unutterable woe!
Yet lefs that anguifh, lefs to her, to me,
Lefs to all Troy, if not depriv'd of thee.   75

the poet does not openly tell us, that Troy was taken
by the Greeks; but that the reader might not be unac-
quainted with what happened after the period of his
poem, he gives us to underftand in this fpeech, that the
city was taken, and that Priam, his wives, his fons, and
daughters, were either killed or made flaves.

Yet ſhun Achilles! enter yet the wall;
And ſpare thy ſelf, thy father, ſpare us all!
Save thy dear life; or if a ſoul ſo brave
Neglect that thought, thy dearer glory ſave.
Pity, while yet I live, theſe ſilver hairs;   80
While yet thy father feels the woes he bears,
Yet curſt with ſenſe! a wretch, whom in his rage
(All trembling on the verge of helpleſs age)
Great Jove has plac'd, ſad ſpectacle of pain!
The bitter dregs of fortune's cup to drain: 85
To fill with ſcenes of death his cloſing eyes,
And number all his days by miſeries!
My heroes ſlain, my bridal bed o'erturn'd,
My daughters raviſh'd, and my city burn'd,
My bleeding infants daſh'd againſt the floor;   90
Theſe I have yet to ſee, perhaps yet more!

ỳ. 76 *Enter yet the wall, And ſpare*, etc.] The argument that Priam uſes (ſays Euſtathius) to induce
Hector to ſecure himſelf in Troy is remarkable. he
draws it not from Hector's fears, nor does he tell him
that he is to ſave his own life but he inſiſts upon
ſtronger motives: he tells him he may preſerve his fel-
low-citizens, his country, and his father; and farther
perſuades him not to add glory to his mortal enemy by
his fall.

ỳ 90 *My bleeding infants daſh'd againſt the floor*.]
Cruelties which the Barbarians uſually exerciſed in the
ſacking of towns Thus Iſaiah foretells to Babylon
that her children ſhall be daſhed in pieces before her
eyes by the Medes *Infantes eorum allidentur in oculis
eorum*, xii. 16 And David ſays to the ſame city, *happy
ſhall he be that taketh and daſheth thy little ones againſt the*
ſtones

Perhaps ev'n I, referv'd by angry fate
The laft fad relick of my ruin'd ftate,
(Dire pomp of fov'reign wretchednefs ') muft fall,
And ftain the pavement of my regal hall;   95
Where famifh'd dogs, late guardians of my door,
Shall lick their mangled mafter's fpatter'd gore.
Yet for my fons I thank ye Gods! 'twas well,
Well have they perifh'd, for in fight they fell.
Who dies in youth, and vigour, dies the beft,   100
Struck thro' with wounds, all honeft on the breaft.
But when the fates, in fulnefs of their rage,
Spurn the hoar head of unrefifting age,
In duft the rev'rend lineaments deform,
And pour to dogs the life-blood fcarcely warm'   105
This, this is mifery' the laft, the worft,
That man can feel; man, fated to be curft!

flores Pfal. cxxxvii. 9. And in the prophet Hofea,
xiii 16. *Their infants fhall be dafhed in pieces.* Dacier.

ᵥ 102 *But when the fates,* etc] Nothing can be
more moving than the image which Homer gives here,
in comparing the different effects produced by the view
of a young man, and that of an old one, both bleeding,
and extended on the duft. The old man, it is certain,
touches us moft, and feveral reafons may be given for
it; the principal is, that the young man defended himfelf, and his death is glorious; whereas an old man has
no defence but his weaknefs, prayers and tears. They
muft be very infenfible of what is dreadful, and have no
tafte in poetry, who omit this paffage in a tranflation,
and fubftitute things of a trivial and infipid nature.
Dacier.

He said, and acting what no words could say,
Rent from his head the silver locks away.
With him the mournful mother bears a part;   110
Yet all their sorrows turn not Hector's heart:
The zone unbrac'd, her bosom she display'd;
And thus, fast-falling the salt tears, she said.

Have mercy on me, O my son! revere
The words of age; attend a parent's pray'r!   115
If ever thee in these fond arms I prest,
Or still'd thy infant clamours at this breast;

℣. 114 *The speech of Hecuba.*] The speech of Hecuba opens with as much tenderness as that of Priam:
the circumstance in particular of her shewing that breast
to her son which had sustained his infancy, is highly
moving: it is a silent kind of oratory, and prepares the
heart to listen, by prepossessing the eye in favour of the
speaker.

Eustathius takes notice of the difference between the
speeches of Priam and Hecuba: Priam dissuades him from
the combate, by enumerating not only the loss of his
own family, but of his whole country: Hecuba dwells
entirely upon his single death; this is a great beauty in
the poet, to make Priam a father to his whole country;
but to describe the fondness of the mother as prevailing
over all other considerations, and to mention that only
which chiefly affects her.

This puts me in mind of a judicious stroke in Milton, with regard to the several characters of Adam and
Eve. When the angel is driving them both out of
paradise, Adam grieves that he must leave a place where
he had conversed with God and his angels; but Eve
laments that she shall never more behold the flowers of
Eden. Here Adam mourns like a man, and Eve like a
woman.

Ah do not thus our helplefs years forego,
But by our walls fecur'd, repel the foe.
Againft his rage if fingly thou proceed,   120
Should'ft thou (but heav'n avert it !) fhould'ft thou bleed,
Nor muft thy corps lie honour'd on the bier,
Nor fpoufe, nor mother, grace thee with a tear;
Far from our pious rites, thofe dear remains
Muft feaft the vultures on the naked plains.   125

  So they, while down their cheeks the torrents roll;
But fix'd remains the purpofe of his foul:
Refolv'd he ftands, and with a fiery glance
Expects the hero's terrible advance
So roll'd up in his den, the fwelling fnake   130
Beholds the traveller approach the brake;
When fed with noxious herbs his turgid veins
Have gather'd half the poifons of the plains;
He burns, he ftiffens with collected ire,
And his red eye-balls glare with living fire.   135
Beneath a turret, on his fhield reclin'd,
He ftood, and queftion'd thus his mighty mind.

  Where lies my way? to enter in the wall?
Honour and fhame th' ungen'rous thought recall:

℣ 138. *The Soliloquy of Hector*] There is much
greatnefs in the fentiments of this whole foliloquy. Hector prefers death to an ignominious life· he knows how
to die with glory, but not how to live with difhonour
The reproach of Polydamas affects him, the fcandals of
the meaneft people have an influence on his thoughts.

  It is remarkable that he does not fay, he fears the infults of the braver Trojans, but of the moft worthlefs

Shall proud Polydamas before the gate   140
Proclaim, his counsels are obey'd too late,

only. Men of merit are always the moſt candid; but
others are ever for bringing all men to a level with themſelves They cannot bear that any one ſhould be ſo
bold as to excel, and are ready to pull him down to
them, upon the leaſt miſcarriage. This ſentiment is
perfectly fine, and agreeable to the way of thinking, natural to a great and ſenſible mind.

There is a very beautiful break in the middle of this
ſpeech Hector's mind fluctuates every way, he is calling a council in his own breaſt, and conſulting what
method to purſue · he doubts if he ſhould not propoſe
terms of peace to Achilles, and grants him very large
conceſſions; but of a ſudden he checks himſelf, and
leaves the ſentence unfiniſhed. The paragraph runs
thus, " If, ſays Hector, I ſhould offer him the largeſt
" conditions, give all that Troy contains"—There he
ſtops, and immediately ſubjoins, " But why do I delude
" myſelf, etc.

It is evident from this ſpeech, that the power of making peace was in Hector's hands : for unleſs Priam had
transferred it to him, he could not have made theſe
propoſitions. So that it was Hector who broke the
treaty in the third book (where the very ſame conditions
were propoſed by Agamemnon.) It is Hector therefore
that is guilty, he is blameable in continuing the war, and
involving the Greeks and Trojans in blood. This conduct in Homer was neceſſary; he obſerves a poetical
juſtice, and ſhews that Hector is a criminal, before he
brings him to death Euſtathius.

y. 140 Shall proud Polydamas, etc.] Hector alludes
to the counſel given him by Polydamas in the eighteenth
book, which he then neglected to follow . it was, to
withdraw to the city, and fortify themſelves there, before Achilles returned to the battel.

Which timely follow'd but the former night,
What numbers had been fav'd by Hector's flight?
That wife advice rejected with difdain,
I feel my folly in my people flain.   145
Methinks my fuff'ring country's voice I hear,
But moft, her worthlefs fons infult my ear,
On my rafh courage charge the chance of war,
And blame thofe virtues which they cannot fhare.
No——if I e'er return, return I muft   150
Glorious, my country's terror laid in duft :
Or if I perifh, let her fee me fall
In field at leaft, and fighting for her wall.
And yet fuppofe thefe meafures I forego,
Approach unarm'd, and parley with the foe,   155
The warrior-fhield, the helm, and lance lay down,
And treat on terms of peace to fave the town :
The wife with-held, the treafure ill-detain'd,
(Caufe of the war, and grievance of the land)
With honourable juftice to reftore ;   160
And add half Ilion's yet remaining ftore,
Which Troy fhall, fworn, produce ; that injur'd Greece
May fhare our wealth, and leave our walls in peace.
But why this thought' unarm'd if I fhould go,   ⎫
What hope of mercy from this vengeful foe,   ⎬ 165
But woman like to fall, and fall without a blow ? ⎭

L 3

We greet not here, as man converfing man,
Met at an oak, or journeying o'er a plain:

ẏ. 167. *We greet not here, as man converfing man,*
        Met at an oak, or journeying o'er a plain, etc.]
The words literally are thefe, " *There is no talking with*
Achilles, ἀπὸ ἐρυὸς ὐδ' ἀπὸ πέτρης, *from an oak, or from a*
rock, [or about an oak or a rock] *as a young man and a*
maiden talk together. It is thought an obfcure paffage,
though I confefs I am either too fond of my own explication in the above cited verfes, or they make it a
very clear one. " There is no converfing with this
" implacable enemy in the rage of battel; as when
" fauntring people talk at leifure to one another on the
" road, or when young men and women meet in a
" field." I think the expofition of Euftathius more
far fetched, though it be ingenious; and therefore I
muft do him the juftice not to fupprefs it. It was a common practice, fays he, with the heathens, to expofe fuch
children as they either could not, or would not educate:
the places where they depofited them, were ufually in
the cavities of *rocks,* or the hollow of *oaks* · thefe children being frequently found and preferved by ftrangers,
were faid to be the offspring of thofe oaks, or rocks
where they were found. This gave occafion to the
poets to feign that men were born of *oaks,* and there was
a famous fable too of Deucalion and Pyrrha's repairing
mankind by cafting *ftones* behind them · it grew at laft
into a proverb, to fignify idle tales, fo that in the prefent paffage it imports, that Achilles *will not liften to*
fuch idle tales as may pafs with filly maids and fond lovers.
For fables and ftories (and particularly fuch ftories as
the prefervation, ftrange fortune, and adventures of expofed children) are the ufual converfation of young
men and maidens Euftathius's explanation may be
corroborated by a parallel place in the Odyffey; where
the poet fays,

No feafon now for calm familiar talk,
Like youths and maidens in an ev'ning walk: 170
War is our bufinefs, but to whom is giv'n
To die, or triumph, that, determine heav'n!

   Thus pond'ring, like a God the Greek drew nigh,
His dreadful plumage nodded from on high;
The Pelian jav'lin, in his better hand,   175
Shot trembling rays that glitter'd o'er the land;
And on his breaft the beamy fplendours fhone
Like Jove's own light'ning, or the rifing fun.
As Hector fees, unufual terrors rife,
Struck by fome God, he fears, recedes, and flies.   180

    Οὐ γάρ ἀπὸ δρυὸς ἴσσι παλαιφάτυ, ἠδ' ἀπὸ πέτρης.

The meaning of which paffage is plainly this, *Tell me
of what race you are, for undoubtedly you had a father and
mother, you are not, according to the old ftory, defcended
from an oak or a rock.* Where the word παλαιφάτυ fhews
that this was become an ancient proverb even in Homer's days.

   ℣. 180. *Struck by fome God, he fears, recedes, and
flies.*] I doubt not moft readers are fhocked at the flight
of Hector: it is indeed a high exaltation of Achilles
(who was the poet's chief hero) that fo brave a man
as Hector durft not ftand him. While Achilles was
at a diftance he had fortified his heart with noble refolu-
tions, but at his approach they all vanifh, and he flies.
This (as exceptionable as fome may think it) may yet
be allowed to be a true portrait of human nature; for
diftance, as it leffens all objects, fo it does our fears: but
where inevitable danger approaches, the ftouteft hearts
will feel fome apprehenfions at certain fate. It was the
faying of one of the braveft men in this age, to one who
told him he feared nothing, *Shew me but a certain dan-*

He leaves the gates, he leaves the walls behind;
Achilles follows like the winged wind.

ger, and I shall be as much afraid as any of you. I do not absolutely pretend to justify this passage in every point, but only to have thus much granted me, that Hector was in this desperate circumstance.

First, It will not be found in the whole Iliad, that Hector ever thought himself a match for Achilles. Homer (to keep this in our minds) had just now made Priam tell him, as a thing known (for certainly Priam would not insult him at that time) that there was no comparison between his own strength, and that of his antagonist:

    ——— ———ἐπειὴ πολὺ φέρτερός ἐσιν

Secondly, We may observe with Dacier, the degrees by which Homer prepares this incident. In the 18th book the mere sight and voice of Achilles unarmed, has terrified and put the whole Trojan army into disorder. In the 19th the very sound of the celestial arms given him by Vulcan, has affrighted his own Myrmidons as they stand about him. In the 20th, he has been upon the point of killing Æneas, and Hector himself was not saved from him but by Apollo's interposing　In that and the following book, he makes an incredible slaughter of all that oppose him, he overtakes most of those that fly from him, and Priam himself opens the gates of Troy to receive the rest.

Thirdly, Hector stays, not that he hopes to overcome Achilles, but because shame and the dread of reproach forbid him to re-enter the city, a shame (says Eustathius) which was a fault that betrayed him out of his life, and ruined his country. Nay, Homer adds farther, that he only stayed by the immediate *will of heaven,* intoxicated and irresistibly bound down by *fate.*

    Ἕκτορα δ᾽ αὐτοῦ μεῖναι ὀλοὴ μοῖρ᾽ ἐπέδησεν.

Thus at the panting dove a falcon flies,
(The swiftest racer of the liquid skies)

Fourthly, He had juft been reflecting on the injuftice
of the war he maintained; his fpirits are depreffed by
heaven, he expects certain death, he perceives himfelf
abandoned by the Gods, (as he directly fays in ẏ. 300,
etc. of the Greek, and 385. of the tranflation) fo that
he might fay to Achilles what Turnus does to Æneas,

Dii me terrent, et Jupiter hoftis.

This indeed is the ftrongeft reafon that can be offered
for the flight of Hector. He flies not from Achilles as
a mortal hero, but from one whom he fees clad in impenetrable armour, feconded by Minerva, and one who
had put to flight the inferior Gods themfelves. This is
not cowardice, according to the conftant principles of
Homer, who thought it no part of a hero's character to
be impious, or to fancy himfelf independent on the
fupreme being.

Indeed it had been a grievous fault, had our author
fuffered the courage of Hector intirely to forfake him
even in this extremity: a brave man's foul is ftill capable of rouzing itfelf, and acting honourably in the laft
ftruggles. Accordingly Hector, though delivered over
to his deftiny, abandoned by the gods, and certain of
death, yet ftops and attacks Achilles, when he lofes his
fpear, he draws his fword: it was impoffible he fhould
conquer, it was only in his power to fall glorioufly; this
he did, and it was all that man could do.

If the reader, after all, cannot bring himfelf to like
this paffage, for his own particular; yet to induce him
to fufpend his abfolute cenfure, he may confider that
Virgil had an uncommon efteem for it, as he has tefti-
fied in transferring it almoft intirely to the death of
Turnus; where there was no neceffity of making ufe of
the like incidents; but doubtlefs he was touched with

Juſt when he holds or thinks he holds his prey, 185
Obliquely wheeling thro' th' aerial way;
With open beak and ſhrilling cries he ſprings,
And aims his claws, and ſhoots upon his wings :

this epiſode, as with one of thoſe which intereſt us moſt
of the whole Iliad, by a ſpectacle at once ſo terrible, and
ſo deplorable. I muſt alſo add the ſuffrage of Ariſtotle,
who was ſo far from looking upon this paſſage as ridiculous or blameable, that he eſteemed it marvellous and
admirable. " The *wonderful*, ſays he, ought to have
" place in tragedy, but ſtill more in epic poetry, which
" proceeds in this point even to the unreaſonable: for
" as in epic poems one ſees not the perſons acting, ſo
" whatever paſſes the bounds of reaſon is proper to pro-
" duce the admirable and the marvellous. For exam-
" ple, what Homer ſays of Hector purſued by Achilles,
" would appear ridiculous on the ſtage; for the ſpecta-
" tors could not forbear laughing to ſee on one ſide the
" Greeks ſtanding without any motion, and on the o-
" ther Achilles purſuing Hector, and making ſigns to
" the troops not to dart at him. But all this does not
" appear when we read the poem: for what is wonder-
" ful is always agreeable, and as a proof of it, we find
" that they who relate any thing, uſually add ſomething
" to the truth, that it may the better pleaſe thoſe who
" hear it."

The ſame great critic vindicates this paſſage in the
chapter following " A poet, ſays he, is inexcuſable
" if he introduces ſuch things as are impoſſible accord-
" ing to the rules of poetry: but this ceaſes to be a
" fault, if by thoſe means he attains to the end pro-
" poſed; for he has then brought about what he intend-
" ed: for example, if he renders by it any part of his
" poem more aſtoniſhing or admirable. Such is the
" place in the Iliad, where Achilles purſues Hector."
Ariſt. poet. chap. 25, 26.

No lefs fore-right the rapid chace they held,
One urg'd by fury, one by fear impell'd;   190
Now circling round the walls their courfe maintain,
Where the high watch-tow'r overlooks the plain;
Now where the fig-trees fpread their umbrage broad,
(A wider compafs) fmoke along the road.
Next by Scamander's double fource they bound,   195
Where two fam'd fountains burft the parted ground;

ɣ. 196. *Where two fam'd fountains.*] Strabo blames
Homer for faying that one of the fources of Scamander
was a warm fountain; whereas (fays he) there is but
one fpring, and that cold, neither is this in the place
where Homer fixes it, but in the mountain.   It is obferved by Euftathius, that though this was not true in
Strabo's days, yet it might in Homer's, greater changes
having happened in lefs time than that which paffed
between thofe two authors, Sandys, who was both a
geographer and critic of great accuracy, as well as a traveller of great veracity, affirms as an eye-witnefs, that
there are yet fome hot-water fprings in that part of the
country, oppofite to Tenedos. I cannot but think that
gentleman muft have been particularly diligent and
curious in his inquiries into the remains of a place fo
celebrated in poetry; as he was not only perhaps the
moft learned, but one of the beft poets of his time: I
am glad of this occafion to do his memory fo much
juftice as to fay, the Englifh verfification owes much of
its improvement to his tranflations, and efpecially that
admirable one of Job.   What chiefly pleafes me in this
place, is to fee the exact landfkip of old Troy; we have
a clear idea of the town itfelf, and of the roads and
country about it; the river, the fig-trees, and every
part is fet before our eyes.

This hot thro' scorching clefts is seen to rise,
With exhalations steaming to the skies;
That the green banks in summer's heat o'erflows,
Like crystal clear, and cold as winter-snows.   200
Each gushing fount a marble cistern fills,
Whose polish'd bed receives the falling rills;
Where Trojan dames (ere yet alarm'd by Greece)
Wash'd their fair garments in the days of peace.
By these they past, one chasing, one in flight,   205
(The mighty fled, pursu'd by stronger might)
Swift was the course; no vulgar prize they play,
No vulgar victim must reward the day,
(Such as in races crown the speedy strife)
The prize contended was great Hector's life.   210
    As when some hero's fun'rals are decreed
In grateful honour of the mighty dead;
Where high rewards the vig'rous youth inflame,
(Some golden tripod, or some lovely dame)
The panting coursers swiftly turn the goal,   215
And with them turns the rais'd spectator's soul.
Thus three times round the Trojan wall they fly;
The gazing Gods lean forward from the sky:

ỿ. 218. *The gazing Gods lean forward from the sky*]
We have here an instance of the great judgment of
Homer.   The death of Hector being the chief action of
the poem, he assembles the gods, and calls a council in
heaven concerning it   it is for the same reason that he
represents Jupiter with the greatest solemnity weighing
in his scales the fates of the two heroes· I have before
observed

To whom, while eager on the chace they look,

The fire of mortals and immortals fpoke   220

  Unworthy fight ! the man, belov'd of heav'n,

Behold, inglorious round yon' city driv'n !

My heart partakes the gen'rous Hector's pain ;

Hector, whofe zeal whole hecatombs has flain,

Whofe grateful fumes the Gods receiv'd with joy, 225

From Ida's fummits, and the tow'rs of Troy ·

Now fee him flying ! to his fears refign'd,

And fate, and fierce Achilles, clofe behind.

Confult, ye pow'rs ! ('tis worthy your debate)

Whether to fnatch him from impending fate,   230

observed at large upon the laft circumftance in a preceding note, fo that there is no occafion to repeat it

I wonder that none of the commentators have taken
notice of this beauty ; in my opinion, it is a very neceffary obfervation, and fhews the art and judgment of
the poet, that he has made the greateft and finifhing a-
ction of the poem of fuch importance that it engages
the gods in debates.

  ℣. 226 *From Ida's fummits——*] It was the cuftom
of the Pagans to facrifice to the gods upon the hills and
mountains, in fcripture language upon the *high places*,
for they were perfuaded that the gods in a particular
manner inhabited fuch eminences : wherefore God ordered his people to deftroy all thofe high places, which
the nations had prophaned by their idolatry *You fhall
utterly deftroy all the places wherein the nations which you
fhall poffefs ferved their gods, upon the high mountains, and
upon the hills, and under every green tree* Deut xii 2.
It is for this reafon that fo many kings are reproached
in fcripture for not *taking away the high places* Dacier

Or let him bear, by stern Pelides slain,
(Good as he is) the lot impos'd on man?

Then Pallas thus: shall he whose vengeance forms
The forky bolt, and blackens heav'n with storms,
Shall he prolong one Trojan's forfeit breath ¹   235
A man, a mortal, pre-ordain'd to death!
And will no murmurs fill the courts above?
No Gods indignant blame their partial Jove?

Go then (return'd the sire) without delay,
Exert thy will. I give the fates their way.   240
Swift at the mandate pleas'd Tritonia flies,
And stoops impetuous from the cleaving skies.

As thro' the forest, o'er the vale and lawn
The well-breath'd beagle drives the flying fawn;
In vain he tries the covert of the brakes,   245
Or deep beneath the trembling thicket shakes;
Sure of the vapour in the tainted dews,
The certain hound his various maze pursues.
Thus step by step, where'er the Trojan wheel'd,
There swift Achilles compass'd round the field.   250

℣. 249. *Thus step by step,* etc.] There is some difficulty in this passage, and it seems strange that Achilles
could not overtake Hector whom he excelled so much in
swiftness, especially when the poet describes him as
running in a narrower circle than Hector. Eustathius
gives us many solutions from the ancients; Homer has
already told us that they run for the life of Hector; and
consequently Hector would exert his utmost speed,
whereas Achilles might only endeavour to keep him
from entering the city: besides, Achilles could not directly pursue him, because he frequently made efforts to

Oft' as to reach the Dardan gates he bends,
And hopes th' affiftance of his pitying friends,
(Whofe fhow'ring arrows, as he cours'd below,
From the high turrets might opprefs the foe)
So oft' Achilles turns him to the plain: 255
He eyes the city, but he eyes in vain.
As men in flumbers feem with fpeedy pace
One to purfue, and one to lead the chace,
Their finking limbs the fancy'd courfe forfake,
Nor this can fly, nor that can overtake.   260

fhelter himfelf under the wall, and he being obliged to
turn him from it, he might be forced to take more fteps
than Hector. But the poet, to take away all grounds
of an objection, tells us afterwards, that Apollo gave
him a fupernatural fwiftnefs.

ỳ. 257. *As men in flumbers.*] This beautiful comparifon has been condemned by fome of the ancients,
even fo far as to judge it unworthy of having a place in
the Iliad · they fay the diction is mean, and the fimilitude itfelf abfurd, becaufe it compares the fwiftnefs of
the heroes to men afleep, who are in a ftate of reft and
inactivity. But there cannot be a more groundlefs criticifm: the poet is fo far from drawing his comparifon
from the repofe of men afleep, that he alludes only to
their dreams: it is a race in fancy that he defcribes; and
furely the imagination is nimble enough to illuftrate the
greateft degree of fwiftnefs: befides the verfes themfelves
run with the utmoft rapidity, and imitate the fwiftnefs
they defcribe. Euftathius.

What fufficiently proves thefe verfes to be genuine,
is, that Virgil has imitated them, Æn. 12.

Ac veluti in fomnis————

M 2

No lefs the lab'ring heroes pant and ftrain;
While that but flies, and this purfues in vain.

What God, O mufe! affifted Hector's force,
With rate itfelf fo long to hold the courfe?
Phœbus it was; who, in his lateft hour,   265
Endu'd his knees with ftrength, his nerves with pow'r:
And great Achilles, left fome Greek's advance
Should fnatch the glory from his lifted lance,
Sign'd to the troops, to yield his foe the way,
And leave untouch'd the honours of the day.   270

v. 269. *Sign'd to the troops*, etc.] The difference
which Homer here makes between Hector and Achilles
deferves to be taken notice of, Hector is running away
towards the walls, to the end that the Trojans who are
upon them may overwhelm Achilles with their darts;
and Achilles in turning Hector towards the plain, makes
a fign to his troops not to attack him. This fhews the
great courage of Achilles Yet this action which appears fo generous has been very much condemned by
the ancients; Plutarch in the life of Pompey gives us to
underftand, that it was looked upon as the action of a
fool too greedy of glory: indeed this is not a fingle
combate of Achilles againft Hector, (for in that cafe
Achilles would have done very ill not to hinder his
troops from affaulting him) this was a rencounter in a
battel, and fo Achilles might, and ought to take all advantages to rid himfelf, the readieft and the fureft way,
of an enemy whofe death would procure an entire victory to his party Wherefore does he leave this victory to chance? Why expofe himfelf to the hazard of
lofing it? Why does he prefer his private glory to the
public weal, and the fafety of all the Greeks, which he
puts to the venture by delaying to conquer, and en-
dangering his own perfon? I grant it is a fault, but it

Jove lifts the golden balances, that show
The fates of mortal men, and things below:
Here each contending hero's lot he tries,
And weighs, with equal hand, their destinies.
Low sinks the scale surcharg'd with Hector's fate; 275
Heavy with death it sinks, and hell receives the weight.

    Then Phœbus left him. Fierce Minerva flies
To stern Pelides, and triumphing, cries:
Oh lov'd of Jove ! this day our labours cease,
And conquest blazes with full beams on Greece. 280
Great Hector falls, that Hector fam'd so far,
Drunk with renown, insatiable of war,
Falls by thy hand, and mine ! not force, nor flight
Shall more avail him, nor his God of light.

must be owned to be the fault of a hero. Euſtathius.
Dacier.

   ℣. 277 *Then Phœbus left him*——] This is a very
beautiful and poetical manner of deſcribing a plain cir-
cumſtance· the hour of Hector's death was now come,
and the poet expreſſes it by ſaying that Apollo, or
Deſtiny, forſakes him: that is, the fates no longer protect him. Euſtathius

   ℣. Ib.——*Fierce Minerva flies To stern Pelides*, etc.]
The poet may ſeem to diminiſh the glory of Achilles, by
aſcribing the victory over Hector to the aſſiſtance of
Pallas, whereas in truth he fell by the hand only of
Achilles but poetry loves to raiſe every thing into a
wonder; it ſteps out of the common road of narration,
and aims to ſurprize, and the poet would farther in-
ſinuate that it is a greater glory to Achilles to be beloved by the gods, than to be only excellent in valour:
for many men have valour, but few the favour of heaven.
Euſtathius.

See, where in vain he supplicates above,   285
Roll'd at the feet of unrelenting Jove !
Rest here: my self will lead the Trojan on,
And urge to meet the fate he cannot shun.

Her voice divine the chief with joyful mind
Obey'd; and rested, on his lance reclin'd.   290
While like Deiphobus the martial dame
(Her face, her gesture, and her arms the same)
In show an aid, by hapless Hector's side
Approach'd, and greets him thus with voice bely'd.

Too long, O Hector ! have I born the sight   295
Of this distress, and sorrow'd in thy flight;
It fits us now a noble stand to make,
And here, as brothers, equal fates partake.

Then he.   O prince ! ally'd in blood and fame,
Dearer than all that own a brother's name;   300
Of all that Hecuba to Priam bore,
Long try'd, long lov'd; much lov'd, but honour'd more!

℣ 290 *Obey'd, and rested.*] The whole passage
where Pallas deceives Hector is evidently an allegory.
Achilles perceiving that he cannot overtake Hector, pre-
tends to be quite spent and wearied in the pursuit, the
stratagem takes effect, and recalls his enemy. this the
poet expresses by saying that Pallas, or Wisdom, came
to assist Achilles   Hector observing his enemy stay to
rest. concludes that he is quite fatigued, and immediately takes courage, and advances upon him; he thinks he
has him at an advantage, but at last finds himself deceived   thus making a wrong judgment, he is betrayed into his death, so that his own *false judgment* is the
treacherous Pallas that deceives him.   Eustathius.

Since you of all our num'rous race, alone
Defend my life, regardless of your own.

Again the Goddess.   Much my father's pray'r, 305
And much my mother's, prest me to forbear:
My friends embrac'd my knees, adjur'd my stay,
But stronger love impell'd, and I obey.
Come then, the glorious conflict let us try,
Let the steel sparkle, and the jav'lin fly;   310
Or let us stretch Achilles on the field,
Or to his arm our bloody trophies yield.

Fraudful she said, then swiftly march'd before;
The Dardan hero shuns his foe no more.
Sternly they met.   The silence Hector broke;   315
His dreadful plumage nodded as he spoke.

Enough, O son of Peleus! Troy has view'd
Her walls thrice circled, and her chief pursu'd.

℣ 317. *The speeches of Hector and of Achilles*] There
is an opposition between these speeches excellently adapted to the characters of both the heroes. that of Hector
is full of courage, but mixt with humanity. that of A-
chilles, of resentment and arrogance· we see the great
Hector disposing of his own remains, and that thirst of
glory which has made him live with honour, now bids
him provide, as Eustathius observes, that what once
was Hector may not be dishonoured. thus we see a se-
date, calm courage, with a contempt of death, in the
speeches of Hector   But in that of Achilles there is a
fierte, and an insolent air of superiority, his magnani-
mity makes him scorn to steal a victory, he bids him prepare to defend himself with all his forces· and that valour and resentment which made him desirous that he
might revenge himself upon Hector with his own hand,

But now fome God within me bids me try
Thine, or my fate. I kill thee, or I die.   320
Yet on the verge of battel let us ftay,
And for a moment's fpace fufpend the day;
Let heav'n's high pow'rs be call'd to arbitrate
The juft conditions of this ftern debate,
(Eternal witneffes of all below,   325
And faithful guardians of the treafur'd vow!)
To them I fwear; if victor in the ftrife,
Jove by thefe hands fhall fhed thy noble life,
No vile difhonour fhall thy corps purfue;
Stript of its arms alone (the conqu'ror's due)   330
The reft to Greece uninjur'd I'll reftore.
Now plight thy mutual oath, I afk no more.

    Talk not of oaths (the dreadful chief replies,
While anger flafh'd from his difdainful eyes)
Detefted as thou art, and ought to be,   335
Nor oath nor pact Achilles plights with thee:

and forbade the Greeks to interpofe, now directs him
not to take any advantage over a brave enemy I think
both their characters are admirably fuftained, and though
Achilles be drawn with a great violence of features, yet
the picture is undoubtedly like him, and it had been the
utmoft abfurdity to have foftened one line upon this occafion, when the foul of Achilles was all on fire to revenge the death of his friend Patroclus.   I muft defire
the reader to carry this obfervation in his memory, and
particularly in that place, where Achilles fays he could
eat the very flefh of Hector, (though I have a little
foftened it in the tranflation,) ỷ. 438.

Such pacts, as lambs and rabid wolves combine,
Such leagues, as men and furious lions join,
To such I call the Gods ! one conftant ftate
Of lafting rancour and eternal hate: 340
No thought but rage, and never-ceafing ftrife,
'Till death extinguifh rage, and thought, and life.
Rouze then thy forces this important hour,
Collect thy foul, and call forth all thy pow'r.
No farther fubterfuge, no farther chance;   345
'Tis Pallas, Pallas gives thee to my lance.
Each Grecian ghoft by thee depriv'd of breath,
Now hovers round, and calls thee to thy death.

    He fpoke, and lanc'd his jav'lin at the foe;
But Hector fhun'd the meditated blow: 350
He ftoop'd, while o'er his head the flying fpear
Sung innocent, and fpent its force in air.
Minerva watch'd it falling on the land,
Then drew, and gave to great Achilles' hand,
Unfeen of Hector, who, elate with joy,   355
Now fhakes his lance, and braves the dread of Troy.

    The life you boafted to that jav'lin giv'n,
Prince ! you have mift.   My fate depends on heav'n.
To thee (prefumptuous as thou art) unknown,
Or what muft prove my fortune, or thy own.   360
Boafting is but an art, our fears to blind,
And with falfe terrors fink another's mind.
But know, whatever fate I am to try,
By no difhoneft wound fhall Hector die;

I shall not fall a fugitive at least,　　　　　365
My soul shall bravely issue from my breast.
But first, try thou my arm; and may this dart
End all my country's woes, deep buried in thy heart!

　The weapon flew, its course unerring held,
Unerring, but the heav'nly shield repell'd　　370
The mortal dart; resulting with a bound
From off the ringing orb, it struck the ground.
Hector beheld his jav'lin fall in vain,
Nor other lance, nor other hope remain;
He calls Deiphobus, demands a spear,　　　375
In vain, for no Deiphobus was there.
All comfortless he stands: then, with a sigh,
'Tis so——heav'n wills it, and my hour is nigh!
I deem'd Deiphobus had heard my call,
But he secure lies guarded in the wall.　　380
A God deceiv'd me; Pallas, 'twas thy deed,
Death, and black fate approach! 'Tis I must bleed.
No refuge now, no succour from above,
Great Jove deserts me, and the son of Jove,
Propitious once, and kind! then welcome fate!　385
'Tis true I perish, yet I perish great:
Yet in a mighty deed I shall expire,
Let future ages hear it, and admire!

　Fierce, at the word, his weighty sword he drew,
And, all collected, on Achilles flew.　　　　390

So Jove's bold bird, high balanc'd in the air,
Stoops from the clouds to trufs the quiv'ring hare,
Nor lefs Achilles his fierce foul prepares,
Before his breaft the flaming fhield he bears,
Refulgent orb! above his fourfold cone   395
The gilded horfe-hair fparkled in the fun,
Nodding at ev'ry ftep: (Vulcanian frame!)
And as he mov'd, his figure feem'd on flame.
As radiant Hefper fhines with keener light,
Far-beaming o'er the filver hoft of night,   400
When all the ftarry train emblaze the fphere:
So fhone the point of great Achilles' fpear.
In his right hand he waves the weapon round,
Eyes the whole man, and meditates the wound;
But the rich mail Patroclus lately wore,   405
Securely cas'd the warrior's body o'er.
One place at length he fpies, to let in fate,
Where 'twixt the neck and throat the jointed plate
Gave entrance: thro' that penetrable part
Furious he drove the well-directed dart: 410

Ῥ. 391. *So Jove's bold bird*, etc.] The poet takes
up fome time in defcribing the two great heroes before
they clofe in fight. The verfes are pompous and magnificent, and he illuftrates his defcription with two beautiful fimiles: he makes a double ufe of this conduct,
which not only raifes our imagination to attend to fo
momentous an action, but by lengthening his narration
keeps the mind in a pleafing fufpence, and divides it
between hopes and fears for the fate of Hector or Achilles.

Ῥ. 409. *Thro' that penetrable part Furious he drove*,
etc.] It was neceffary that the poet fhould be very par-

Nor pierc'd the wind-pipe yet, nor took the pow'r
Of speech, unhappy! from thy dying hour.
Prone on the field the bleeding warrior lies,
While thus triumphing, stern Achilles cries.

At last is Hector stretch'd upon the plain,   415
Who fear'd no vengeance for Patroclus slain:
Then, prince! you should have fear'd, what now you feel;
Achilles absent, was Achilles still.
Yet a short space the great avenger stay'd,
Then low in dust thy strength and glory lay'd.   420
Peaceful he sleeps, with all our rites adorn'd,
For ever honour'd, and for ever mourn'd:
While cast to all the rage of hostile pow'r,
Thee, birds shall mangle, and the dogs devour.

Then Hector fainting at th' approach of death.   425
By thy own soul! by those who gave thee breath!
By all the sacred prevalence of pray'r;
Ah, leave me not for Grecian dogs to tear!
The common rites of sepulture bestow,
To soothe a father's and a mother's woe;   430

ticular in this point, because the arms that Hector wore,
were the arms of Achilles, taken from Patroclus; and
consequently as they were the work of Vulcan, they
would preserve Hector from the possibility of a wound:
the poet therefore to give an air of probability to his
story, tells us that they were Patroclus's arms, and as
they were not made for Hector they might not exactly
fit his body so that it is not improbable but there
might be some place about the neck of Hector so open,
as to admit the spear of Achilles. Eustathius.

Let

Let their large gifts procure an urn at least,
And Hector's ashes in his country rest.

No, wretch accurst; relentless he replies,
(Flames, as he spoke, shot flashing from his eyes)
Not those who gave me breath shou'd bid me spare,　435
Nor all the sacred prevalence of pray'r.
Could I myself the bloody banquet join!
No——to the dogs that carcase I resign.
Should Troy, to bribe me, bring forth all her store,
And giving thousands, offer thousands more;　440

℣. 347. *Could I myself the bloody banquet join!*] I have
before hinted that there is something very fierce and
violent in this passage; but I fancy that what I there
observed will justify Homer in his relation, though not
Achilles in his savage sentiments: yet the poet softens
the expression by making Achilles only wish that his
heart would permit him to devour him, this is much
more tolerable than a passage in the Thebais of Statius,
where Tydeus in the very pangs of death is represented
as gnawing the head of his enemy.

℣ 439. *Should Troy, to bribe me, etc*] Such reso-
lutions as Achilles here makes, are very natural to men
in anger, he tells Hector that no motives shall ever prevail with him to suffer his body to be ransom'd, yet
when time had cooled his heat, and he had so come hot
satisfied his revenge by insulting his remains, he restores
them to Priam. This perfectly agrees with his conduct
in the ninth book, where at first he gives a rough de-
nial, and afterwards softens into an easier temper. And
this is very agreeable to the nature of Achilles, his anger abates very slowly; it is stubborn, yet still it returns.
had the poet drawn him as never to be pacified, he had
outraged nature, and not represented his hero as a man,
but as a monster. Eustathius

Should Dardan Priam, and his weeping dame
Drain their whole realm to buy one fun'ral flame:
Their Hector on the pile they should not see,
Nor rob the vultures of one limb of thee.

Then thus the chief his dying accents drew;⠀⠀⠀445
Thy rage, implacable ! too well I knew:
The furies that relentless breast have steel'd,
And curst thee with a heart that cannot yield.
Yet think, a day will come, when fate's decree
And angry Gods, shall wreak this wrong on thee;⠀⠀450
Phœbus and Paris shall avenge my fate,
And stretch thee here, before this Scæan gate.

He ceas'd⠀⠀The fates suppreſt his lab'ring breath,
And his eyes stiffened at the hand of death;
To the dark realm the spirit wings its way,⠀⠀⠀455
(The manly body left a load of clay)
And plaintive glides along the dreary coast,
A naked, wand'ring, melancholy ghost !

Achilles, musing as he roll'd his eyes
O'er the dead hero, thus (unheard) replies.⠀⠀⠀460
Die thou the first ! when Jove and heav'n ordain,
I follow thee——He said, and stripp'd the slain.

⠀⠀⠀ỳ. 449. *A day will come——*] Hector *prophesies* at
his death that Achilles shall fall by the hand of Paris.
This confirms an obfervation made in a former note,
that the words of dying men were looked upon as pro-
phecies, but whether such conjectures are true or false,
it appears from hence, that such opinions have prevailed
in the world above three thousand years.

Then forcing backward from the gaping wound
The reeking jav'lin, caft it on the ground
The thronging Greeks behold with wond'ring eyes 465
His manly beauty and fuperior fize:
While fome ignobler, the great dead deface
With wounds ungen'rous, or with taunts difgrace.
" How chang'd that Hector! who like Jove of late
" Sent light'ning on our fleets, and fcatter'd fate?" 470
High o'er the flain the great Achilles ftands,
Begirt with heroes, and furrounding bands;

Ŷ 467. *The great dead defce With wounds, etc*]
Euftathius tells us that Homer introduces the foldiers
wounding the dead body of Hector, in order to mitigate
the cruelties which Achilles exercifes upon it. For if
every common foldier takes a pride in giving him a
wound, what infults may we not expect from the inexorable, inflamed Achilles? But I muft confefs myfelf
unable to vindicate the poet in giving us fuch an idea of
his countrymen. I think the former courage of their
enemy fhould have been fo far from moving them to revenge, that it fhould have recommended him to their
efteem what Achilles afterwards acts is fuitable to his
character, and confequently the poet is juftified, but
furely all the Greeks were not of his temper? Patroclus
was not fo dear to them all, as he was to Achilles It is
true, the poet reprefents Achilles (as Euftathius obferves)
enumerating the many ills they had fuffered from Hector, and feems to endeavour to infect the whole army
with his refentment Had Hector been living, they
had been acted by a generous indignation againft him
but thefe men feem as if they only dared approach him
dead, in fhort, what they fay over his body is a mean
infult, and the ftabs they give it are cowardly and barbarous.

And thus aloud, while all the hoft attends.

Princes and leaders! countrymen and friends!

Since now at length the pow'rful will of heav'n   475

The dire deftroyer to our arm has giv'n,

Is not Troy fall'n already? Hafte, ye pow'rs!

See, if already their deferted tow'rs

Are left unmann'd; or if they yet retain

The fouls of heroes, their great Hector flain?   480

But what is Troy, of glory what to me?

Or why reflects my mind on ought but thee,

Divine Patroclus! death has feal'd his eyes;

Unwept, unhonour'd, uninterr'd he lies!

v. 474. *The fpeech of Achilles.*] We have a very fine obfervation of Euftathius on this place, that the judgment and addrefs of Homer here is extremely worthy of remark: he knew, and had often faid, that the gods and fate had not granted Achilles the glory of taking Troy: there was then no reafon to make him march againft the town after the death of Hector, fince all his efforts muft have been ineffectual. What has the poet done in this conjuncture? It was but reafonable that the firft thought of Achilles fhould be to march directly to Troy, and to profit himfelf of the general confternation into which the death of Hector had thrown the Trojans. We here fee he knows the duty, and does not want the ability, of a great general; but after this on a fudden he changes his defign, and derives a plaufible pretence from the impatience he has to pay the laft devoirs to his friend. The manners of Achilles, and what he has already done for Patroclus, make this very natural. At the fame time, this turning off to the tender and pathetic has a fine effect; the reader in the very fury of the hero's vengeance, perceives that Achilles is ftill a man, and capable of fofter paffions.

Can his dear image from my foul depart,   485
Long as the vital fpirit moves my heart?
If, in the melancholy fhades below,
The fames of friends and lovers ceafe to glow,
Yet mine fhall facred laft, mine undecay'd,
Burn on thro' death, and animate my fhade.   490
Meanwhile, ye fons of Greece, in triumph bring
The corps of Hector, and your Pæans fing.
Fe this the fong, flow-moving tow'rd the fhore,
" Hector is dead, and Ilion is no more."

Then his fell foul a thought of vengeance bred,   495
(Unworthy of himfelf, and of the dead)

ɣ̷ 494   " Hector is dead, and Ilion is no more."]   I
have followed the opinion of Euftathius, who thought
that what Achilles fays here was the chorus or burden of
a fong of triumph, in which his troops bear a part with
him, as he returns from this glorious combate. Dacier
obferves that this is very correfpondent to the manners
of thofe times, and inftances in that paffage of the book
of Kings, when David returns from the conqueft of
Goliah the women there go out to meet him from all
the cities of Ifrael, and fing a triumphal fong, the chorus
whereof is, Saul has killed his thoufands, and David his
ten thoufands.

ɣ̷ 496. Unworthy of himfelf, and of the dead.] This
inhumanity of Achilles in dragging the dead body of
Hector, has been feverely (and I think indeed not without fome juftice) cenfured by feveral, both ancients and
moderns Plato in his third book de republica, fpeaks
of it with deteftation but methinks it is a great injuftice to Homer, to reflect upon the morals of the author himfelf, for things which he only paints as the manners of a vicious hero

N 3

The nervous ancles bor'd, his feet he bound
With thongs inserted thro' the double wound;
These fix'd up high behind the rolling wain,
His graceful head was trail'd along the plain.   500
Proud on his car th' insulting victor stood,
And bore aloft his arms, distilling blood.
He smites the steeds; the rapid chariot flies;
The sudden clouds of circling dust arise.

It may justly be observed in general of all Plato's objections against Homer, that they are still in a view to
morality, constantly blaming him for representing ill
and immortal things as the opinions or actions of his
persons   To every one of these, one general answer
will serve, which is, that Homer as often describes ill
things, in order to make us avoid them, as good, to induce us to follow them, (which is the case with all writers
whatever)   But what is extremely remarkable, and e-
vidently shews the injustice of Plato's censure, is, that
many of those very actions for which he blames him, are
expresly characterized and marked by Homer himself as
evil and detestable, by previous expressions or cautions.
Thus in the present place, before he describes this barbarity of Achilles, he tells us it was a most unworthy
action.

- - - - - - Καὶ Ἕκτορα δῖον ἀεικία μήδετο ἔργα.

When Achilles sacrifices the twelve young Trojans in
l. 23. he repeats the same words   When Pandarus
broke the truce in l. 4. he told us it was a mad, unjust
deed;

- - - - - - - - τὰ δὲ φρεσὶ ἄφρονι τύβεν.

And so of the rest.

Now loft is all that formidable air; 505
The face divine, and long defcending hair
Purple the ground, and ftreak the fable fand;
Deform'd, difhonour'd, in his native land!
Giv'n to the rage of an infulting throng!
And, in his parent's fight, now dragg'd along! 510
    The mother firft beheld with fad furvey;
She rent her treffes, venerably grey,
And caft, far off, the regal veils away.
With piercing fhrieks his bitter fate fhe moans,
While the fad father anfwers groans with groans, 515
Tears after tears his mournful cheeks o'erflow,
And the whole city wears one face of woe.
No lefs than if the rage of hoftile fires
From her foundations curling to her fpires,

℣. 506. *The face divine, and long-defcending hair.*]
It is impoffible to read the actions of great men without
having our curiofity raifed to know the leaft circumftance that relates to them. Homer, to fatisfy it, has
taken care in the procefs of his poem to give us the fhape
of his heroes, and the very colour of their hair; thus
he has told us that Achilles's locks were yellow, and
here the epithet Κυάνεαι fhews us that thofe of Hector
were of a darker colour· as to his perfon, he told us a
little above, that it was fo handfome, that all the Greeks
were furprized to fee it Plutarch recites a remarkable
ftory of the beauty of Hector it was reported in Lace-
dæmon, that a handfome youth who very much refem-
bled Hector was arrived there; immediately the whole
city run in fuch numbers to behold him, that he was
trampled to death by the croud. Euftathius.

O'er the proud citadel at length should rise, 420
And the laft blaze fend Ilion to the fkies.
The wretched monarch of the falling ftate,
Diftracted, preffes to the Dardan gate.
Scarce the whole people ftop his defp'rate courfe,
While ftrong affliction gives the feeble force : 525
Grief tears his heart, and drives him to and fro,
In all the raging impotence of woe.
At length he roll'd in duft, and thus begun :
Imploring all, and naming one by one.
Ah! let me, let me go where forrow calls; 530
I, only I, will iffue from your walls,
(Guide or companion, friends! I afk ye none)
And bow before the murd'rer of my fon.
My grief perhaps his pity may engage;
Perhaps at leaft he may refpect my age: 535
He has a father too; a man like me;
One, not exempt from age and mifery,
(Vig'rous no more, as when his young embrace
Begot this peft of me, and all my race)
How many valiant fons, in early bloom, 540
Has that curft hand fent headlong to the tomb!
Thee, Hector! laft: thy lofs (divinely brave)
Sinks my fad foul with forrow to the grave.

℣. 543. *Sinks my fad foul with forrow to the grave*]
It is in the Greek,

'Ου μ' άχος ὀξύ κατοισεται ἀΐδος ἴσω.

It is needlefs to obferve to the reader with what a
beautiful *pathos* the wretched father laments his fon

Oh had thy gentle spirit paſt in peace,
The ſon expiring in the ſire's embrace,   545
While both thy parents wept the fatal hour,
And bending o'er thee, mix'd the tender ſhow'r!
Some comfort that had been, ſome ſad relief,
To melt in full ſatiety of grief!

 Thus wail'd the father; grov'ling on the ground, 550
And all the eyes of Ilion ſtream'd around.

 Amidſt her matrons Hecuba appears,
(A mourning princeſs, and a train in tears)
Ah why has heav'n prolong'd this hated breath,
Patient of horrors, to behold thy death?   555
Oh Hector! late thy parents pride and joy,
The boaſt of nations! the defence of Troy!
To whom her ſafety and her fame ſhe ow'd,
Her chief, her hero, and almoſt her God!
O fatal change! become in one ſad day   560
A ſenſeleſs corſe! inanimated clay!

 But not as yet the fatal news had ſpread
To fair Andromache, of Hector dead;

Hector: it is impoſſible not to join with Priam in his
ſorrows. But what I would chiefly point out to my
reader, is the beauty of this line, which is particularly
tender, and almoſt word for word the ſame with that of
the patriarch Jacob; who upon a like occaſion breaks
out into the ſame complaint, and tells his children, that
if they deprive him of his ſon Benjamin, they will *bring
down his grey hairs with ſorrow to the grave.*

 v. 563, etc] The grief of Andromache, which is
painted in the following part, is far beyond all the
praiſes that can be given it; but I muſt take notice of

As yet no meſſenger had told his fate,
Nor ev'n his ſtay without the Scæan gate.   565
Far in the cloſe receſſes of the dome,
Penſive ſhe ply'd the melancholy loom;
A growing work employ'd her ſecret hours,
Confus'dly gay with intermingled flow'rs.
Here fair-hair'd handmaids heat the brazen urn,   570
The bath preparing for her Lord's return:
In vain: alas! her Lord returns no more!
Unbath'd he lies, and bleeds along the ſhore!
Now from the walls the clamours reach her ear,
And all her members ſhake with ſudden fear;   575
Forth from her iv'ry hand the ſhuttle falls,
As thus, aſtoniſh'd, to her maids ſhe calls.

Ah follow me! (ſhe cry'd) what plaintive noiſe
Invades my ear? 'Tis ſure my mother's voice.
My fault'ring knees their trembling frame deſert,   580
A pulſe unuſual flutters at my heart.
Some ſtrange diſaſter, ſome reverſe of fate
(Ye Gods avert it) threats the Trojan ſtate.

one particular which ſhews the great art of the poet.
In order to make the wife of Hector appear yet more
afflicted than his parents, he has taken care to increaſe
her affliction by *ſurprize*: it is finely prepared by the
circumſtances of her being retired to her innermoſt a-
partment, of her employment in weaving a robe for her
huſband, (as may be conjectured from what ſhe ſays
afterward, ℣. 657.) and of her maids preparing the bath
for his return: all which (as the critics have obſerved)
augment the ſurprize, and render this reverſe of fortune
much more dreadful and afflicting.

Far be the omen which my thoughts suggest!
But much I fear my Hector's dauntless breast   585
Confronts Achilles; chas'd along the plain,
Shut from our walls! I fear, I fear Him slain!
Safe in the croud he ever scorn'd to wait,
And sought for glory in the jaws of fate:
Perhaps that noble heat has cost his breath,   590
Now quench'd for ever in the arms of death.

She spoke; and furious, with distracted pace,
Fears in her heart, and anguish in her face,
Flies thro' the dome, (the maids her steps pursue)
And mounts the walls, and sends around her view. 595
Too soon her eyes the killing object found,
The god-like Hector dragg'd along the ground.
A sudden darkness shades her swimming eyes.
She faints, she falls; her breath, her colour flies.
Her hair's fair ornaments, the braids that bound, 600
The net that held them, and the wreath that crown'd,

♈. 600. *Her hair's fair ornaments*] Eustathius remarks, that in speaking of Andromache and Hecuba,
Homer expatiates upon the ornaments of dress in Andromache, because she was a beautiful young princess; but
is very concise about that of Hecuba, because she was
old, and wore a dress rather suitable to her age and
gravity, than to her state, birth, and condition. I cannot pass over a matter of such importance as a lady's
dress, without endeavouring to explain what sort of
heads were worn above three thousand years ago.
It is difficult to describe particularly every ornament
mentioned by the poet, but I shall lay before my female
readers the bishop's explanation. The Ἄμπυξ was used,

The veil and diadem, flew far away;
(The gift of Venus on her bridal day)
Around a train of weeping sisters stands
To raise her sinking with assistant hands.   605
Scarce from the verge of death recall'd again,
She faints, or but recovers to complain.

O wretched husband of a wretched wife!
Born with one fate, to one unhappy life!
For sure one star its baneful beam display'd   610
On Priam's roof, and Hippoplacia's shade.
From diff'rent parents, diff'rent climes we came,
At diff'rent periods, yet our fate the same!
Why was my birth to great Aetion ow'd,
And why was all that tender care bestow'd?   615

το τὰς ἐμπροσθίας τρίχας ἀναδεῖν, that is, to tie backwards
the hair that grew on the forepart of the head· the
Κεκρύφαλος was a veil of net-work that covered the hair
when it was so tied: Ἀναδέσμη was an ornament used
κύκλω περὶ τὰς κροτάφυς ἀναδεῖν, to tie backwards the hair
that grew on the temples; and the Κρήδεμνον was a fillet,
perhaps embroidered with gold, (from the expression of
χρυσῆ Ἀφροδίτη) that bound the whole, and compleated
the dress.

The ladies cannot but be pleased to see so much learn-
ing and Greek upon this important subject.

Homer is in nothing more excellent than in that di-
stinction of characters which he maintains through his
whole poem: what Andromache here says, cannot be
spoken properly by any but Andromache: there is nothing general in her sorrows, nothing that can be tranf-
ferred to another character: the mother laments the
son, and the wife weeps over the husband.

Would

Would I had never been!—O thou, the ghost
Of my dead husband! miferably loft!
Thou to the difmal realms for ever gone!
And I abandon'd, defolate, alone!
An only child, once comfort of my pains,   ·   620
Sad product now of haplefs love remains!
No more to fmile upon his fire! no friend
To help him now! no father to defend!
For fhould he 'fcape the fword, the common doom!
What wrongs attend him, and what griefs to come? 625
Ev'n from his own paternal roof expell'd,   ·
Some ftranger plows his patrimonial field.
The day, that to the fhades the father fends,
Robs the fad orphan of his father's friends:

x. 628. *The day, that to the fhades,* etc.] The following verfes, which fo finely defcribe the condition of
an orphan, have been rejected by fome ancient critics:
it is a proof there were always critics of no manner of
tafte; it being impoffible any where to meet with a
more exquifite paffage. I will venture to fay, there
are not in all Homer any lines more worthy of him:
the beauty of this tender and compaffionate image is
fuch, that it even makes amends for the many cruel ones,
with which the Iliad is too much ftained. Thefe cenfurers
imagined this defcription to be of too abject and mean
a nature of one of the quality of Aftyanax, but had they
confidered (fays Euftathius) that thefe are the words of
a fond mother, who feared every thing for her fon;
that women are by nature timorous, and think all mif-
fortunes will happen, becaufe there is a poffibility that
they may; that Andromache is in the very height of
her forrows, in the inftant fhe is fpeaking; I fancy they
would have altered their opinion.

He, wretched outcaſt of mankind! appears   630
For ever ſad, for ever bath'd in tears;
Amongſt the happy, unregarded he,
Hangs on the robe, or trembles at the knee,
While thoſe his father's former bounty fed,
Nor reach the goblet, nor divide the bread: 635
The kindeſt but his preſent wants allay,
To leave him wretched the ſucceeding day.
Frugal compaſſion! heedleſs they who boaſt
Both parents ſtill, nor feel what he has loſt,
Shall cry, " Be gone! thy father feaſts not here: ' 640
The wretch obeys, retiring with a fear.
Thus wretched, thus retiring all in tears,
To my ſad ſoul Aſtyanax appears!
Forc'd by repeated inſults to return,
And to his widow'd mother vainly mourn.   645
He, who with tender delicacy bred,
With princes ſported, and on dainties fed,

It is undoubtedly an aggravation to our misfortunes
when they ſink us in a moment from the higheſt flow of
proſperity to the loweſt adverſity: the poet judiciouſly
makes uſe of this circumſtance, the more to excite our
pity, and introduces the mother with the utmoſt tenderneſs, lamenting this reverſe of fortune in her ſon;
changed all at once into a ſlave, a beggar, an orphan!
have we not examples in our own times of unhappy
princes, whoſe condition renders this of Aſtyanax but too
probable?

   ẏ. 647. *On dainties fed.*] It is in the Greek, " Who
" upon his father's knees, uſed to eat marrow and the
" fat of ſheep." This would ſeem groſs if it were literally tranſlated, but it is a figurative expreſſion; in

And when ſtill ev'ning gave him up to reſt,
Sunk ſoft in down upon the nurſe's breaſt,
Muſt—ah what muſt he not? Whom Ilion calls   650
Aſtyanax, from her well-guarded walls,
Is now that name no more, unhappy boy!
Since now no more the father guards his Troy.
But thou, my Hector, ly'ſt expos'd in air,
Far from thy parent's and thy conſort's care,   655
Whoſe hand in vain, directed by her love,
The martial ſcarf and robe of triumph wove.

the ſtyle of the orientals, marrow and fatneſs are taken for whatever is beſt, tendereſt, and moſt delicious. Thus in Job xxi. 24. *Viſcera ejus plena ſunt adipe, et medullis oſſa ejus irrigantur.* And xxxvi 16. *Requies autem menſæ tuæ erit plena pinguedine.* In Jer. xxxi. 14. God ſays, that he will ſatiate the ſoul of the prieſts with fatneſs. *Inebriabo animam ſacerdotum pinguedine.* Dacier.

Ў. 657. *The martial ſcarf and robe of triumph wove.*] This idea very naturally offers itſelf to a woman, who rep.eſents to herſelf the body of her huſband daſhed to pieces, and all his limbs dragged upon the ground uncovered, and nothing is more proper to excite pity. It is well known, that it was anciently the cuſtom among princeſſes and great ladies to have large quantities of ſtuffs and moveables. This proviſion was more neceſſary in thoſe times than now, becauſe of the great conſumption made of them on thoſe occaſions of mourning Dacier.

I am of opinion that Homer had a farther view in expatiating thus largely upon the death of Hector. Every word that Hecuba, Priam, and Andromache ſpeak, ſhews us the importance of Hector: every word adds a weight to the concluding action of the poem, and at the ſame time repreſents the ſad effects of the anger of Achilles, which is the ſubject of it.

Now to devouring flames be thefe a prey,
Ufelefs to thee, from this accurfed day!
Yet let the facrifice at leaft be paid,   660
An honour to the living, not the dead!

  So fpake the mournful dame: her matrons hear,
Sigh back her fighs, and anfwer tear with tear.

THE

I L I A D.

B O O K XXIII.

THE ARGUMENT.

ACHILLES and the *Myrmidons do honours to the body
of Patroclus. After the funeral feaſt he retires to the
ſea-ſhore, where falling aſleep, the ghoſt of his friend
appears to him, and demands the rites of burial; the next
morning the ſoldiers are ſent with mules and waggons to
fetch wood for the pyre. The funeral proceſſion, and the
offering their hair to the dead. Achilles ſacrifices ſeveral animals, and laſtly twelve Trojan captives at the
pile, then ſets fire to it. He pays libations to the
winds, which (at the inſtance of Iris) riſe, and raiſe
the flames. When the pile has burned all night, they
gather the bones, place them in an urn of gold, and
raiſe the tomb. Achilles inſtitutes the funeral games:
the chariot-race, the fight of the Cæſtus, the wreſt-
ling, the foot-race, the ſingle combate, the Diſcus, the
ſhooting with arrows, the darting the javelin: the
various deſcriptions of which, and the various ſucceſs
of the ſeveral antagoniſts, make the greateſt part of
the book.*

*In this book ends the thirtieth day. The night following,
the ghoſt of Patroclus appears to Achilles. the one and
thirtieth day is employed in felling the timber for the
pile, the two and thirtieth in burning it; and the three
and thirtieth in the games. The ſcene is generally on
the ſea ſhore.*

THUS humbled in the duft, the penfive train
   Thro' the fad city mourn'd her hero flain.
The body foil'd with duft, and black with gore,
Lies on broad Hellefpont's refounding fhore:

This, and the following book, which contain the
defcription of the funeral of Patroclus and other matters
relating to Hector, are undoubtedly fuper-added to the
grand cataftrophe of the poem; for the ftory is com-
pleatly finifhed with the death of that hero in the twen-
ty-fecond book. Many judicious critics have been of
opinion, that Homer is blameable for protracting it.
Virgil clofes the whole fcene of action with the death of
Turnus, and leaves the reft to be imagined by the mind
of the reader. he does not draw the picture at full length,
but delineates it fo far, that we cannot fail of imagining
the whole draught. There is however one thing to be
faid in favour of Homer, which may perhaps juftify him
in his method, that what he undertook to paint was the
anger of Achilles: and as that anger does not die with
Hector, but perfecutes his very remains, fo the poet
ftill keeps up to his fubject; nay, it feems to require
that he fhould carry down the relation of that refentment, which is the foundation of his poem, till it is fully
fatisfied · and as this furvives Hector, and gives the
poet an opportunity of ftill fhewing many fad effects of
Achilles's anger, the two following books may be thought
not to be excrefcencies, but effential to the poem.

Virgil had been inexcufable had he trod' in Homer's
footfteps; for it is evident that the fall of Turnus, by
giving Æneas a full power over Italy, anfwers the whole
defign and intention of the poem, had he gone farther,
he had overfhot his mark · and though Homer proceeds
after Hector's death, yet the fubject is ftill the *anger of*
Achilles.

We are now paft the war and violence of the Ilias,
the fcenes of blood are clofed during the reft of the

The Grecians feek their fhips, and clear the ftrand, 5
All, but the martial Myrmidonian band:
Thefe yet affembled great Achilles holds,
And the ftern purpofe of his mind unfolds.

Not yet (my brave companions of the war)
Releafe your fmoking courfers from the car; 10
But, with his chariot each in order led,
Perform due honours to Patroclus dead.
Ere yet from reft or food we feek relief,
Some rites remain, to glut our rage of grief.

The troops obey'd; and thrice in order led 15
(Achilles firft) their courfers round the dead;
And thrice their forrows and laments renew;
Tears bathe their arms, and tears the fands bedew.

poem; we may look back with a pleafing kind of horror
upon the anger of Achilles, and fee what dire effects it
has wrought in the compafs of nineteen days: Troy
and Greece are both in mourning for it, heaven and
earth, gods and men, have fuffered in the conflict. The
reader feems landed upon the fhore after a violent ftorm;
and has leifure to furvey the confequences of the tempeft, and the wreck occafioned by the former commo-
tions, Troy weeping for Hector, and Greece for Patroclus.
Our paffions have been in an agitation fince the opening
of the poem: wherefore the poet, like fome great mafter
in mufic, foftens his notes, and melts his readers into
tendernefs and pity.

℣. 18. *Tears bathe their arms, and tears the fands
bedew,*
——— ——*Thetis aids their woe*——]
It is not eafy to give a reafon why Thetis fhould be faid
to excite the grief of the Myrmidons and of Achilles; it
had feemed more natural for the mother to have com-

For fuch a warrior Thetis aids their woe,
Melts their ftrong hearts, and bids their eyes to flow. 20

pofed the forrows of the fon, and reftored his troubled
mind to tranquillity

But fuch a procedure would have outraged the character of Achilles, who is all along defcribed to be of
fuch a violence of temper, that he is not eafy to be pacified at any time, much lefs upon fo great an incident
as the death of his friend Patroclus   Perhaps the poet
made ufe of this fiction in honour of Achilles; he makes
every paffion of his hero confiderable; his forrow as
well as anger is important, and he cannot grieve but a
goddefs attends him, and a whole army weeps.

Some commentators fancy that Homer animates the
very fands of the fea, and the arms of the Myrmidons,
and makes them fenfible of the lofs of Patroclus; the
preceding words feem to ftrengthen that opinion, becaufe the poet introduces a goddefs to raife the forrow
of the army.   But Euftathius feems not to give into
this conjecture, and I think very judicioufly; for what
relation is there between the fands of the fhores, and
the arms of the Myrmidons ? It would have been more
poetical to have faid, the fands and the rocks, than the
fands and the arms, but it is very natural to fay, that
the foldiers wept fo bitterly, that their armour and the
very fands were wet with their tears.   I believe this
remark will appear very juft by reading the verfe, with
a comma after τ ι χ α, thus,

Δ ι δο.-ο Δ αυαβοι, δ δοι-ο δι τ ι χ α, φατων
Δ αγ υσι

Then the conftruction will be natural and eafy, period
will anfwer period in the Greek, and the fenfe in Englifh
will be, the fands were wet, and the arms were wet,
with the tears of the mot rners.

But however this be, there is a very remarkable
beauty in the run of the verfe in Homer, every word

But chief, Pelides: thick-fucceeding fighs
Burft from his heart, and torrents from his eyes:
His flaught'ring hands, yet red with blood, he laid
On his dead friend's cold breaft, and thus he faid.

All hail, Patroclus! let thy honour'd ghoft   25
Hear, and rejoice on Pluto's dreary coaft;
Behold! Achilles' promife is compleat;
The bloody Hector ftretch'd before thy feet.
Lo! to the dogs his carcafs I refign;
And twelve fad victims of the Trojan line,   30
Sacred to vengeance, inftant fhall expire,
Their lives effus'd around thy fun'ral pyre.

Gloomy he faid, and (horrible to view)
Before the bier the bleeding Hector threw,

has a melancholy cadence, and the poet has not only
made the fands and the arms, but even his very verfe,
to lament with Achilles.

℣. 23. *His flaught'ring hands, yet red with blood, he*
laid
On his dead friend's cold breaft——]
I could not pafs by this paffage without obferving to my
reader the great beauty of this epithet, ανδροφονυς An
ordinary poet would have contented himfelf with faying,
he laid his hand upon the breaft of Patroclus; but Homer knows how to raife the moft trivial circumftance,
and by adding this one word, he laid his *deadly* hands,
or his *murderous* hands, he fills our minds with great
ideas, and by a fingle epithet recalls to our thoughts all
the noble atchievements of Achilles through the Iliad.

℣. 25. *All hail, Patroclus, etc*] There is in this a-
poftrophe of Achilles to the ghoft of Patroclus, a fort of
favagenefs, and a mixture of foftnefs and atrocity, which
are highly conformable to his character. Dacier.

Prone on the duft.   The Myrmidons around   35
Unbrac'd their armour, and the fteeds unbound.
All to Achilles' fable fhip repair,
Frequent and full, the genial feaft to fhare.
Now from the well-fed fwine black fmoaks afpire,
The briftly victims hiffing o'er the fire: 40
The huge ox bellowing falls; with feebler cries
Expires the goat; the fheep in filence dies.
Around the hero's proftrate body flow'd,
In one promifcuous ftream, the reeking blood.
And now a band of Argive monarchs brings   45
The glorious victor to the king of kings.
From his dead friend the penfive warrior went,
With fteps unwilling, to the regal tent.
Th' attending heralds, as by office bound,
With kindled flames the tripod-vafe furround;   50
To cleanfe his conqu'ring hands from hoftile gore,
They urg'd in vain; the chief refus'd, and fwore.

    No drop fhall touch me, by almighty Jove [1]
The firft and greateft of the Gods above [1]
'Till on the pyre I place thee; 'till I rear   55
The graffy mound, and clip thy facred hair.

    ẏ 51. *To cleanfe his conqu'ring hands* ————
            ———— *The chief refus'd*————]
This is conformable to the cuftom of the orientals: A-
chilles will not be induced to wafh, and afterwards retires to the fea-fhore, and fleeps on the ground.   It is
juft thus that David mourns in the fcriptures; he refufes to wafh, or to take any repaft, but retires from
company, and lies upon the earth.

Some eafe at leaft thofe pious rites may give,
And foothe my forrows, while I bear to live.
Howe'er, reluctant as I am, I ftay,
And fhare your feaft; but, with the dawn of day, 60
(O king of men!) it claims thy royal care,
That Greece the warrior's fun'ral pile prepare,
And bid the forefts fall: (fuch rites are paid
To heroes flumb'ring in eternal fhade)
Then, when his earthly part fhall mount in fire, 65
Let the leagu'd fquadrons to their pofts retire.

He fpoke; they hear him, and the word obey;
The rage of hunger and of thirft allay,
Then eafe in fleep the labours of the day.
But great Pelides, ftretch'd along the fhore 70
Where dafh'd on rocks the broken billows rore,
Lies inly groaning; while on either hand
The martial Myrmidons confus'dly ftand:
Along the grafs his languid members fall,
Tir'd with his chafe around the Trojan wall; 75
Hufh'd by the murmurs of the rolling deep,
At length he finks in the foft arms of fleep.
When lo! the fhade before his clofing eyes
Of fad Patroclus rofe, or feem'd to rife;

$\dot{y}$. 78. *The ghoft of Patroclus.*] Homer has introduced into the former parts of the poem the perfonages of
gods and goddeffes from heaven, and of furies from hell.
He has embellifhed it with ornaments from earth, fea,
and air; and he here opens a new fcene, and brings to
the view a ghoft, the fhade of the departed friend · by
thefe methods he diverfifies his poem with new and fur-

In the fame robe he living wore, he came,   80
In ftature, voice, and pleafing look, the fame.
The form familiar hover'd o'er his head,   }
And fleeps Achilles (thus the phantom faid)   }
Sleeps my Achilles, his Patroclus dead?   }
Living, I feem'd his deareft, tend'reft care,   85
But now forgot, I wander in the air;
Let my pale corfe the rites of burial know,
And give me entrance in the realms below:
'Till then, the fpirit finds no refting-place,
But here and there th' unbody'd fpectres chace   90
The vagrant dead around the dark abode,
Forbid to crofs th' irremeable flood.

prizing circumftances, and awakens the attention of the
reader; at the fame time he very poetically adapts his
language to the circumftances of this imaginary Patroclus, and teaches us the opinions that prevailed in his
time, concerning the ftate of feparate fouls.

ỳ 92 *Forbid to crofs th' irremeable flood.*] It was
the common opinion of the ancients, that the fouls of
the departed were not admitted into the number of the
happy till their bodies had received the funeral rites;
they fuppofed thofe that wanted them wandered an hundred years before they were wafted over the infernal
river, Virgil perhaps had this paffage of Homer in his
view in the fixth Æneis, at leaft he coincides with his
fentiments concerning the ftate of the departed fouls.

Hæc omnis, quam cernis, inops inhumataque turba eft:
Nec ripas datur horrendas, nec rauca fluenta
Tranfportare prius, quam fedibus offa quierunt;
Centum errant annos, volitantque hæc littora circum;
Tum demum admiffi ftagna exoptata revifunt.

It

Now give thy hand; for' to' the farther shore
When once we pass,'the soul returns no more.
When once the last funereal flames ascend,   95
No more shall meet Achilles and his friend,
No more our thoughts to thofe we lov'd make known,
Or quit the deareft, to converfe alone.
Me fate has fever'd from the fons of earth,
The fate fore-doom'd that waited from my birth: 100
Thee too it waits, before the Trojan wall
Ev'n great and godlike thou art doom'd to fall.
Hear then; and as in fate and love we join,
Ah fuffer that my bones may reft with thine!

It was during this interval between death and the rites
of funeral, that they fuppofed the only time allowed for
feparate fpirits to appear to men, therefore Patroclus
here tells his friend,

> ———To the farther fhore
> When once we pafs, the foul retuins no more.

For the fuller underftanding of Homer, it is neceffary
to be acquainted with his notion of the ftate of the foul
after death: he followed the philofophy of the Ægyptians, who fuppofed man to be compounded of three
parts, an intelligent mind, a vehicle for that mind, and
a body; the mind they call φρὴν, or ψυχὴ, the vehicle
εἴδωλον, *image* or *foul*, and the grofs body σᾶμα The
foul, in which the mind was lodged, was fuppofed exactly to refemble the body in fhape, magnitude, and
features; for this being in the body, as the ftatue in its
mold, fo foon as it goes forth is properly the image of
that body in which it was inclofed: this it was that appeared to Achilles, with the full refemblance of his
friend Patroclus. Vid. Dacier's life of Pythagoras, p. 71.

    ℣. 104. *Ah fuffer that my bones may reft with thine.*]

Together have we liv'd, together bred,   105
One houfe receiv'd us, and one table fed:
That golden urn thy goddefs-mother gave,
May mix our afhes in one common grave.

And is it thou? (he anfwers) to my fight
Once more return'ft thou from the realms of night?   110
Oh more than brother! think each office paid,
Whate'er can reft a difcontented fhade;
But grant one laft embrace, unhappy boy!
Afford at leaft that melancholy joy.

There is fomething very pathetical in this whole fpeech
of Patroclus; he begins it with kind reproaches, and
blames Achilles with a friendly tendernefs; he recounts
to him the infeparable affection that had been between
them in their lives, and makes it his laft requeft, that
they may not be parted even in death, but that their
bones may reft in the fame urn. The fpeech itfelf is
of a due length; it ought not to be very fhort, becaufe
this apparition is an incident intirely different from any
other in the whole poem, and confequently the reader
would not have been fatisfied with a curfory mention
of it; neither ought it to be long, becaufe this would
have been contrary to the nature of fuch apparitions,
whofe ftay upon earth has ever been defcribed as very
fhort, and confequently they cannot be fuppofed to ufe
many words.

The circumftance of being buried in the fame urn, is
intirely conformable to the eaftern cuftom: there are
innumerable inftances in the fcriptures of great perfonages being buried with their fathers fo Jofeph would
not fuffer his bones to reft in Ægypt, but commands his
brethren to carry them into Canaan, to the burying-
place of his father Jacob.

He faid, and with his longing arms effay'd   115
In vain to grafp the vifionary fhade;
Like a thin fmoke he fees the fpirit fly,
And hears a feeble lamentable cry
Confus'd he wakes; amazement breaks the bands ⎫
Of golden fleep, and ftarting from the fands,   ⎬ 120
Penfive he mufes with uplifted hands.   ⎭

  'Tis true, 'tis certain; man tho' dead, retains
Part of himfelf, th' immortal mind remains
The form fubfifts without the body's aid,
Aerial femblance, and an empty fhade!   125

    ℣. 124. *The form fubfifts, without the body's aid,*
        Aerial femblance, and an empty fhade.]

The words of Homer are,

        Ἀτὰρ φρίνες ὐκ ἔνι πάμπαν.

In which there feems to be a great difficulty; it being
not eafy to explain how Achilles can fay that the ghoft
of his friend had no underftanding, when it had but
juft made fuch a rational and moving fpeech; efpecially
when the poet introduces the apparition with the very
fhape, air, and voice of Patroclus.

  But this paffage will be clearly underftood, by explaining the notion which the ancients entertained of
the fouls of the departed, according to the fore-cited
triple divifion of *mind*, *image*, and *body* They imagined
that the foul was not only feparated from the body at
the hour of death, but that there was a farther feparati-
on of the φρὴν, or underftanding, from its ἐιδωλόν, or vehicle; fo that while the ἐιδωλον, or image of the body,
was in hell, the φρὴν or underftanding might be in
heaven: and that this is a true explication, is evident
from a paffage in the Odyffey, book 11. ℣. 600

This night my friend, so late in battel loſt,
Stood at my ſide, a penſive, plaintive ghoſt;
Ev'n now familiar, as in life, he came,
Alas! how diff'rent! yet how like the ſame!

Thus while he ſpoke, each eye grew big with tears; 130
And now the roſy-finger'd morn appears,
Shews ev'ry mournful face with tears o'erſpread,
And glares on the pale viſage of the dead.

Τὸν δ' μ τ', ̉ στένσα ϐίην, Ἡρακληΐην
Εἴδωλον αὐτὸς δὲ μιτ' ἀθανάτοισι θεοῖσι
Τέρπεται ἐν θαλίης, καὶ ἔχει καλλίσφυρον Ἥϐην,

Now I the ſtrength of Hercules behold,
A tow'ring ſpectre of gigantic mold,
A ſhadowy form! for high in heav'n's abodes
Himſelf reſides, a God among the Gods:
There in the bright aſſemblies of the ſkies
He Nectar quaffs, and Hebe crowns his joys.

By this it appears that Homer was of opinion that Hercules was in heaven, while his εἴδωλον, or image, was in
hell ſo that when this ſecond ſeparation is made, the
image or vehicle becomes a mere thoughtleſs form.
We have this whole doctrine very diſtinctly delivered
by Plutarch in theſe words. " Man is a compound ſub-
" ject; but not of two parts, as is commonly believed,
" becauſe the underſtanding is generally accounted a
" part of the ſoul, whereas indeed it as far exceeds the
" ſoul, as the ſoul is diviner than the body. Now the
" ſoul, when compounded with the underſtanding,
" makes reaſon, and when compounded with the body,
" paſſion: whereof the one is the ſource or principle
" of pleaſure or pain, the other of vice or virtue. Man
" therefore properly dies two deaths, the firſt death
" makes him two of three, and the ſecond makes him
" one of two." Plutarch, *of the face in the moon.*

But Agamemnon, as the rites demand,

With mules and waggons sends a chosen band;   135

To load the timber, and the pile to rear,

A charge consign'd to Merion's faithful care.

With proper instruments they take the road,

Axes to cut, and ropes to sling the load,

First march the heavy mules, securely slow,   140

O'er hills, o'er dales, o'er crags, o'er rocks they go:

♈. 141. *O'er hills, o'er dales, o'er crags, o'er rocks*
   they go————
  On all sides round the forest hurls her oaks
  Headlong———— ————]

The numbers in the original of this whole passage are
admirably adapted to the images the verses convey to
us   Every ear must have felt the propriety of sound
in this line,

Πολλὰ δ' ἄναντα, κάταντα, πάρανταί τι, δόχμιά τ' ἦλθην.

The other in its kind is no less exact,

Τάμνον ἐπειγόμενοι, ταὶ δὲ μεγάλα κτυπέουσι
Πίπτον ------------

Dionysius of Halicarnassus has collected many instances
of these sorts of beauties in Homer.   This description
of felling the forests, so excellent as it is, is comprehended in a few lines, which has left room for a larger
and more particular one in Statius, one of the best (I
think) in that author.

  ————*Cadit ardua fagus,*
Chaoniumque nemus, brumæque illæsa cupressus;
Procumbunt piceæ, flammis alimenta supremis,
Ornique,iliciæque trabes, metuandaque sulco

B 3

Jumping, high o'er the fhrubs of the rough ground,
Rattle the clatt'ring cars, and the fkockt axles bound
But when arriv'd at Ida's fpreading woods,
(Fair Ida, water'd with defcending floods)   145
Loud founds the axe, redoubling ftrokes on ftrokes,
On all fides round the foreft hurls her oaks
Headlong   Deep-echoing groan the thickets brown;
Then ruftling, crackling, crafhing, thunder down.

Taxus, et infandos belli potura cruores
Fraxinus, atque fitu non expugrabile robur.
Hic audax abies, et odoro vulnere pinus
Sordiuur, cecinant irtonfa cacumina terræ
Amis amica fretis, nec inhofpita vitibus ulmus, etc.

I the rather cite this fine paffage, becaufe I find it copied by two of the greateft poets of our own nation,
Chaucer and Spenfer.   The firft in the *affembly of fouls,*
the fecond in his *fairy queen,* lib. 1.

The failing pine, the cedar proud and tall,
The sire-prop elm, the poplar never dry,
The builder oak, fole king of forefts all,
The afpin good for flaves, the cyprefs funeral.
The Laurel, meed of mighty conquerors,
And poets fage, the fir that weepeth ftill,
The willow, worn of forlorn paramours,
The yew obedient to the bender's will,
The birch for fhafts, the fallow for the mill,
The myrrh, fweet-bleeding in the bitter wound,
The warlike beech, the afh for nothing ill,
The fruitful olive, and the platane round,
The carver holme, the maple feldom inward found.

The wood the Grecians cleave, prepar'd to burn; 150
And the flow mules the fame rough road return.
The fturdy woodmen equal burdens bore
(Such charge was giv'n 'em) to the fandy fhore;
There on the fpot which great Achilles fhow'd,
They eas'd their fhoulders, and difpos'd the load; 155
Circling around the place, where times to come
Shall view Patroclus' and Achilles' tomb.
The hero bids his martial troops appear
High on their cars in all the pomp of war,
Each in refulgent arms his limbs attires, 160
All mount their chariots, combatants and fquires.
The chariots firft proceed, a fhining train,
Then clouds of foot that fmoke along the plain;
Next thefe the melancholy band appear,
Amidft, lay dead Patroclus on the bier · 165
O'er all the corfe their fcatter'd locks they throw;
Achilles next, oppreft with mighty woe,

℣. 160 *Each in refulgent arms*, etc] It is not to be
fuppofed that this was a general cuftom ufed at all funerals, but Patroclus being a warrior, he is buried like a
foldier, with military honours. Euftathius.

℣. 166. *O'er all the corfe their fcatter'd locks they
throw*]
The ceremony of cutting off the hair in honour of the
dead, was practifed not only among the Greeks, but alfo among other nations, thus Statius Thebaid 6.

————*Tergoque et pectore fufam*
Cefariem ferro minuit, fectifque jacentis
Obnubit tenuia ora comis.

Supporting with his hands the hero's head,
Bends o'er th' extended body of the dead.

This cuſtom is taken notice of in holy ſcripture: Eze-
kiel deſcribing a great lamentation, ſays, *They ſhall make
themſelves utterly bald for thee*, ch xxvii ⱨ. 31. I believe it was done not only in token of ſorrow, but perhaps had a concealed meaning, that as the hair was cut
from the head, and was never more to be joined to it,
ſo was the dead for ever cut off from the living, never
more to return.

I muſt obſerve that this ceremony of cutting off the
hair was not always in token of ſorrow; Lycophron in
his Caſſandra, ⱨ. 976. deſcribing a general lamentation,
ſays,

Κρατὸς δ᾽ ἄκυρος νῶτα καλλίνει ζόβη

A length of unſhorn hair adorn'd their backs.

And that the ancients ſometimes had their hair cut off
in token of *joy*, is evident from Juvenal, Sat. 12. ⱨ. 82.

————*Gaudent ibi vertice raſo
Garrula ſecuri narrare pericula nautæ.*

This ſeeming contradiction will be ſolved by having reſpect to the different practices of different nations. If
it was the general cuſtom of any country to wear long
hair, then the cutting it off was a token of ſorrow, but
if it was the cuſtom to wear ſhort hair, then the letting
it grow long and neglecting it, ſhewed that ſuch people
were mourners.

ⱨ 163 *Supporting with his hands the hero's head*].
Achilles follows the corſe as chief mourner, and ſuſtains
the head of his friend: this laſt circumſtance ſeems to
be general, thus Euripides in the funeral of Rheſus,
ⱨ. 886.

Patroclus decent on th' appointed ground   170
They place, and heap the fylvan pile around.
But great Achilles ftands apart in pray'r,
And from his head divides the yellow hair;
Thofe curling locks which from his youth he vow'd,
And facred grew, to Sperchius' honour'd flood: 175
Then fighing, to the deep his looks he caft,
And roll'd his eyes around the wat'ry wafte.

Sperchius! whofe waves in mazy errors loft
Delightful roll along my native coaft! '
To whom we vainly vow'd, at our return,   180
Thefe locks to fall, and hecatombs to burn:

> Τίς ὑπὲρ κεφαλῆς θεὸς, ὦ Βασιλεῦ,
> Τὸν νεόδμητον ἐν χεροῖν
> Φοράδην πέμπει,

What God, O king, with his hands fupports the head of the
deceafed?

♯. 175. *And facred grew to Sperchius' honour'd flood.*]
It was the cuftom of the ancients not only to offer their
own hair, but likewife to confecrate that of their children to the river-gods of their country. This is what
Paufanias fhews in his Attics: *Before you pafs the Ce-*
phifa (fays he) *you find the tomb of Theodorus, who was*
the moft excellent actor of his time for tragedy, and on
the banks you fee two ftatues, one of Mnefimachus, and the
other of his fon, who cut off his hair in honour of the rivers:
for that this was in all ages the cuftom of the Greeks, may
be inferred from Homer's poetry, where Peleus promifes by
a folemn vow to confecrate to the river Sperchius the hair
of his fon, if he returns fafe from the Trojan war. This
cuftom was likewife in Ægypt, where Philoftratus tells
us, that Memnon confecrated his hair to the Nile. This
practice of Achilles was imitated by Alexander at the
funeral of Hephæftion. Spondanus.

Full fifty rams to bleed in sacrifice,
Where to the day thy silver fountains rise,
And where in shade of confecrated bow'rs
The altars stand, perfum'd with native flow'rs!   185
So vow'd my father, but he vow'd in vain;
No more Achilles sees his native plain;
In that vain hope these hairs no longer grow,
Patroclus bears them to the shades below.

 Thus o'er Patroclus while the hero pray'd,   190
On his cold hand the facred lock he laid.
Once more afresh the Grecian forrows flow:
And now the fun had fet upon their woe;
But to the king of men thus spoke the chief.
Enough Atrides! give the troops relief: 195
Permit the mourning legions to retire,
And let the chiefs alone attend the pyre;
The pious care be ours, the dead to burn——
He said: the people to their ships return:
While those deputed to interr the flain,   200
Heap with a rising pyramid the plain.
A hundred foot in length, a hundred wide,
The growing structure spreads on ev'ry fide;
High on the top the manly corfe they lay,
And well-fed sheep, and fable oxen flay: 205
Achilles cover'd with their fat the dead,
And the pil'd victims round the body spread.
Then jars of honey, and of fragrant oil
Sufpends around, low-bending o'er the pile.

Four fprightly courfers, with a deadly groan   210
Pour forth their lives, and on the pyre are thrown.
Of nine large dogs, domeftic at his board,
Fall two, felected to attend their Lord.
Then laft of all, and horrible to tell,
Sad facrifice ! twelve Trojan captives fell.   215
On thefe the rage of fire victorious preys,
Involves and joins them in one common blaze.
Smear'd with the bloody rites, he ftands on high,
And calls the fpirit with a dreadful cry.

 All hail, Patroclus ! let thy vengeful ghoft   220
Hear, and exult on Pluto's dreary coaft.
Behold, Achilles' promife fully paid,
Twelve Trojan heroes offer'd to thy fhade;
But heavier fates on Hector's corfe attend,
Sav'd from the flames, for hungry dogs to rend.   225
 So fpake he, threat'ning : but the Gods made vain
His threat, and guard inviolate the flain :
Celeftial Venus hover'd o'er his head,
And rofeate unguents, heav'nly fragrance ! fhed :

ẏ. 228 *Celeftial Venus*, etc.] Homer has here introduced a *feries* of allegories in the compafs of a few lines :
the body of Hector may be fuppofed to continue beautiful even after he was flain ; and Venus being the pre-
fident of beauty, the poet by a natural fiction tells us
it was preferved by that goddefs.

Apollo's covering the body with a cloud is a very
natural allegory · for the fun (fays Euftathius) has a
double quality which produces contrary effects, the
heat of it caufes a drynefs, but at the fame time it ex-
hales the vapours of the earth, from whence the clouds

She watch'd him all the night, and all the day,   230
And drove the bloodhounds from their deftin'd prey.
Nor facred Phœbus lefs employ'd his care;
He pour'd around a veil of gather'd air,
And kept the nerves undrv'd, the flefh intire,
Againft the folar beam and Sirian fire.   235

 Nor yet the pile where dead Patroclus lies,
Smokes, nor as yet the fullen flames arife;
But faft befide Achilles ftood in pray'r,
Inv o'n the Gods whofe fpirit moves the air,
Ar victims promis'd, and libations caft,   240
To g n'k Zephyr and the Boreal blaft.
He call'd th aerial pow'rs, along the fkies
To breathe, and whifper to the fires to rife.
The winged Iris heard the hero's call,
And inftant haften'd to their airy hall,   245
Where, in old Zephyr's open courts on high,
Sate all the bluft'ring brethren of the fky.
She fhone amidft them, on her painted bow;
The rocky pavement glitter'd with the fhow.
All from the banquet rife, and each invites   250
The various Goddefs to partake the rites.
Not fo, (the dame reply'd) I hafte to go
To facred Ocean, and the floods below:

of heaven are formed. This allegory may be founded
upon truth, there might happen to be a cool feafon
while Hector lay unburied, and Apollo, or the fun, raifing clouds which intercept the heat of his beams, by a
very eafy fiction in poetry may be introduced in perfon
to preferve the body of Hector.

Ev'n now our folemn hecatombs attend,

And heav'n is feafting on the world's green end,   255

With righteous Æthiops (uncorrupted train ')

Far on th' extremeft limits of the main.

But Peleus' fon intreats, with facrifice,

The Weftern Spirit, and the North to rife;

Let on Patroclus' pile your blaft be driv'n,   260

And bear the blazing honours high to heav'n.

Swift as the word, fhe vanifh'd from their view;

Swift as the word the winds tumultuous flew;

𝓎 263 *The allegory of the winds*] A poet ought
to exprefs nothing vulgarly, and fure no poet ever tref-
paffed lefs againft this rule than Homer, the fruitful-
nefs of his invention is continually raifing incidents new
and furprifing   Take this paffage out of its poetical
drefs, and it will be no more than this   a ftrong gale
of wind blew, and fo increafed the flame that it foon
confumed the pile   But Homer introduces the gods of
the winds in perfon   and Iris, or the rain bow, being
(as Euftathius obferves) a fign not only of fhowers, but
of winds, he makes them come at her fummons

Every circumftance is well adapted as foon as the
winds fee Iris, they rife, that is, when the rainbow appears, the wind rifes   fhe refufes to fit, and immediately returns, that is, the rainbow is never feen long at
one time, but foon appears, and foon vanifhes: fhe returns over the ocean, that is, the bow is compofed of
waters, and it would have been an unnatural fiction to
have defcribed her as paffing by land

The winds are all together in the cave of Zephyrus,
which may imply that they were there as at their general rendezvous, or that the nature of all the winds is
the fame; or that the weftern wind is in that country the
moft conftant, and confequently it may be faid that at

Forth burſt the ſtormy band with thund'ring rore,
And heaps on heaps the clouds are toſt before.   265
To the wide main then ſtooping from the ſkies,
The heaving deeps in wat'ry mountains riſe:
Troy feels the blaſt along her ſhaking walls,
'Till on the pile the gather'd tempeſt falls.
The ſtructure crackles in the roaring fires,   270
And all the night the plenteous flame aſpires.
All night Achilles hails Patroclus' ſoul,
With large libation from the golden bowl.
As a poor father, helpleſs and undone,
Mourns o'er the aſhes of an only ſon,   275
Takes a ſad pleaſure the laſt bones to burn,
And pour in tears, ere yet they cloſe the urn:
So ſtay'd Achilles, circling round the ſhore,
So watch'd the flames, 'till now they flame no more.
'Twas when, emerging thro' the ſhades of night,   280
The morning planet told th' approach of light;

ſuch ſeaſons all the winds are aſſembled in one corner,
or rendezvous with Zephyrus.

Iris will not enter the cave it is the nature of the
rainbow to be ſtretched intirely upon the ſurface, and
therefore this fiction is agreeable to reaſon

When Iris ſays that the gods are partaking heca‐
tombs in Æthiopia, it is to be remembered that the
gods are repreſen ed there in the firſt book, before the
ſcenes of war were opened, and now they are cloſed,
they return hither Euſtathius ———Thus Homer
makes the anger of his hero ſo important, that it rouſed
heaven to arms; and now when it is almoſt appeaſed,
Achilles as it were gives peace to the gods.

And faſt behind, Aurora's warmer ray
O'er the broad ocean pour'd the golden day:
Then funk the blaze, the pile no longer burn'd,
And to their caves the whiſtling winds return'd. 285
Acroſs the Thracian feas their courſe they bore;
The ruffled feas beneath their paſſage rore.

Then parting from the pile he ceas'd to weep,
And funk to quiet in th' embrace of ſleep,
Exhauſted with his grief· meanwhile the croud 290
Of thronging Grecians round Achilles ſtood;
The tumult wak'd him: from his eyes he ſhook
Unwilling ſlumber, and the chiefs befpoke.

Ye kings and princes of th' Achaian name!
Firſt let us quench the yet remaining flame 295
With fable wine; then, (as the rites direct)
The hero's bones with careful view felect:
(Apart, and eafy to be known they lie,
Amidſt the heap, and obvious to the eye:
The reſt around the margins will be feen, 300
Promiſcuous, ſteeds, and immolated men)
Theſe wrapt in double cawls of fat, prepare;
And in the golden vafe difpofe with care;
There let them reſt with decent honour laid,
'Till I ſhall follow to th' infernal ſhade. 305
Meantime erect the tomb with pious hands,
A common ſtructure on the humble fands;

Hereafter Greece fome nobler work may raife,
And late pofterity record our praife.

The Greeks obey; where yet the embers glow   310
Wide o'er the pile the fable wine they throw,
And deep fubfides the afhy heap below.
Next the white bones his fad companions place
With tears collected, in the golden vafe.
The facred relicks to the tent they bore;   315
The urn a veil of linen cover'd o'er.
That done, they bid the fepulchre afpire,
And caft the deep foundations round the pyre;
High in the midft they heap the fwelling bed
Of rifing earth, memorial of the dead.   320

The fwarming populace the chief detains,
And leads amidft a wide extent of plains;

℣. 308. *Hereafter Greece a nobler pile fhall raife.*] We fee how Achilles confults his own glory; the defire of it prevails over his tendernefs for Patroclus, and he will not permit any man, not even his beloved Patroclus, to fhare an equality of honour with himfelf, even in the grave. Euftathius.

℣ 321. *The games for Patroclus.*] The conduct of Homer in inlarging upon the games at the funeral of Patroclus is very judicious there had undoubtedly been fuch honours paid to feveral heroes during this war, as appears from a paffage in the ninth book, where Agamemnon to enhance the value of the horfes which he offers Achilles, fays, that any perfon would be rich that had treafures equal to the value of the prizes they had won, which races muft have been run during the fiege. for had they been before it, the horfes would now have been too old to be of any value, this being the tenth.

There plac'd 'em round: then from the ſhips proceeds
A train of oxen, mules, and ſtately ſteeds,
Vaſes and tripods, for the fun'ral games,   325
Reſplendent braſs, and more reſplendent dames.
Firſt ſtood the prizes to reward the force
Of rapid racers in the duſty courſe.
A woman for the firſt, in beauty's bloom,
Skill'd in the needle, and the lab'ring loom;   330
And a large vaſe, where two bright handles riſe,
Of twenty meaſures its capacious ſize.
The ſecond victor claims a mare unbroke,
Big with a mule, unknowing of the yoke;   •

year of the war. But the poet paſſes all thoſe games
over in ſilence, and reſerves them for this ſeaſon, not
only in honour of Patroclus, but alſo of his hero A-
chilles; who exhibits games to a whole army; great
generals are candidates for the prizes, and he himſelf
ſits the judge and arbitrator thus in peace as well as
war the poet maintains the ſuperiority of the character
of Achilles.

But there is another reaſon why the poet deferred to
relate any games that were exhibited at any preceding
funerals the death of Patroclus was the moſt eminent
period; and conſequently the moſt proper time for ſuch
games

It is farther obſervable, that he chuſes this peculiar
time with great judgment. When the fury of the war
raged, the army could not well have found leiſure for
the games, and they might have met with interruption
from the enemy but Hector being dead, all Troy was
in confuſion · they are in too great a conſternation to
make any attempts, and therefore the poet could not poſ-
ſibly have choſen a more happy opportunity. Euſtathius.

Q 3

The third, a charger yet untouch'd by flame; 335
Four ample meafures held the fhining frame -
Two golden talents for the fourth were plac'd;
An ample double bowl contents the laft.
Thefe in fair order rang'd upon the plain,
The hero, rifing, thus addreft the train. 340

Behold the prizes, valiant Greeks ! decreed
To the brave rulers of the racing fteed;
Prizes which none befide ourfelf could gain,
Should our immortal courfers take the plain;
(A race unrivall'd, which from Ocean's God 345
Peleus receiv'd, and on his fon beftow'd.)
But this no time our vigour to difplay,
Nor fuit, with them, the games of this fad day:
Loft is Patroclus now, that wont to deck
Their flowing manes, and fleek their gloffy neck. 350

ɣ 349 Loft is Patroclus now, etc] I am not ignorant that Homer has frequently been blamed for fuch
little digreffions as thefe; in this paffage he gives us the
genealogy of his horfes, which he has frequently told
us in the preceding part of the poem. But Fuftathius
juftifies his conduct, and fays that it was very proper to
commend the virtue of thefe horfes upon this occafion,
when horfes were to contend for victory at the fame
time he takes an opportunity to make an honourable
mention of his friend Patroclus, in whofe honour thefe
games were exhibited

It may be added as a farther juftification of Homer,
that this laft circumftance is very natural; Achilles,
while he commends is horfes, remembers how careful
Patroclus had been of them - his love for his friend is
fo great, that the minuteft circumftance recalls him to

Sad, as they ſhar'd in human grief, they ſtand,
And trail thoſe graceful honours on the ſand.
Let others for the noble taſk prepare,
Who truſt the courſer, and the flying car.

Fir'd at his word, the rival racers riſe;   355
But far the firſt, Eumelus hopes the prize,
Fam'd thro' Pieria for the fleeteſt breed,
And ſkill'd to manage tne high-bounding ſteed.
With equal ardour bold Tydides ſwell'd
The ſteeds of Tros beneath his yoke compell'd,   360
(Which late obey'd the Dardan chief's command,
When ſcarce a God redeem'd him from his hand)
Then Menelaus his Podargus brings,
And the fam'd courſer of the king of kings:
Whom rich Echepolus, (more rich than brave)   365
To 'ſcape the wars, to Agamemnon gave,

his mind; and ſuch little digreſſions, ſuch avocations of thought as theſe, very naturally proceed from the overflows of love and ſorrow,

℣. 365. *Whom rich Echepolus, etc.*] One would think that Agamemnon might be accuſed of avarice, in diſpenſing with a man from going to the war for the ſake of a horſe; but Ariſtotle very well obſerves, that this prince is praiſe-worthy for having preferred a horſe to a perſon ſo cowardly, and ſo uncapable of ſervice. It may be alſo conjectured from this paſſage, that even in thoſe elder times it was the cuſtom, that thoſe who were willing to be excuſed from the war, ſhould give either a horſe or a man, and often both. Thus Scipio going to Africa, ordered the Sicilians either to attend him, or to give him horſes or men. and Ageſilaus being at Epheſus and wanting cavalry, made a proclamation,

(Æthe her name) at home to end his days,
Bafe wealth preferring to eternal praife.
Next him Antilochus demands the courfe,
With beating heart, and chears his Pylian horfe.   370
Experienc'd Neftor gives his fon the reins,
Directs his judgment, and his heat reftrains ;

that the rich men who would not ferve in the war
fhould be difpenfed with, provided they furnifhed a man
and a horfe in their ftead. in which, fays Plutarch, he
wifely followed the example of king Agamemnon, who
excufed a very rich coward from ferving in perfon, for
a prefent of a good mare   Euftathius. Dacier.

λ 371 *Experienc'd Neftor*, etc] The poet omits
ro opportunity of paying honour to his old favourite
Neftor, and I think he is no where more particularly
complemented than in this book. His age had difabled
him from bearing any fbare in the games, and yet he
artfully introduces him not as a mere fpectator, but as
an actor in the fports   Thus he as it were wins the
prize for Antilochus; Antilochus wins not by the fwiftnefs of his horfes, but by the wifdom of Neftor.

This fatherly tendernefs is wonderfully natural: we
fee him in all imaginable inquietude and concern for his
fon ; he comes to the barrier, ftands befide the chariot,
animates his fon by his praifes, and directs him by his
leffons· you think the old man's foul mounts on the
chariot with his Antilochus, to partake the fame dangers,
and run the fame career

Nothing can be better adapted to the character than
this fpeech, he expatiates upon the advantages of wifdom over ftrength, which is a tacit complement to himfelf. and had there been a prize for wifdom, undoubtedly the old man would have claimed it as his right.
Euftathius.

Nor idly warns the hoary fire, nor hears
The prudent fon with unattending ears.

My fon, tho' youthful ardour fire thy breaft,   375
The Gods have lov'd thee, and with arts have bleft.
Neptune and Jove on thee conferr'd the fkill,
Swift round the goal to turn the flying wheel.
To guide thy conduct, little precept needs;
But flow, and paft their vigour, are my fteeds.   380
Fear not thy rivals, tho' for fwiftnefs known,
Compare thofe rivals judgment, and thy own:
It is not ftrength, but art, obtains the prize,
And to be fwift is lefs than to be wife;
'Tis more by art, than force of num'rous ftrokes, 385
The dext'rous woodman fhapes the ftubborn oaks;
By art the pilot, thro' the boiling deep
And howling tempeft, fteers the fearlefs fhip:
And 'tis the artift wins the glorious courfe,
Not thofe, who truft in chariots, and in horfe.   390
In vain unfkilful to the goal they ftrive,
And fhort, or wide, th' ungovern'd courfer drive:
While with fure fkill, tho' with inferior fteeds,
The knowing racer to his end proceeds;
Fix'd on the goal his eye fore-runs the courfe,   395
His hand unerring fteers the fteady horfe,
And now contracts, or now extends the rein,
Obferving ftill the foremoft on the plain.
Mark then the goal, 'tis eafy to be found;
Yon' aged trunk, a cubit from the ground;   400

Of some once stately oak the last remains,
Or hardy fir, unperish'd with the rains.
Inclos'd with stones conspicuous from afar,
And round, a circle for the wheeling car.
(Some tomb perhaps of old, the dead to grace;   405
Or then, as now, the limit of a race)
Bear close to this, and warily proceed,
A little bending to the left hand steed;
But urge the right, and give him all the reins;
While thy strict hand his fellow's head restrains,   410
And turns him short; 'till, doubling as they roll,
The wheel's round naves appear to brush the goal.
Yet (not to break the car, or lame the horse)
Clear of the stony heap direct the course;
Lest thro' incaution failing, thou may'st be   415
A joy to others, a reproach to me.
So shalt thou pass the goal, secure of mind,
And leave unskilful swiftness far behind.
Tho' thy fierce rival drove the matchless steed
Which bore Adrastus, of celestial breed;   420
Or the fam'd race thro' all the regions known,
That whirl'd the car of proud Laomedon.

Thus, (nought unsaid) the much-advising sage
Concludes; then sate, stiff with unwieldy age.
Next bold Meriones was seen to rise,   425
The last, but not least ardent for the prize.

They mount their feats; the lots their place difpofe;
(Roll'd in his helmet, thefe Achilles throws.)
Young Neftor leads the race : Eumelus then;
And next the brother of the king of men :   430
Thy lot, Meriones, the fourth was caft ;
And far the braveft, Diomed, was laft.

℣. 427. *The lots their place difpofe.*] According to
thefe lots the char.oteers took their places; but to know
whether they ftood all in an equal front, or one behind
another, is a difficulty· Euftathius fays, the ancients
were of opinion that they did not ftand in one front;
becaufe it is evident that he who had the firft lot, had
a great advantage of the other charioteers: if he had
not, why fhould Achilles caft lots ? Madam Dacier is
of opinion that they all ftood a-breaft at the barrier,
and that the firft would ftill have a fufficient advantage,
as he was nearer the bound, and ftood within the reft;
whereas the others muft take a larger circle, and confequently were forced to run a greater compafs of ground.
Phœnix was placed as an infpector of the race, that is,
fays Euftathius, he was to make report whether they had
obferved the laws of the race in their feveral turnings.

Sophocles obferves the fame method with Homer in
relation to the lots and infpectors, in his Electra.

-- ----- ------ Οἱ τιταγμένοι βραβεῖς
Κλήροις ἔπηλαν και κατίστησαν δίφρον

The conftituted judges affigned the places according to the lots.
The ancients fay that the charioteers ftarted at the Si-
gæum, where the fhips of Achilles lay, and ran towards
the Rhætcum, from the fhips towards the fhores   But
Ariftarchus affirmed that they run in the compafs of
ground five *ftadia,* which lay between the wall and the
tents toward the fhore.   Euftathius.

They ftand in order an impatient train;
Pelides points the barrier on the plain,
And fends before old Phœnix to the place,   435
To mark the racers, and to judge the race
At once the courfers from the barrier bound;
The lifted fcourges all at once refound;
Their heart, their eyes, their voice, they fend before;
And up the champain thunder from the fhore: 440
Thick, where they drive, the dufty clouds arife,
And the loft courfer in the whirlwind flies;
Loofe on their fhoulders the long manes reclin'd,
Float in their fpeed, and dance upon the wind.
The fmoaking chariots, rapid as they bound,   445
Now feem to touch the fky, and now the ground.
While hot for fame, and conqueft all their care,
(Each o'er his flying courfer hung in air)
Erect with ardour, pois'd upon the rein,
They pant they ftretch, they fhout along the plain. 450
Now (the laft compafs fetch'd around the goal)
At the near prize each gathers all his foul,
Each burns with double hope, with double pain,
Tears up the fhore, and thunders tow'rd the main.
Firft flew Eumelus on Pheretrian fteeds;   455
With thofe of Tros, bold Diomed fucceeds:
Clofe on Eumelus' back they puff the wind,
And feem juft mounting on his car behind;

Ỷ. 458. And feem juft mounting on his car behind.] A
more natural image than this could not be thought of.
The poet makes us fpectators of the race, we fee Diomed

Full on his neck he feels the fultry breeze,

And hov'ring o'er, their ftretching fhadows fees. 460

Then had he loft, or left a doubtful prize;

But angry Phœbus to Tydides flies,

Strikes from his hand the fcourge, and renders vain

His matchlefs horfes labour on the plain.

Rage fills his eye with anguifh, to furvey 465

Snatch'd from his hope, the glories of the day.

med preffing upon Eumelus fo clofely, that his chariot feems to climb the chariot of Eumelus.

℣. 465. *Rage fills his eye with anguifh to furvey*, etc.] We have feen Diomed furrounded with innumerable dangers acting in the moft perilous fcenes of blood and death, yet never fhed one tear. and now he weeps on a fmall occafion, for a mere trifle. this muft be afcribed to the nature of mankind, who are often tranfported with trifles, and there are certain unguarded moments in every man's life; fo th t he who could meet the greateft dangers with intrepidity, may through anger be betrayed into an indecency. Euftathius.

The reafon why Apollo is angry at Diomed, according to Euftathius, is becaufe he was interefted for Eumelus, whofe mares he had fed, when he ferved Admetus; but I fancy he is under a miftake. this indeed is a reafon why he fhould favour Eumelus, but not why he fhould be angry at Diomed I rather think that the quarrel of Apollo with Diomed was perfonal, becaufe he offered him a violence in the fifth book, and Apollo ftill refents it.

The fiction of Minerva's affifting Diomed is grounded upon his being fo wife as to take a couple of whips to prevent any mifchance: fo that Wifdom, or Pallas, may be faid to lend him one. Euftathius.

The fraud celeftial Pallas fees with pain,
Springs to her knight, and gives the fcourge again,
And fills his fteeds with vigour.   At a ftroke,
She breaks his rival's chariot from the yoke;   470
No more their way the ftartled horfes held ;
The car revers'd came ratling on the field ;
Shot headlong from his feat, befide the wheel,
Prone on the duft th' unhappy mafter fell;
His batter'd face and elbows ftrike the ground ;   475
Nofe, mouth and front, one undiftinguifh'd wound;
Grief ftops his voice, a torrent drowns his eyes ;
Before him far the glad Tydides flies;
Minerva's fpirit drives his matchlefs pace,
And crowns him victor of the labour'd race.   480

   The next, tho' diftant, Menelaus fucceeds ;
While thus young Neftor animates his fteeds.
Now, now, my gen'rous pair, exert your force:
Not that we hope to match Tydides' horfe,
Since great Minerva wings their rapid way,   485
And gives their lord the honours of the day.

   y̆. 483 The fpeech of Antilochus to his horfes.] I fear
Antilochus his fpeech to his horfes is blameable; Euftathius himfelf feems to think it a fault that he fhould
fpeak fo much in the very heat of the race   He commands and fooths, counfels and threatens his horfes,
as if they were reafonable creatures   The fubfequent
fpeech of Menelaus is more excufable as it is more fhort,
but both of them are fpoken in a paffion, and anger we
know makes us fpeak to every thing, and we difcharge
it upon the moft fenfelefs objects.

But reach Atrides! fhall his mare out-go
Your fwiftnefs' vanquifh'd by a female foe?
Thro' your negleĉt, if lagging on the plain
The laſt ignoble gift be all we gain;   490
No more fhall Neſtor's hand your food fupply,
The old man's fury rifes, and ye die.
Haſte then, yon' narrow road before our fight
Trefents th' occafion, could we ufe it right.

Thus he. The courfers at their maſter's threat 495
With quicker ſteps the founding champain beat.
And now Antilochus with nice furvey,
Obferves the compafs of the hollow way.
'Twas where by force of wintry torrents torn,
Faſt by the road a precipice was worn: 500
Here, where but one could pafs, to fhun the throng
The Spartan hero's chariot fmoak'd along.
Clofe up the vent'rous youth refolves to keep,
Still edging near, and bears him tow'rd the ſteep.
Atrides, trembling caſts his eye below,   505
And wonders at the rafhnefs of his foe.
Hold, ſtay your ſteeds—What madnefs thus to ride
This narrow way; take larger field (he cry'd)
Or both muſt fall—Atrides cry'd in vain;
He flies more faſt, and throws up all the rein   510
Far as an able arm the difk can fend,
When youthful rivals their full force extend,
So far, Antilochus! thy chariot flew
Before the king: he cautious, backward drew

R 2

His horfe compell'd; foreboding in his fears   515
The rattling ruin of the clafhing cars,
The flound'ring courfers rolling on the plain,
And conqueft loft thro' frantic hafte to gain:
But thus upbraids his rival as he flies;
Go, furious youth, ungen'rous and unwife!   520
Go, but expeçt not I'll the prize refign :
Add perjury to fraud, and make it thine——
Then to his fteeds with all his force he cries;
Be fwift, be vig'rous, and regain the prize !
Your rivals, deftitute of youthful force,   525
With fainting knees fhall labour in the courfe,
And yield the glory yours—The fteeds obey;
Already at their heels they wing their way,
And feem already to retrieve the day.

   Meantime the Grecians in a ring beheld   530
The courfers bounding o'er the dufty field.
The firft who mark'd them was the Cretan king ;
High on a rifing ground, above the ring,
The monarch fate: from whence with fure furvey
He well obferv'd the chief who led the way,   535
And heard from far his animating cries,
And faw the foremoft fteed with fharpen'd eyes ;
On whofe broad front, a blaze of fhining white
Like the full moon, ftood obvious to the fight.
He faw ; and rifing, to the Greeks begun.   540
Are yonder horfe difcern'd by me alone?
Or can ye, all, another chief furvey,
And other fteeds, than lately led the way?

Thofe, tho' the fwifteft, by fome God with-held,
Lie fure difabled in the middle field: 545
For fince the goal they doubled, round the plain
I fearch to find them, but I fearch in vain.
Perchance the reins forfook the driver's hand,
And, turn'd too fhort, he tumbled on the ftrand,
Shot from the chariot; while his courfers ftray   550
With frantic fury from the deftin'd way.
Rife then fome other, and inform my fight,
(For thefe dim eyes, perhaps, difcern not right)
Yet fure he feems, (to judge by fhape and air,)
The great Ætolian chief, renown'd in war.   555

Old man! (Oileus rafhly thus replies)
Thy tongue too haftily confers the prize.
Of thofe who view the courfe, not fharpeft ey'd,
Nor youngeft, yet the readieft to decide.
Eumelus' fteeds high-bounding in the chace,   560
Still, as at firft, unrivall'd lead the race:
I well difcern him, as he fhakes the rein,
And hear his fhouts victorious o'er the plain.
Thus he.   Idomeneus incens'd rejoin'd.
Barb'rous of words! and arrogant of mind!   565

ỳ. 565. *The difpute between Idomeneus and Ajax*]
Nothing could be more naturally imagined than this
contention at a horfe-race the leaders were divided
into parties, and each was interefted for his friend: the
poet had a two-fold defign, not only to embellifh and
diverfify his poem by fuch natural circumftances, but alfo to fhew us, as Euftathius obferves, from the conduct
of Ajax, that paffionate men betray themfelves into

Contentious prince, of all the Greeks befide

The laft in merit, as the firft in pride.

To vile reproach what anfwer can we make?

A goblet or a tripod let us ftake,

And be the king the judge.   The moft unwife   570

Will learn their rafhnefs, when they pay the price.

He faid: and Ajax by mad paffion born,

Stern had reply'd; fierce fcorn enhancing fcorn

follies, and are themfelves guilty of the faults of which they accufe others.

It is with a particular decency that Homer makes Achilles the arbitrator between Idomeneus and Ajax: Agamemnon was his fuperior in the army, but as Achilles exhibited the fhows, he was the proper judge of any difference that fhould arife about them.   Had the conteft been between Ajax and Idomeneus, confidered as foldiers, the caufe muft have been brought before Agamemnon; but as they are to be confidered as fpectators of the games, they ought to be determined by Achilles.

It may not be unneceffary juft to obferve to the reader the judicioufnefs of Homer's conduct in making Achilles exhibit the games, and not Agamemnon: Achilles is the hero of the poem, and confequently muft be the chief actor in all the great fcenes of it: he had remained inactive during a great part of the poem, yet the poet makes his very inactivity contribute to the carrying on the defign of his Ilias: and to fupply his abfence from many of the bufy fcenes of the preceding parts of it, he now in the conclufion makes him almoft the fole agent. by thefe means he leaves a noble idea of his hero upon the mind of his reader; as he raifed our expectations when he brought him upon the ftage of action, fo he makes him go off with the utmoft pomp and applaufe.

To fell extreams. But Thetis' god-like fon.
Awful amidft them rofe, and thus begun.   575
    Forbear, ye chiefs! reproachful to contend;
Much would ye blame, fhould others thus offend.
And lo ! th' approaching fteeds your conteft end.
No fooner had he fpoke, but thund'ring near,
Drives, thro' a ftream of duft, the charioteer;   580
High o'er his head the circling lafh he wields;
His bounding horfes fcarcely touch the fields:
His car amidft the dufty whirlwind roll'd,
Bright with the mingled blaze of tin and gold,
Refulgent thro' the cloud · no eye could find   585
The track his flying wheels had left behind:
And the fierce courfers urg'd their rapid pace
So fwift, it feem'd a flight, and not a race.
Now victor at the goal Tydides ftands,
Quits his bright car, and fprings upon the fands;   590
From the hot fteeds the fweaty torrents ftream;
The well-ply'd whip is hung athwart the beam:

    ⍦ 581. High o'er his head the circling lafh he wields.]
I am perfuaded that the common tranflation of the word
Καταμαδὸν, in the original of this verfe, is faulty: it is
rendered, *he lafhed the horfes continually over the fhoulders;*
whereas I fancy it fhould be tranflated thus, *affidue*
(equos) *agitabat feutica ab humero ducta.* This naturally
expreffes the very action, and whirl of the whip over
the driver's fhoulder, in the act of lafhing the horfes,
and agrees with the ufe of the fame word in the 431ft
line of this book, where *ꭓρα δίσκυ καταμαδιοιο* muft be
tranflated *jactus difci ab humero vibrati.*

With joy brave Sthenelus receives the prize,
The tripod-vafe, and dame with radiant eyes:
Thefe to the fhips his train triumphant leads,   595
The chief himfelf unyokes the panting fteeds.

   Young Neftor follows (who by art, not force,
O'er-paft Atrides) fecond in the courfe.
Behind, Atrides urg'd the race, more near
Than to the courfer in his fwift career   600
The following car, juft touching with his heel
And brufhing with his tail the whirling wheel.
Such, and fo narrow now the fpace between
The rivals, late fo diftant on the green;
So foon fwift Æthe her loft ground regain'd,   605
One length, one moment had the race obtain'd.

   Merion purfu'd, at greater diftance ftill,
With tardier courfers, and inferior fkill.
Laft came, Admetus! thy unhappy fon;
Slow dragg'd the fteeds his batter'd chariot on: 610
Achilles faw, and pitying thus begun.

   Behold! the man whofe matchlefs art furpaft
The fons of Greece! the ableft, yet the laft!
Fortune denies, but juftice bids us pay
(Since great Tydides bears the firft away)   615
To him, the fecond honours of the day.

ỳ 614 *Fortune denies, but juftice,* etc] Achilles
here intends to fhew, that it is not juft, fortune fhould
rule over virtue, but that a brave man who had performed his duty, and who did not bring upon himfelf
his misfortune, ought to have the recompence he has
deferved. and this principle is juft, provided we do not

The Greeks confent with loud applauding cries,
And then Eumelus had receiv'd the prize,
But youthful Neftor, jealous of his fame,
Th' award oppofes, and afferts his claim.   620
Think not (he cries) I tamely will refign
O Peleus' fon! the mare fo juftly mine.
What if the Gods, the fkilful to confound,
Have thrown the horfe and horfeman to the ground!
Perhaps he fought not heav'n by facrifice,   625
And vows omitted forfeited the prize.
If yet, (diftinction to thy friend to fhow,
And pleafe a foul defirous to beftow,)
Some gift muft grace Eumelus, view thy ftore
Of beauteous handmaids, fteeds, and fhining ore,   630
An ample prefent let him thence receive,
And Greece fhall praife thy gen'rous thirft to give.
But this, my prize, I never fhall forego;
This, who but touches, warriors! is my foe.

reward him at the expence of another's right: Eumelus
is a Theffalian, and it is probable Achilles has a par-
tiality to his countryman.   Dacier.

ẏ. 633. *But this, my prize, I never fhall forego.*—]
There is an air of bravery in this difcourfe of Antilochus: he fpeaks with the generofity of a gallant foldier,
and prefers his honour to his intereft; he tells Achilles
if he pleafes he may make Eumelus a richer prefent than
his prize; he is not concerned for the value of it; but
as it was the reward of victory, he would not refign it,
becaufe that would be an acknowlegement that Eumelus
deferved it.

The character of Antilochus is admirably fuftained
through this whole epifode; he is a very fenfible man,

. Thus fpake the youth; nor did his words offend; 635
Pleas'd with the well-turn'd flatt'ry of a friend,
Achilles fmil'd: the gift propos'd (he cry'd)
Antilochus! we fhall ourfelf provide.
With plates of brafs the corfelet cover'd o'er,
(The fame renown'd Afteropæus wore)   640
Whofe glitt'ring margins rais'd with filver fhine,
(No vulgar gift) Eumelus, fhall be thine.

He faid: Automedon at his command
The corfelet brought, and gave it to his hand.
Diftinguifh'd by his friend, his bofom glows   645
With gen'rous joy: then Menelaus rofe;
The herald plac'd the fceptre in his hands,
And ftill'd the clamour of the fhouting bands.
Not without caufe incens'd at Neftor's fon,
And inly grieving, thus the king begun·   650
  The praife of wifdom, in thy youth obtain'd,
An act fo rafh (Antilochus) has ftain'd.
Robb'd of my glory and my juft reward,
To you, O Grecians! be my wrong declar'd:
So not a leader fhall our conduct blame,   655
Or judge me envious of a rival's fame;
But fhall not we, ourfelves, the truth maintain?
What needs appealing in a fact fo plain?

but tranfported with youthful heat, and ambitious of
glory his rafhnefs in driving fo furioufly againft Menelaus muft be imputed to this; but his paffions being
gratified by the conqueft in the race, his reafon again
returns, he owns his error, and is full of refignation to
Menelaus.

What *Greek* fhall blame me, if I bid thee rife,
And vindicate by oath th' ill-gotten prize ?   660
Rife if thou dar'ft, before thy chariot ftand,
The driving fcourge high-lifted in thy hand,
And touch thy fteeds, and fwear, thy whole intent
Was but to conquer, not to circumvent.
Swear by that God whofe liquid arms furround   665
The globe, and whofe dread earthquakes heave the ground.

    The prudent chief with calm attention heard;
Then mildly .thus   Excufe, if youth have err'd;
Superior as thou art, forgive th' offence,
Nor I thy equal, or in years, or fenfe.   670
Thou know'ft the errors of unripen'd age,
Weak are its counfels, headlong is its rage.
The prize I quit, if thou thy wrath refign;
The mare, or ought thou afk'ft, be freely thine,
Ere I become (from thy dear friendfhip torn)   675
Hateful to thee, and to the Gods forfworn.

    So fpake Antilochus; and at the word
The mare contefted to the king reftor'd.

    ẏ. 663. *And touch thy fteeds, and fweat* ——] It is
evident, fays Euftathius, from hence, that all fraud was
forbid in the chariot race; but it is not very plain what
unlawful deceit Antilochus ufed againft Menelaus· perhaps Antilochus in his hafte had declined from the race-
ground, and avoided fome of the uneven places of it,
and confequently took an unfair advantage of his adver-
fary; or perhaps his driving fo furioufly againft Menelaus, as to endanger both their chariots and their lives,
might be reckoned foul play; and therefore Antilochus
refufes to take the oath.

Joy fwells his foul, as when the vernal grain
Lifts the green ear above the fpringing plain,   680
The fields their vegetable life renew,
And laugh and glitter with the morning dew;
Such joy the Spartan's fhining face o'er-fpread
And lifted his gay heart, while thus he faid.

   Still may our fouls, O gen'rous youth! agree,   685
'Tis now Atrides' turn to yield to thee.
Rafh heat perhaps a moment might controul,
Not break, the fettled temper of thy foul.
Not but (my friend) 'tis ftill the wifer way
To wave contention with fuperior fway;   690
For ah! how few, who fhould like thee offend,
Like thee, have talents to regain the friend?
To plead indulgence, and thy fault atone,
Suffice thy father's merit and thy own:

   ̵. 679 Joy fwells his foul, as when the vernal
      grain, etc.]
Euftathius is very large in the explication of this fimilitude, which at the firft view feems obfcure: his words
are thefe·

As the dew raifes the blades of corn, that are for
want of it weak and depreffed, and by pervading the
pores of the corn animates and makes it flourifh, fo did
the behaviour of Antilochus raife the dejected mind of
Menelaus, exalt his fpirits, and reftore him to a full
fatisfaction.

I have given the reader his interpretation, and tranflated it with the liberty of poetry: it is very much in
the language of fcripture, and in the fpirit of the
orientals.

Gen'rous

Gen'rous alike, for me, the fire and fon   695
Have greatly fuffer'd, and have greatly done.
I yield; that all may know, my foul can bend,
Nor is my pride preferr'd before my friend.

He faid, and pleas'd his paffion to command,
Refign'd the courfer to Noeman's hand,   700
Friend of the youthful chief: himfelf content,
The fhining charger to his veffel fent.
The golden talents Merion next obtain'd;
The fifth reward, the double bowl, remain'd.
Achilles this to rev'rend Neftor bears,   705
And thus the purpofe of his gift declares.

Accept thou this, O facred fire ! (he faid)
In dear memorial of Patroclus dead;
Dead, and for ever loft Patroclus lies,
For ever fnatch'd from our defiring eyes !   710

�{\psi}. 707. *Accept thou this, O facred fire*] The poet
in my opinion preferves a great deal of decency towards
this old hero and venerable counfellor: he gives him
an honorary reward for his fuperior wifdom, and therefore Achilles calls it ἀέθλον, and not δῶρον, a prize, and
not a prefent. The moral of Homer is, that princes
ought no lefs to honour and recompence thofe who excel in wifdom and counfel, than thofe who are capable
of actual fervice.

Achilles, perhaps, had a double view in paying him
this refpect, not only out of deference to his age, and
wifdom, but alfo becaufe he had in a manner won the
prize by the advice he gave his fon; fo that Neftor
may be faid to have conquered in the perfon of Antilochus. Euftathius.

Take thou this token of a grateful heart,
Tho' 'tis not thine to hurl the diftant dart,
The quoit to tofs, the pond'rous mace to wield,
Or urge the race, or wreftle on the field.
Thy prefent vigour age has overthrown,   715
But left the glory of the paft thy own.

　　He faid, and plac'd the goblet at his fide;
With joy, the venerable king reply'd.

　　Wifely and well, my fon, thy words have prov'd
A fenior honour'd, and a friend belov'd!   720

　　ỳ. 719. *Neftor's fpeech to Achilles.*] This fpeech is
admirably well adapted to the character of Neftor · he
aggrandizes, with an infirmity peculiar to age, his own
exploits, and one would think Horace had him in
his eye,

　　——*Laudatur temporis acti*
　　Se puero————

Neither is it any blemifh to the character of Neftor thus
to be a little talkative about his own atchievements: to
have defcribed him otherwife, would have been an outrage to human nature, in as much as the wifeft man living is not free from the infirmities of man; and as every
ftage of life has fome imperfection peculiar to itfelf.

　　-- ------ Ὁ μὲν ἔμπεδον ἡνιόχευεν.
　　———————— Ἔμπεδον ἡνιόχευ

　　The reader may obferve that the old man takes a-
bundance of pains to give reafons how his rivals came
to be victors in the chariot-race · he is very follicitous
to make it appear that it was not through any want of
fkill or power in himfelf · and in my opinion Neftor is
never more vain-glorious than in this recital of his own
difappointment.

Too true it is, deferted of my ftrength,

Thefe wither'd arms and limbs have fail'd at length.

Oh! had I now that force I felt of yore,

Known thro' Buprafium and the Pylian fhore!

Victorious then in ev'ry folemn game,   725

Ordain'd to Amarynces' mighty name;

The brave Epeians gave my glory way,

Ætolians, Pylians, all refign'd the day.

It is for the fame reafon he repeats the words I have cited above: he obtrudes (by that repetition) the difadvantages under which he laboured, upon the obfervation of the reader, for fear he fhould impute the lofs of the victory to his want of fkill.

Neftor fays that thefe Moliones overpowered him by their *number*. The critics, as Euftathius remarks, have laboured hard to explain this difficulty; they tell us a formal ftory, that when Neftor was ready to enter the lifts againft thefe brothers, he objected againft them as unfair adverfaries, (for it muft be remembered that they were monfters that grew together, and confequently had four hands to Neftor's two) but the judges would not allow his plea, but determined, that as they grew together, fo they ought to be confidered as one man.

Others tells us that they brought feveral chariots into the lifts, whofe charioteers combined together in favour of Eurytus and Cteatus, thefe brother-monfters.

Others fay, that the multitude of the fpectators confpired to difappoint Neftor.

I thought it neceffary to give my reader thefe feveral conjectures that he might underftand why Neftor fays he was overpowered by πληθει, or *numbers;* and alfo, becaufe it confirms my former obfervation, that Neftor is very careful to draw his own picture in the ftrongeft colours, and to fhew it in the faireft light.

I quell'd Clytomedes in fights of hand,
And backward hurl'd Ancæus on the fand,   730
Surpaft Iphyclus in the fwift career,
Phyleus and Polydorus, with the fpear.
The fons of Aftor won the prize of horfe,
But won by numbers, not by art or force:
For the fam'd twins, impatient to furvey,   735
Prize after prize by Neftor born away,
Sprung to their car, and with united pains
One lafh'd the courfers, while one rul'd the reins.
Such once I was ! now to thefe tafks fucceeds
A younger race, that emulate our deeds: 740
I yield alas ! (to age who muft not yield ?)
Tho' once the foremoft hero of the field.
Go thou ! my fon ! by gen'rous friendfhip led,
With martial honours decorate the dead ;
While pleas'd I take the gift thy hands prefent, 745
(Pledge of benevolence, and kind intent)
Rejoic'd, of all the num'rous Greeks, to fee
Not one but honours facred age and me ·
Thofe due diftinftions thou fo well can'ft pay,
May the juft Gods return another day.   750
   Proud of the gift, thus fpake the full of days ·
Achilles heard him, prouder of the praife.
   The prizes next are ordered to the field,
For the bold champions who the Cæftus wield.
A ftately mule, as yet by toils unbroke,   755
Of fix years age, unconfcious of the yoke,

Is to the Circus led, and firmly bound;
Next stands a goblet, massy, large and round.
Achilles rising thus: Let Greece excite
Two heroes equal to this hardy fight;　　　　760
Who dares his foe with lifted arms provoke,
And rush beneath the long-descending stroke?
On whom Apollo shall the palm bestow,
And whom the Greeks supreme by conquest know,
This mule his dauntless labour shall repay;　　765
The vanquish'd bear the massy bowl away.

This dreadful combate great Epeus chose,
High o'er the croud, enormous bulk! he rose,
And seiz'd the beast, and thus began to say:
Stand forth some man, to bear the bowl away!　770
(Price of his ruin.) for who dares deny
This mule my right? th' undoubted victor I.
Others, 'tis own'd, in fields of battel shine,
But the first honours of this fight are mine;
For who excels in all? Then let my foe　　　775
Draw near, but first his certain fortune know,
Secure, this hand shall his whole frame confound,
Mash all his bones, and all his body pound:
So let his friends be nigh, a needful train
To heave the batter'd carcase off the plain.　　780

The giant spoke; and in a stupid gaze
The host beheld him, silent with amaze!
'Twas thou, Euryalus! who durst aspire
To meet his might, and emulate thy sire,

The great Mecistheus; who in days of yore   785
In Theban games the noblest trophy bore,
(The games ordain'd dead Oedipus to grace)
And singly vanquish'd the Cadmean race.
Him great Tydides urges to contend,
Warm with the hopes of conquest for his friend,   790
Officious with the cincture girds him round;
And to his wrist the gloves of death are bound.
Amid the circle now each champion stands,
And poises high in air his iron hands;
With clashing gantlets now they fiercely close,   } 795
Their crackling jaws re-echo to the blows,
And painful sweat from all their members flows.
At length Epeus dealt a weighty blow,
Full on the cheek of his unwary foe;
Beneath that pond'rous arm's resistless sway   800
Down dropt he, nerveless, and extended lay.
As a large fish, when winds and waters rore,
By some huge billow dash'd against the shore,
Lies panting: not less batter'd with his wound,
The bleeding hero pants upon the ground.   · 805
To rear his fallen foe, the victor lends,
Scornful, his hand; and gives him to his friends;
Whose arms support him, reeling thro' the throng,
And dragging his disabled legs along,
Nodding, his head hangs down his shoulder o'er;   810
His mouth and nostrils pour the clotted gore;
Wrapt round in mists he lies, and lost to thought;
His friends receive the bowl, too dearly bought.

The third bold game Achilles next demands,
And calls the wreftlers to the level fands: 815
A maffy tripod for the victor lies,
Of twice fix oxen its reputed price;
And next, the lofers fpirits to reftore,
A female captive, valu'd but at four
Scarce did the chief the vig'rous ftrife propofe,   820
When tow'r-like Ajax and Ulyffes rofe.
Amid the ring each nervous rival ftands,
Embracing rigid with implicit hands:
Clofe lock'd above, their heads and arms are mixt;
Below, their planted feet, at diftance fixt: 825
Like two ftrong rafters which the builder forms
Proof to the wintry wind and howling ftorms,

℣. 819   *A female captive, valu'd but at four*] I cannot in civility neglect a remark made upon this paffage
by Madam Dacier, who highly refents the affront put
upon her fex by the ancients, who fet (it feems) thrice
the value upon a Tripod as upon a beautiful female
flave. nay, fhe is afraid the value of women is not raifed
even in our days; for fhe fays there are curious perfons
now living, who had rather have a true antique kettle,
than the fineft woman alive   I confefs I intirely agree
with the lady, and muft impute fuch opinions of the
fair fex to want of tafte in both ancients and moderns:
the reader may remember that thefe tripods were of no
ufe, but made intirely for fhow; and confequently the
moft fatirical critic could only fay, the woman and Tripod ought to have born an equal value

℣. 826   *Like two ftrong rafters*, etc.] I will give the
reader the words of Fuftathius upon this fimilitude,
which very happily reprefents the wreftlers in the pofture of wreftling.   Their heads leaned one againft the

Their tops connected, but at wider fpace
Fixt on the centre ftands their folid bafe.
Now to the grafp each manly body bends;   830
The humid fweat from ev'ry pore defcends;
Their bones refound with blows · fides, fhoulders, thighs,
Swell to each gripe, and bloody tumours rife.
Nor could Ulyffes, for his art renown'd,
O'erturn the ftrength of Ajax on the ground;   835
Nor could the ftrength of Ajax overthrow
The watchful caution of his artful foe
While the long ftrife ev'n tir'd the lookers-on,
Thus to Ulyffes fpoke great Telamon.
Or let me lift thee, chief, or lift thou me: 840
Prove we our force, and Jove the reft decree.

He faid, and ftraining, heav'd him off the ground
With matchlefs ftrength ; that time Ulyffes found
The ftrength t' evade, and where the nerves combine
His ankle ftrook: the giant fell fupine;   845
Ulyffes following, on his bofom lies ;
Shouts of applaufe run ratt'ling thro' the fkies.
Ajax to lift, Ulyffes next effays,
He barely ftirr'd him, but he could not raife :

other, like the rafters that fupport the roof of a houfe ;
at the foot they are disjoined, and ftand at a greater
diftance, which naturally paints the attitude of body in
thefe two wreftlers, while they contend for victory.

ỷ. 849 *He barely ftirr'd him, but he could not raife.*]
The poet by this circumftance excellently maintains the
character of Ajax, who has all along been defcribed as a
ftrong, unwieldy warrior: he is fo heavy, that Ulyffes

His knee look'd faft, the foe's attempt deny'd;   850
And grappling clofe, they tumbled fide by fide.
Defil'd with honourable duft, they roll
Still breathing ftrife, and unfubdu'd of foul:
Again they rage, again to combate rife;
When great Achilles thus divides the prize.   855

Your nobler vigour, oh my friends, reftrain;
Nor weary out your gen'rous ftrength in vain.
Ye both have won: let others who excel,
Now prove that prowefs you have prov'd fo well.

The hero's words the willing chiefs obey,   860
From their tir'd bodies wipe the duft away,
And, cloath'd anew, the following games furvey.
And now fuceeed the gifts, ordain'd to grace
The youths contending in the rapid race.
A filver urn that full fix meafures held,   865
By none in weight or workmanfhip excell'd:

can fcarce lift him   The words that follow will bear a
different meaning, either that Ajax locked his leg within that of Ulyffes, or that Ulyffes did it.   Euftathius
obferves, that if Ajax give Ulyffes this fhook, then he
may be allowed to have fome appearance of an equality
in the conteft; but if Ulyffes gave it, than Ajax muft be
acknowleged to have been foiled. but (continues he) it
appeared to be otherwife to Achilles, who was the judge
of the field, and therefore he gives them an equal prize,
becaufe they were equal in the conteft.

Madam Dacier mifreprefents Euftathius on this place,
in faying he thinks it was Ulyffes who gave the fecond
ftroke to Ajax, whereas it appeais by the foregoing note
that he rather determines otherwife in confent with the
judgment given by Achilles.

Sidonian artifts taught the frame to fhine,
Elaborate, with artifice divine;
Whence Tyrian failors did the prize tranfport,
And gave to Thoas at the Lemnian port: 870
From him defcended good Eunæus heir'd
The glorious gift; and, for Lycaon fpar'd,
To brave Patroclus gave the rich reward.
Now, the fame hero's fun'ral rites to grace,
It ftands the prize of fwiftnefs in the race.   875
A well-fed ox was for the fecond plac'd;
And half a talent muft content the laft.
Achilles rifing then befpoke the train:
Who hope the palm of fwiftnefs to obtain,
Stand forth, and bear thefe prizes from the plain.   880
    The hero faid, and ftarting from his place,
Oilean Ajax rifes to the race;
Ulyffes next; and he whofe fpeed furpaft
His youthful equals, Neftor's fon the laft.
Rang'd in a line the ready racers ftand;   885
Pelides points the barrier with his hand;
All ftart at once, Oileus led the race;
The next Ulyffes, meas'ring pace with pace;
Behind him, diligently clofe, he fped,
As clofely following as the running thread   890
The fpindle follows, and difplays the charms
Of the fair fpinfter's breaft, and moving arms:
Graceful in motion thus, his foe he plies,
And treads each footftep ere the duft can rife:

His glowing breath upon his fhoulders plays; 895
Th' admiring Greeks loud acclamations raife,
To him they give their wifhes, hearts, and eyes,
And fend their fouls before him as he flies.
Now three times turn'd in profpect of the goal,
The panting chief to Pallas lifts his foul : 900
Affift, O Goddefs ! (thus in thought he pray'd)
And prefent at his thought, defcends the maid.
Buoy'd by her heav'nly force, he feems to fwim,
And feels a pinion lifting ev'ry limb.
All fierce, and ready now the prize to gain, 905
Unhappy Ajax ftumbles on the plain,
(O'erturn'd by Pallas) where the flipp'ry fhore
Was clogg'd with flimy dung, and mingled gore.
(The felf-fame place befide Patroclus' pyre,
Where late the flaughter'd victims fed the fire) 910
Befmear'd with filth, and blotted o'er with clay,
Obfcene to fight, the rueful racer lay ;
The well fed bull (the fecond prize) he fhar'd,
And left the urn Ulyffes' rich reward.

ỷ . 901. *Affift, O Goddefs !* (*thus in thought he pray'd.*)]
Nothing could be better adapted to the prefent circumftances of Ulyffes than this prayer it is fhort, and ought
to be fo, becaufe the time would not allow him to make
a longer: nay he prefers this petition mentally, ὸν κατὰ
θυμόν, all his faculties are fo bent upon the race, that he
does not call off his attention from it, even to fpeak fo
fhort a petition as feven words, which comprehend the
whole of it: fuch paffages as thefe are inftances of great
judgment in the poet.

Then, grafping by the horn the mighty beaft,   915
The baffled hero thus the Greeks addreft.

Accurfed fate ! the conqueft I forego;
A mortal I, a Goddefs was my foe;
She urg'd her fav'rite on the rapid way,
And Pallas, not Ulyffes, won the day.   920

Thus fourly wail'd he, fputt'ring dirt and gore,
A burft of laughter echo'd thro' the fhore.
Antilochus, more hum'rous than the reft,
Takes the laft prize, and takes it with a jeft.

Why with our wifer elders fhould we ftrive ?   925
The Gods ftill love them, and they always thrive
Ye fee, to Ajax I muft yield the prize
He to Ulyffes, ftill more aged and wife,
(A green old age unconfcious of decays,
That proves the hero born in better days !)   930
Behold his vigour in this active race !
Achilles only boafts a fwifter pace:
For who can match Achilles ? He who can,
Muft yet be more than hero, more than man.

℣ 924 *And takes it with a jeft*] Antilochus comes
off very well, and wittily prevents raillery, by attribu-
ting the victory of his rivals to the protection which the
gods gave to age   By this he infinuates, that he has
fomething to comfort himfelf with, (for youth is better
than the prize) and that he may pretend hereafter to
the fame protection, fince it is a privilege of feniority.
Dacier.

℣ 933 *For who can match Achilles ?*] There is
great art in thefe tranfient complements to Achilles.
that hero could not poffibly fhew his own fuperiority

Th' effect succeeds the speech.   Pelides cries,   935
Thy artful praise deserves a better prize.
Nor Greece in vain shall hear thy friend extoll'd;
Receive a talent of the purest gold.
The youth departs content.   The host admire
The son of Nestor, worthy of his sire   940

Next these a buckler, spear and helm, he brings,
Cast on the plain the brazen burthen rings:
Arms, which of late divine Sarpedon wore,
And great Patroclus in short triumph bore.
Stand forth the bravest of our host! (he cries)   945
Whoever dares deserve so rich a prize,
Now grace the lists before our army's sight,
And sheath'd in steel, provoke his foe to fight.
Who first the jointed armour shall explore,
And stain his rival's mail with issuing gore;   950

in these games by contending for any of the prizes, because he was the exhibiter of the sports· but Homer
has found out a way to give him the victory in two of
them.   In the chariot-race Achilles is represented as
being able to conquer every opponent, and though he
speaks it himself, the poet brings it in so happily, that
he speaks it without any indecency· and in this place
Antilochus with a very good grace tells Achilles, that in
the foot-race no one can dispute the prize with him
Thus though Diomed and Ulysses conquer in the chariot
and foot-race, it is only because Achilles is not their
antagonist.

ᴠ. 949 *Who first the jointed armour shall explore.*]
Some of the ancients have been shocked at this combate,
thinking it a barbarity that men in sport should thus

The fword, Afteropeus poffeft of old,
(A Thracian blade, diftinct with ftuds of gold)
Shall pay the ftroke, and grace the ftriker's fide:
Thefe arms in common let the chief divide:
For each brave champion, when the combate ends,   955
A fumptuous banquet at our tent attends.

   Fierce at the word, uprofe great Tydeus' fon,
And the huge bulk of Ajax Telamon.
Clad in refulgent fteel, on either hand,
The dreadful chiefs amid the circle ftand: 960
Low'ring they meet, tremendous to the fight;
Each Argive bofom beats with fierce delight.
Oppos'd in arms not long they idly ftood,
But thrice they clos'd, and thrice the charge renew'd.
A furious pafs the fpear of Ajax made   965
Thro' the broad fhield, but at the corflet ftay'd:

contend for their lives ; and therefore Ariftophanes the
grammarian made this alteration in the verfes.

'Οπότερός κεν πρῶτος ἐπιγράψας χρόα καλ᾽ν
Φθήη ἐπιυξάμε ος δια δ᾽ ἔντια, etc.

But it is evident that they intirely miftook the meaning
and intention of Achilles; for he that gave the firft
wound was to be accounted the victor.   How could
Achilles promife to entertain them both in his tent after
the combate, if he intended that one of them fhould
fall in it? This duel therefore was only a trial of fkill,
and as fuch fingle combates were frequent in the wars of
thofe ages againft adverfaries, fo this was propofed only
to fhew the dexterity of the combatants in that exercife.
Euftathius.

Not thus the foe: his jav'lin aim'd above
The buckler's margin, at the neck he drove.
But Greece now trembling for her hero's life,
Bade fhare the honours, and furceafe the ftrife.   970
Yet ftill the victor's due Tydides gains,
With him the fword and ftudded belt remains.

Then hurl'd the hero, thund'ring on the ground
A mafs of iron, (an enormous round)
Whofe weight and fize the circling Greeks admire, 975
Rude from the furnace, and but fhap'd by fire.
This mighty quoit Aetion wont to rear,
And from his whirling arm difmifs in air:
The giant by Achilles flain, he ftow'd
Among his fpoils this memorable load.   980

ỿ. 971 *Yet ftill the victor's due Tydides gains.*] A-
chilles in this place acts the part of a very juft arbitrator. though the combate did not proceed to a full
iffue, yet Diomed had evidently the advantage, and
confequently ought to be rewarded as victor, becaufe
he would have been victorious, had not the Greeks in-
terpofed.

I could have wifhed that the poet had given Ajax
the prize in fome of thefe contefts.   He undoubtedly
was a very gallant foldier, and has been defcribed as
repulfing a whole army: yet in all thefe fports he is
foiled.   But perhaps the poet had a double view in this
reprefentation, not only to fhew, that ftrength without
conduct is ufually unfuccefsful, but alfo his defign might
be to complement the Greeks his countrymen, by fhewing that this Ajax, who had repelled a whole army of
Trojans, was not able to conquer any one of the Grecian
worthies· for we find him overpowered in three of
thefe exercifes.

For this, he bids thofe nervous artifts vie,

That teach the difk to found along the fky.

Let him whofe might can hurl this bowl, arife,

Who fartheft hurls it, take it as his prize:

If he be one, inrich'd with large domain　　　　985

Of downs for flocks, and arable for grain,

Small ftock of iron needs that man provide;

His hinds and fwains whole years fhall be fupply'd

From hence: nor afk the neighb'ring city's aid,

For plowfhares, wheels, and all the rural trade.　990

　Stern Polypœtes ftept before the throng;

And great Leonteus, more than mortal ftrong;

Whofe force with rival forces to oppofe,

Uprofe great Ajax; up Epeus rofe.

Each ftood in order. firft Epeus threw;　　　　995

High o'er the wond'ring crouds the whirling circle flew.

℣ 985 *If he be one inrich'd*, etc] The poet in this
place fpeaks in the fimplicity of ancient times the prodigious weight and fize of the quoit is defcribed with a
noble plainnefs, peculiar to the oriental way, and agreeable to the manners of thofe heroic ages. He does not
fet down the quantity of this enormous piece of iron,
neither as to its bignefs nor weight, but as to the ufe it
will be of to him who fhall gain it. We fee from hence,
that the ancients in the prizes they propofed, had in
view not only the honourable, but the ufeful; a captive
for work, a bull for tillage, a quoit for the provifion of
iron. Befides, it muft be remembered, that in thofe
times iron was very fcarce; and a fure fign of this
fcarcity, is, that their arms were brafs. Euftathius.
Dacier.

Leonteus next a little space surpast,
And third, the strength of god-like Ajax cast.
O'er both their marks it flew; 'till fiercely flung
From Polypœtes' arm, the Discus sung: 1000
Far, as a swain his whirling sheephook throws,
That distant falls among the grazing cows,
So past them all the rapid circle flies:
His friends (while loud applauses shake the skies)
With force conjoin'd heave off the weighty prize.   1005
   Those, who in skilful archery contend,
He next invites the twanging bow to bend:
And twice ten axes casts amidst the round,
(Ten double edg'd, and ten that singly wound.)
The mast, which late a first-rate galley bore,   1010
The hero fixes in the sandy shore:
To the tall top a milk-white dove they tie,
The trembling mark at which their arrows fly
Whose weapon strikes yon' flutt'ring bird, shall bear
These two edg'd axes, terrible in war;   1015
The single, he, whose shaft divides the cord.
He said experienc'd Merion took the word;
And skilful Teucer. in the helm they threw
Their lots inscrib'd, and forth the latter flew.
Swift from the string the sounding arrow flies;   1020
But flies unblest! no grateful sacrifice,
No firstling lambs, unheedful! didst thou vow
To Phœbus, patron of the shaft and bow.
For this, thy well aim'd arrow, turn'd aside,
Err'd from the dove, yet cut the cord that ty'd: 1025

A-down the main-maft fell the parted ftring,
And the free bird to heav'n difplays her wing:
Seas, fhores, and fkies with loud applaufe refound,
And Merion eager meditates the wound:
He takes the bow, directs the fhaft above,   1030
And following with his eye the foaring dove,

὎ . 1030 *He takes the bow*] There having been
many editions of Homer, that of Marfeilles reprefents
thefe two rivals in archery as ufing two bows in the
conteft; and reads the verfes thus,

Σπε-χόμενος δ' ἄρα Μηριόνης ἐπίθη κατ' ὄϊσὸν
Τοξν ἐν γαρ χιεσιν ἐχε παλα, ὡς ἴθυνεν.

Our common editions follow the better alteration of
Antimachus, with this only difference, that he reads it

Ἐξείρυσε τεύχεν τόξον   And they, Ἐξείρυσε χειρὸς τόξον.

It is evident that thefe archers had but one bow, as
they that threw the quoit had but one quoit, by thefe
means the one had no advantage over the other, becaufe both of them fhot with the fame bow. So that
the common reading is undoubtedly the beft, where the
lines ftand thus,

Σπερχόμενος δ' ἄρα Μηριόνες ἐξ ἐρυσε χειρὸς or Τεύχρυ
Τόξον, ἀτάρ δη οϊσὰν ἐχε παλαι ὡς ἴθυνεν   Euftathius.

This Teucer is the moft eminent man for archery of any
through the whole Iliad, yet he is here excelled by Meriones, and the poet afcribes his mifcarriages to the
reglect of invoking Apollo, the God of archery, whereas Meriones, who invokes him, is crowned with fuccefs.
There is an excellent moral in this paffage, and the
poet would teach us, that without addreffing to heaven
we cannot fucceed Meriones does not conquer becaufe
he is the better archer, but becaufe he is the better man.

Implores the God, to fpeed it thro' the fkies,
With vows of firftling lambs, and grateful facrifice.
The dove, in airy circles as fhe wheels,
Amid the clouds the piercing arrow feels;   1035
Quite thro' and thro' the point its paffage found,
And at his feet fell bloody to the ground.
The wounded bird, ere yet fhe breath'd her laft,
With flagging wings alighted on the maft,
A moment hung, and fpread her pinions there,   1040
Then fudden dropt, and left her life in air.
From the pleas'd croud new peals of thunder rife,
And to the fhips brave Merion bears the prize.

To clofe the fun'ral games, Achilles laft
A maffy fpear amid the circle plac'd,   1045
And ample charger of unfullied frame,
With flow'rs high-wrought, not blacken'd yet by flame.
For thefe he bids the heroes prove their art,
Whofe dextrous fkill directs the flying dart.
Here too great Merion hopes the noble prize;   1050
Nor here difdain'd the king of men to rife.

Ᵽ 1051. *Nor here difdain'd the king of men to rife.*]
There is an admirable conduct in this paffage; Agamemnon never contended for any of the former prizes,
though of much greater value; fo that he is a candidate
for this, only to hono r Patroclus and Achilles. The
decency which the poet ufes both in the choice of the
game, in which Agamemnon is about to contend, and
the giving him the prize without a conteft, is very remarkable the game was a warlike exercife, fit for the
general of an army; the giving him the prize without
a conteft is a decency judicioufly obferved, becaufe no

With joy Pelides faw the honour paid,
Rofe to the monarch, and refpectful faid.

    Thee firft in virtue, as in pow'r fupreme,
O king of nations! all thy Greeks proclaim;   1055.
In ev'ry martial game thy worth atteft,
And know thee both their greateft, and their beft.
Take then the prize, but let brave Merion bear
This beamy jav'lin in thy brother's war.

    Pleas'd from the hero's lips his praife to hear, 1060
The king to Merion gives the brazen fpear:
But, fet apart for facred ufe, commands
The glitt'ring charger to Talthybius' hands,

one ought to be fuppofed to excel the general in any military art: Agamemnon does juftice to his own character; for whereas he had been reprefen ed by Achilles in the opening of the poem as a covetous perfon, he now puts in for the prize that is of the leaft value, and generoufly gives even that to Talthybius.   Euftathius.

    As to this laft particular, of Agamemnon's prefenting the charger to Talthybius, I cannot but be of a different opinion. It had been an affront to Achilles not to have accepted of his prefent on this occafion, and I believe the words of Homer,

Ταρ θυτα κηρυκι δ δυ περικαλλες αεθλον,

mean no more, than that he put it into the hands of this herald to carry it to his fhips, Talthybius being by his office an attendant upon Agamemnon.

I T will be expected I should here say something tending to a comparison between the games of Homer and those of Virgil. If I may own my private opinion, there is in general more variety of natural incidents, and a more lively picture of natural passions, in the games and persons of Homer. On the other hand, there seems to me more art, contrivance, gradation, and a greater pomp of verse in those of Virgil. The *chariot-race* is that which Homer has most laboured, of which Virgil being sensible, he judiciously avoided the imitation of what he could not improve, and substituted in its place the *naval course*, or *ship-race*. It is in this the Roman poet has employed all his force, as if on set purpose to rival his great master; but it is extremely observable how constantly he keeps Homer in his eye, and is afraid to depart from his very track, even when he had varied the subject itself. Accordingly the accidents of the naval course have a strange resemblance with those of Homer's chariot-race. He could not forbear at the very beginning to draw a part of that description into a simile. Do not we see he has Homer's chariots in his head, by these lines;

Non tam præcipites bijugo certamine campum
Corripuere, ruuntque effusi carcere currus.
Nec sic immissis aurigæ undantia lora
Concussere jugis, pronique in verbera pendent.

Æn. v *ỳ*. 144.

What is the encounter of Cloanthus and Gyas in the strait between the rocks, but the same with that of Menelaus and Antilochus in the hollow way? Had the galley of Sergestus been broken, if the chariot of Eumelus had not been demolished? Or Mnestheus been cast from the helm, had not the other been thrown from his seat? Does not Mnestheus exhort his rowers in the very words Antilochus had used to his horses?

Non jam prima peto Mnestheus, neque vincere certo.
Quamquam O! sed superent quibus hoc Neptune dedisti,

Extremos pudeat rediiſſe! hoc vincite, cives,
Et prohibete nefas————

Ἔμβητον, καὶ σφῶϊ τιταίνετον ὅττι τάχιστα.
Ἤ τοι μὲν κείνοισιν ἐριζέμεν ὔτι κελεύω
Τυδείδεω ἵπποισι δαΐφρονος, οἷσιν Ἀθήνη
Νῦν ὤρεξε τάχος————————
Ἵππυς δ᾽ Ἀτρείδαο κιχάνετε, μηδὲ λίπησθον,
Καρπαλίμως, μὴ σφῶιν ἐλεγχείην καταχεύῃ
Αἴθη θῆλυς ἐῦσα.————————

Upon the whole, the deſcription of the ſea-race I think
has the more poetry and majeſty, that of the chariots
more nature and lively incidents.   There is nothing in
Virgil ſo picturesque, ſo animated, or which ſo much
marks the characters, as the epiſodes of Antilochus and
Menelaus, Ajax and Idomeneus, with that beautiful in-
terpoſition of old Neſtor, (ſo naturally introduced into
an affair where one ſo little expects him) On the other
ſide, in Virgil the deſcription itſelf is nobler; it has
ſomething more oſtentatiouſly grand, and ſeems a ſpectacle more worthy the preſence of princes and great
perſons.

In three other games we find the Roman poet contending openly with the Grecian.   That of the Cæſtus
is in great part a verbal tranſlation: but it muſt be owned
in favour of Virgil, that he has varied from Homer in
the event of the combate with admirable judgment and
with an improvement of the moral.   Epeus and Dares
are deſcribed by both poets as vain boaſters; but Virgil
with more poetical juſtice puniſhes Dares for his arro-
gance, whereas the preſumption and pride of Epeus is
rewarded by Homer.

On the contrary, in the *foot-race*, I am of opinion,
that Homer has ſhewn more judgment and morality than
Virgil Niſus in the latter is unjuſt to his adverſary in
favour of his friend Euryalus; ſo that Euryalus wins the
race by a palpable fraud, and yet the poet gives him the
firſt prize; whereas Homer makes Ulyſſes victorious,

purely through the mifchance of Ajax, and his own piety in invoking Minerva.

The *fhooting* is alfo a direct copy, but with the addition of two circumftances which make a beautiful gradation. In Homer the firft archer cuts the ftring that held the bird, and the other fhoots him as he is mounting. In Virgil the firft only hits the maft which the bird was fixed upon, the fecond cuts the ftring, the third fhoots him, and the fourth to vaunt the ftrength of his arm directs his arrow up to heaven, where it kindles into a flame, and makes a prodigy. This laft is certainly fuperior to Homer in what they call the *wonderful* but what is the *intent* or *effect* of this prodigy, or whether a reader is not at leaft as much furprized at it, as at the moft unreafonable parts in Homer, I leave to thofe critics who are more inclined to find faults than I am: nor fhall I obferve upon the many literal imitations in the Roman poet, to object againft which were to derogate from the merit of thofe fine paffages, which Virgil was fo very fenfible of, that he was refolved to take them, at any rate, to himfelf

There remain in Homer three games untouched by Virgil, the *wreftling*, the *combate*, and the Difcus. In Virgil there is only the Lufus Trojæ added, which is purely his own, and muft be confeft to be inimitable: I do not know whether I may be allowed to fay, it is worth all thofe three of Homer?

I could not forgive myfelf if I omitted to mention in this place the funeral games in the fixth Thebaid of Statius; it is by much the moft beautiful book of that poem. It is very remarkable, that he has followed Homer through the whole courfe of his games · there is the *chariot-race*, the *foot-race*, the Difcus, the Cæftus, the *wreftling*, the *fingle combate* (which is put off in the fame manner as in Homer) and the *fhooting*, which laft ends (as in Virgil) with a prodigy · yet in the particular defcriptions of each of thefe games this poet has not borrowed from either of his predeceffors, and his poem is fo much the worfe for it.

THE

I L I A D.

B O O K XXIV.

THE ARGUMENT.

The redemption of the body of Hector.

*THE Gods deliberate about the redemption of Hector's
body.   Jupiter sends Thetis to Achilles to dispose him
for the restoring it, and Iris to Priam, to encourage him
to go in person, and treat for it.   The old king, notwith-
standing the remonstrances of his queen, makes ready for
the journey, to which he is encouraged by an omen from
Jupiter.   He sets forth in his chariot, with a waggon
loaded with presents under the charge of Idæus the
herald.   Mercury descends in the shape of a young man,
and conducts him to the pavilion of Achilles.   Their conversation on the way.   Priam finds Achilles at his table,
casts himself at his feet, and begs for the body of his son.
Achilles, moved with compassion, grants his request, detains him one night in his tent, and the next morning
sends him home with the body   the Trojans run out to
meet him.   The lamentations of Andromache, Hecuba,
and Helen, with the solemnities of the funeral.*

*The time of twelve days is employed in this book, while the body
of Hector lies in the tent of Achilles.   And as* many more
*are spent in the truce allowed for his interment.   The
scene is partly in Achilles's camp, and partly in Troy.*

NOW from the finish'd games the Grecian band
    Seek their black ships, and clear the crouded strand:

All ſtretch'd at eaſe the genial banquet ſhare,
And pleaſing ſlumbers quiet all their care.
Not ſo Achilles: he, to grief reſign'd,   5
His friend's dear image preſent to his mind,
Takes his ſad couch, more unobſerv'd to weep,
Nor taſtes the gifts of all-compoſing ſleep.
Reſtleſs he roll'd around his weary bed,
And all his ſoul on his Patroclus fed: 10
The form ſo pleaſing, and the heart ſo kind,
That youthful vigour, and that manly mind,
What toils they ſhar'd, what martial works they wrought,
What ſeas they meaſur'd, and what fields they fought;

ẏ. 14. *What ſeas they meaſur'd*, etc] There is ſomething very noble in theſe ſentiments of Achilles. he
does not recollect any ſoft moments, any tenderneſſes
that had paſſed between him and Patroclus, but he re-
volves the many difficulties, the toils by land, and the
dangers by ſea, in which they had been companions ·
thus the poet on all occaſions admirably ſuſtains the
character of Achilles, when he played upon the harp in
the ninth book, he ſung the atchievements of kings;
and in this place there is an air of greatneſs in his very
ſorrows Achilles is as much a hero when he weeps, as
when he fights.

This paſſage in Homer has not eſcaped the cenſure
of Plato, who thought it a diminution to his character
to be thus tranſported with grief, but the objection will
vaniſh, if we remember that all the paſſions of Achilles
are in the extreme; his nature is violent, and it would
have been an outrage to his general character to have
repreſented him as mourning moderately for his friend.
Plato ſpoke more like a philoſopher than a critic when
he blamed the behaviour of Achilles as unmanly: theſe

All paſt before him in remembrance dear,   15
Thought follows thought, and tear ſucceeds to tear.
And now ſupine, now prone, the hero lay,
Now ſhifts his ſide, impatient for the day .
Then ſtarting up, diſconſolate he goes
Wide on the lonely beach to vent his woes.   20
There as the ſolitary mourner raves,
The ruddy morning riſes o'er the waves :
Soon as it roſe, his furious ſteeds he join'd ;
The chariot flies, and Hector trails behind.
And thrice Patroclus ! round thy monument   25
Was Hector dragg'd, then hurry'd to the tent.
There ſleep at laſt o'ercomes the hero's eyes :
While foul in duſt th' unhonour'd carcaſe lies,
But not deſerted by the pitying ſkies.
For Phœbus watch'd it with ſuperior care,   30
Preſerv'd from gaping wounds, and tainting air ;

tears would have ill become Plato, but they are graceful in Achilles.

Beſides, there is ſomething very inſtructive in this
whole repreſentation, it ſhews us the power of a ſincere
friendſhip, and ſoftens and recommends the character
of Achilles ; the violence he uſed towards his enemy is
alleviated by the ſincerity he expreſſes towards his friend ;
he is a terrible enemy, but amiable friend

ỷ. 30 _For Phœbus watch'd it_, etc] Euſtathius ſays,
that by this ſhield of Apollo are meant the clouds that
are drawn up by the beams of the ſun, which cooling
and qualifying the ſultrineſs of the air, preſerved the
body from decay. but perhaps the poet had ſomething
farther in his eye when he introduced Apollo upon this
occaſion : Apollo is a phyſician and the God of medi-

And ignominious as it fwept the field,

Spread o'er the facred corfe his golden fhield.

All heav'n was mov'd, and Hermes will'd to go

By ftealth to fnatch him from th' infulting foe :   35

But Neptune this, and Pallas this denies,

And th' unrelenting emprefs of the fkies :

caments, if therefore Achilles ufed any arts to preferve
Hector from decay, that he might be able the longer to
infult his remains, Apollo may properly be faid to protect
it with his Ægis.

℣ 36 *But Neptune this, and Pallas this denies.*] It
is with excellent art that the poet carries on this part of
the poem   he fhews that he could have contrived another way to recover the body of Hector, but as a God
is never to be introduced but when human means fail,
he rejects the interpofition of Mercury, makes ufe of
ordinary methods, and Priam redeems his fon. this gives
an air of probability to the relation, at the fame time
that it advances the glory of Achilles; for the greateft
of his enemies labours to purchafe his favour, the gods
hold a confultation, and a king becomes his fuppliant.
Euftathius

Thofe feven lines, from Κλίδαι δ' ἀρρύτισκον to Μαχ-
λοσυνην ἀπέτεινην have been thought fpurious by fome of
the ancients: they judged it as an indecency that the
goddefs of wifdom and Achilles fhould be equally inexorable; and that it was below the majefty of the gods to
be faid to fteal   Befides, fay they, had Homer been
acquainted with the judgment of Paris, he would undoubtedly have mentioned it before this time in his
poem, and confequently that ftory was of a later invention · and Ariftarchus affirms that Μαχλοσύνη is a more
modern word, and never known before the time of Hefiod, who ufes it when he fpeaks of the daughters of
Prætus; and adds, that it is appropriated to fignify the

E'er fince that day implacable to Troy,
What time young Paris, fimple fhepherd boy,
Won by deftructive luft (reward obfcene)   40
Their charms rejected for the Cyprian queen.
But when the tenth celeftial morning broke;
To heav'n affembled, thus Apollo fpoke.

    Unpitying pow'rs! how oft each holy fane
Has Hector ting'd with blood of victims flain?   45

incontinence of women, and cannot be at all applied to
men. therefore others read the laft verfe,

*Η οἱ κεχαρισμένα δῶρ ὀνόμηνε

Thefe objections are entirely gathered from Euftathius;
to which we may add, that Macrobius feems to have
been one of thofe who rejected thefe verfes, fince he affirms that our author never mentions the judgment of
Paris. It may be anfwered, that the filence of Homer
in the foregoing part of the poem, as to the judgment
of Paris, is no argument that he was ignorant of that
ftory perhaps he might think it moft proper to unfold
the caufe of the deftruction of Troy in the conclufion of
the Ilias, that the reader feeing the wrong done, and
the punifhment of that wrong immediately following,
might acknowlege the juftice of it.

    The fame reafon will be an anfwer to the objection
relating to the anger of Pallas. Wifdom cannot be fatisfied without juftice, and confequently Pallas ought
not to ceafe from refentment, till Troy has fuffered the
deferts of her crimes

    I cannot think that the objection about the word
Μαχλοσυνη is of any weight, the date of words is utterly
uncertain, and as no one has been able to determine the
ages of Homer and Hefiod, fo neither can any perfon
be affured that fuch words were not in ufe in Homer's
days,

And can ye ſtill his cold remains purſue?
Still grudge his body to the Trojans view?
Deny to confort, mother, ſon, and ſire,
The laſt ſad honours of a fun'ral fire?
Is then the dire Achilles all your care?　　　　　50
That iron heart, inflexibly ſevere;
A lion, not a man, who ſlaughters wide
In ſtrength of rage and impotence of pride,
Who haſtes to murder with a ſavage joy,
Invades around, and breathes but to deſtroy.　　　55
Shame is not of his ſoul, nor underſtood,
The greateſt evil and the greateſt good.
Still for one loſs he rages unreſign'd,
Repugnant to the lot of all mankind;
To loſe a friend, a brother, or a ſon,　　　　　60
Heav'n dooms each mortal, and its will is done:
A while they ſorrow, then diſmiſs their care;
Fate gives the wound, and man is born to bear.
But this inſatiate the commiſſion giv'n
By fate, exceeds; and tempts the wrath of heav'n: 65

ỷ. 52. *A lion, not a man,* etc.] This is a very formal condemnation of the morals of Achilles, which Homer puts into the mouth of a God　One may ſee from
this alone that he was far from deſigning his hero a virtuous character, yet the poet artfully introduces Apollo
in the midſt of his reproaches, intermingling the hero's
praiſes with his blemiſhes· *Brave though he be,* etc.
Thus what is the real merit of Achilles is diſtinguiſhed
from what is blameable in his character, and we ſee A-
pollo or the God of wiſdom, is no leſs impartial than
juſt in his repreſentation of Achilles.

Lo how his rage difhoneft drags along
Hector's dead earth infenfible of wrong!
Brave tho' he be, yet by no reafon aw'd,
He violates the laws of man and God.

  If equal honours by the partial fkies   70
Are doom'd both heroes, (Juno thus replies)
If Thetis' fon muft no diftinction know,
Then hear, ye Gods! the patron of the bow.
But Hector only boafts a mortal claim;
His birth deriving from a mortal dame: 75
Achilles of your own æthereal race
Springs from a Goddefs by a man's embrace;
(A Goddefs by our felf to Peleus giv'n,
A man divine, and chofen friend of heav'n)
To grace thofe nuptials, from the bright abode 80
Your felves were prefent, where this minftrel-God
(Well pleas'd to fhare the feaft,) amid the quire
Stood proud to hymn, and tune his youthful lyre.

  Then thus the thund'rer checks th'imperial dame:
Let not thy wrath the court of heav'n inflame; 85
Their merits, not their honours, are the fame.
But mine, and ev'ry God's peculiar grace
Hector deferves, of all the Trojan race:
Still on our fhrines his grateful off'rings lay,
(The only honours men to Gods can pay)   90
Nor ever from our fmoking altar ceaft
The pure libation, and the holy feaft.
Howe'er by ftealth to fnatch the corfe away,
We will not: Thetis guards it night and day.

But hafte, and fummon to our courts above   95
The azure queen; let her perfuafion move
Her furious fon from Priam to receive
The proffer'd ranfom, and the corfe to leave.

He added not · and Iris from the fkies,
Swift as a whirlwind on the meffage flies,   100
Meteorous the face of Ocean fweeps,
Refulgent gliding o'er the fable deeps.

Between where Samos wide his forefts fpreads,
And rocky Imbrus lifts its pointed heads,
Down plung'd the maid, (the parted waves refound) 105
She plung'd, and inftant fhot the dark profound.
As bearing death in the fallacious bait
From the bent angle finks the leaden weight;
So paft the Goddefs thro' the clofing wave,
Where Thetis forrow'd in her fecret cave: 110
There plac'd amidft her melancholy train
(The blue-hair'd fifters of the facred main)
Penfive fhe fate, revolving fates to come,
And wept her God-like fon's approaching doom.

ỳ. 114. *And wept her God-like fon's approaching doom.*]
Thefe words are very artfully inferted by the poet.
The poet could not proceed to the death of Achilles
without breaking the action, and therefore to fatisfy
the curiofity of the reader concerning the fate of this
great man, he takes care to inform us that his life draws
to a period, and as it were celebrates his funeral before
his death.

Such circumftances as thefe greatly raife the character
of Achilles, he is fo truly valiant, that though he knows
he muft fall before Troy, yet he does not abftain from

Then thus the Goddefs of the painted bow. 115
Arife, O Thetis, from thy feats below,
'Tis Jove that calls   And why (the dame replies)
Calls Jove his Thetis to the hated fkies?
Sad object as I am for heav'nly fight!
Ah may my forrows ever fhun the light! 120
Howe'er be heav'n's almighty fire obey'd————
She fpake, and veil'd her head in fable fhade,
Which, flowing long, her graceful perfon clad;
And forth fhe pac'd, majeftically fad.

Then thro' the world of waters, they repair 125
(The way fair Iris led) to upper air.
The deeps dividing, o'er the coaft they rife,
And touch with momentary flight the fkies.
There in the light'nings blaze the fire they found,
And all the Gods in fhining fynod round. 130
Thetis approach'd with anguifh in her face,
(Minerva rifing, gave the mourner place)

the war, but couragioufly meets his death: and here I
think it proper to infert an obfervation that ought to
have been made before, which is, that Achilles did not
know that Hector was to fall by his hand, if he had
known it, where would have been the mighty courage
in engaging him in a fingle combate, in which he was
fure to conquer? The contrary of this is evident from
the words of Achilles to Hector juft before the combate,

-------- -Πρὶν γ' ἢ ἕτερον γε πισόντα
Αἵματος ἆσαι ἄρηα, etc

I will make no compacts with thee, fays *Achilles*, *but one
of us fhall fall.*

Ev'n Juno fought her forrows to confole,
And offer'd from her hand the nectar bowl:
She tafted, and refign'd it: Then began   135
The facred fire of Gods and mortal man·

Thou com ft, fair Thetis, but with grief o'ercaft,
Maternal forrows long, ah long to laft!
Suffice, we know and we partake thy cares:
But yield to fate, and hear what Jove declares.   140
Nine days are paft, fince all the court above
In Hector's caufe have mov'd the ear of Jove;

⅋ 141. *Nine days are paft, fince all the court above,*
etc] It may be thought that fo many interpofitions of
the gods, fuch meffages from heaven to earth, and down
to the feas, are needlefs machines, and it may be imagined that it is an offence againft probability that fo
many deities fhould be employed to pacify Achilles:
but I am of opinion that the poet conducts this whole
affair with admirable judgment.   The poem is now almoft at the conclufion, and Achilles is to pafs from a
ftate of an almoft inexorable refentment to a ftate of
perfect tranquillity, fuch a change could not be brought
about by human means; Achilles is too ftubborn to
obey any thing lefs than a God   this is evident from
his rejecting the perfuafion of the whole Grecian army
to return to the battel   fo that it appears that this machinery was neceffary, and confequently a beauty to the
poem
    It may be farther added that thefe feveral incidents
proceed from Jupiter it is by his appointment that fo
many gods are employed to attend Achilles.   By thefe
means Jupiter fulfils the promife mentioned in the firft
book, of honouring the fon of Thetis, and Homer excellently fuftains his character by reprefenting the inexora-

'Twas voted, Hermes from his god-like foe
By stealth should bear him, but we will'd not so:
We will, thy son himself the corse restore,   145
And to his conquest add this glory more.
Then hye thee to him, and our mandate bear;
Tell him he tempts the wrath of heav'n too far:
Nor let him more (our anger if he dread)
Vent his mad vengeance on the sacred dead: 150
But yield to ransom and the father's pray'r.
The mournful father Iris shall prepare,
With gifts to sue; and offer to his hands
Whate'er his honour asks, or heart demands.

His word the silver-footed queen attends,   155
And from Olympus' snowy tops descends.
Arriv'd, she heard the voice of loud lament,
And echoing groans that shook the lofty tent.
His friends prepare the victim, and dispose
Repast unheeded, while he vents his woes.   160
The Goddess seats her by her pensive son,
She prest his hand, and tender thus begun.

ble Achilles as not parting with the body of his mortal
enemy, but by the immediate command of Jupiter.

If the poet had conducted these incidents merely by
human means, or supposed Achilles to restore the body
of Hector entirely out of compassion, the draught had
been unnatural, because unlike Achilles· such a violence
of temper was not to be pacified by ordinary methods.
Besides, he has made use of the properest personages to
carry on the affair, for who could be supposed to have
so great an influence upon Achilles as his own mother,
who is a goddess?

How long, unhappy ! fhall thy forrows flow !
And thy heart wafte with life-confuming woe ?
Mindlefs of food, or love whofe pleafing reign   165
Soothes weary life, and foftens human pain.
O fnatch the moments yet within thy pow'r,
Nor long to live, indulge the am'rous hour !

☿ 164 *And thy heart wafte with life-confuming woe.*]
This expreffion in the original is very particular. Were
it to be tranflated literally, it muft be rendered, how
long wilt thou *eat, or prey upon thy own heart* by thefe
forrows ? And it feems that it was a common way of
expreffing a deep forrow; and Pythagoras ufes it in this
fenfe, μὴ ἐσθ'ειν καρδίαν, that is, grieve not exceffively,
let not forrow make too great an impreffion upon thy
heart.   Euftathius

☿ 168 ——*Indulge the am'rous hour* !] The ancients
(fays Euftathius) rejected thefe verfes becaufe of the in-
decent idea they convey the goddefs in plain terms
advifes Achilles to go to bed to his miftrefs, and tells
him a woman will be a comfort   The good bifhop is
of opinion, that they ought to be rejected, but the reafon he gives is as extraordinary as that of Thetis   foldiers, fays he, have more occafion for fomething to
ftrengthen themfelves with, than for women   and this
is the reafon, continues he, why wreftlers are forbid all
commerce with that fex during the whole time of their
exercife

Dionyfius of Halicarnaffus endeavours to juftify Homer by obferving that this advice of Thetis was not given
him to induce him to any wantonnefs, but was intended
to indulge a nobler paffion, his defire of glory · fhe advifes him to go to that captive who was reftored to him
in a public manner to fatisfy his honour   to that captive, the detention of whom had been fo great a punifhment to the whole Grecian army. And therefore Thetis
ufes

Lo! Jove himſelf (for Jove's command I bear)
Forbids to tempt the wrath of heav'n too far, 170

uſes a very proper motive to comfort her ſon, by advi-
ſing him to gratify at once both his love and his glory.

Plutarch has likewiſe laboured in Homer's juſtification;
he obſerves that the poet has ſet the picture of Achilles
in this place in a very fair and ſtrong point of light:
though Achilles had ſo lately received his beloved Briſeis
from the hands of Agamemnon; though he knew that
his own life drew to a ſudden period, yet the hero prevails over the lover, and he does not haſte to indulge
his love. he does not lament Patroclus like a common
man by neglecting the duties of life, but he abſtains from
all pleaſure by an exceſs of ſorrow, and the love of his
miſtreſs is loſt in that of his friend

This obſervation excellently juſtifies Achilles, in not
indulging himſelf with the company of his miſtreſs the
hero indeed prevails ſo much over the lover, that Thetis
thinks herſelf obliged to recall Briſeis to his memory
Yet ſtill the indecency remains. All that can be ſaid
in favour of Thetis is, that ſhe was mother to Achilles,
and conſequently might take the greater freedom with
her ſon.

Madam Dacier diſapproves of both the former obſervations: ſhe has recourſe to the lawfulneſs of ſuch a
practice between Achilles and Briſeis; and becauſe ſuch
commerces in thoſe times were repute honeſt therefore
ſhe thinks the advice was decent: the married ladies
are obliged to her for this obſervation, and I hope all
tender mothers, when their ſons are afflicted, will adviſe
them to comfort themſelves in this manner

In ſhort, I am of opinion that this paſſage outrages
decency, and it is a ſign of ſome weakneſs to have ſo
much occaſion of juſtification Indeed the whole paſſage is capable of a ſerious conſtruction, and of ſuch a
ſenſe as a mother might expreſs to a ſon with decency:
and then it will run thus, " Why art thou, my ſon,

No longer then (his fury if thou dread)
Detain the relics of great Hector dead;
Nor vent on fenfelefs earth thy vengeance vain,
But yield to ranfom, and reftore the flain.

To whom Achilles: be the ranfom giv'n,   175
And we fubmit, fince fuch the will of heav'n.

While thus they commun'd, from th' Olympian bow'rs
Jove orders Iris to the Trojan tow'rs.
Hafte, winged Goddefs! to the facred town,
And urge her monarch to redeem his fon;   180
Alone, the Ilian ramparts let him leave,
And bear what ftern Achilles may receive:
Alone, for fo we will. no Trojan near;
Except to place the dead with decent care,
Some aged herald, who with gentle hand,   185
May the flow mules and fun'ral car command.
Nor let him death, nor let him danger dread,
Safe thro' the foe by our protection led ·

' thus afflicted? Why thus refigned to forrow? Can
" neither fleep nor love divert you? Short is thy date
" of life, fpend it not all in weeping, but allow fome
" part of it to love and pleafure!" But ftill the indecency
lies in the marner of the expreffion, which muft be allow ed to be almoft obfcene, 'for fuch is the word μισγεσθ'
 τι ferι) All that can be faid in defence of it is, that as
we are not competent judges of what ideas words might
carry in Homer's time, fo we ought not intirely to condemn him, becaufe it is poffible the expreffion might not
found fo indecently in ancient, as in modern ears.

Him Hermes to Achilles shall convey,

Guard of his life, and partner of his way. 190

Fierce as he is, Achilles' self shall spare

His age, nor touch one venerable hair:

ỹ 189. *Him Hermes to Achilles shall convey.*] The intervention of Mercury was very necessary at this time, and by it the poet not only gives an air of probability to the relation, but also pays a complement to his countrymen the Grecians. they kept so strict a guard that nothing but a God could pass unobserved; this highly recommends their military discipline; and Priam not being able to carry the ransom without a chariot, it would have been an offence against probability to have supposed him able to have passed all the guards of the army in his chariot, without tne assistance of some deity: Horace had this passage in his view, ode the 10th of the first book,

Iniqua Trojæ castra fefellit.

ỹ. 191. ——*Achilles' self shall spare*
        His age, nor touch one venerable hair, etc]
It is observable that every word here is a negative, ἄφρων, ἄσκοπος, ἀλιτήμων, Achilles is still so angry that Jupiter cannot say he is wise, judicious, and merciful; he only commends him negatively, and barely says he is not a madman, nor perversely wicked

It is the observation of the ancients, says Eustathius, that all the causes of the sins of man are included in those three words: man offends either out of ignorance, and then he is ἄφρων, or through inadvertency, then he is ἄσκοπος, or wilfully and maliciously, and then he is ἀλιτήμων So that this description agrees very well with the present disposition of Achilles; he is not ἄφρων, because his resentment begins to abate, he is not ἄσκοπος, because his mother has given him instructions, nor

Some thought there muſt be, in a ſoul ſo brave,
Some ſenſe of duty, ſome deſire to ſave.

Then down her bow the winged Iris drives, 195
And ſwift at Priam's mournful court arrives·
Where the ſad ſons beſide their father's throne
Sate bath'd in tears, and anſwer'd groan with groan.
And all amidſt them lay the hoary ſire,
(Sad ſcene of woe!) His face his wrapt attire 200

ἐλιτζε· becauſe he will not offend againſt the injunctions of Jupiter.

⟩ 195 *The winged Iris flies*, etc] Monſ Rapin has been very free upon this paſſage, where ſo many ma-chines are made uſe of, to cauſe Priam to obtain the body of Hector from Achilles, " This father (ſays he) ' who has ſo much tenderneſs for this ſon, who is ſo " ſuperſtitious in obſerving the funeral ceremonies, and " ſaving thoſe precious remains from the dogs and " vultures, ought not he to have thought of doing this " himſelf without being thus expreſly commanded by " the gods? Was there need of a machine to make ' him remember that he was a father?' But this cri-tic intirely forgets what rendered ſuch a conduct of ab-ſolute neceſſity, namely, the extreme danger and (in all probability) imminent ruin both of the king and ſtate, upon Priam's putting himſelf into the power of his moſt inveterate enemy. There was no other method of re-covering Hector, and of diſcharging his funeral rites (which were looked upon by the ancients of ſo high importance) and therefore the meſſage from Jupiter to encourage Priam, with the aſſiſtance of Mercury to con-duct him, and to prepare Achilles to receive him with favour, was far from impertinent it was *aigrus vindice rc*, as Horace expreſſes it.

200 *His face his wrapt attire Conceal'd from* ſs ·] The poet has obſerved a great decency in this

Conceal'd from fight; with frantic hands he fpread
A fhow'r of afhes o'er his neck and head.
From room to room his penfive daughters roam;
Whofe fhrieks and clamours fill the vaulted dome;
Mindful of thofe, who, late their pride and joy,   205
Lie pale and breathlefs round the fields of Troy !
Before the king Jove's meffenger appears,
And thus in whifpers greets his trembling ears.

   Fear not, oh father ! no ill news I bear,
From Jove I come, Jove makes thee ftill his care ·   210
For Hector's fake thefe walls he bids thee leave,
And bear what ftern Achilles may receive;
Alone, for fo he wills   no Trojan near,
Except to place the dead with decent care,
Some aged herald, who with gentle hand,   215
May the flow mules and fun'ral car command.
Nor fhalt thou death, nor fhalt thou danger dread;
Safe thro' the foe by his protection led;
Thee Hermes to Pelides fhall convey,
Guard of thy life, and partner of thy way.   220
Fierce as he is, Achilles' felf fhall fpare
Thy age, nor touch one venerable hair;

place, he was not able to exprefs the grief of his royal
mourner, and fo covers what he could not reprefent.
From this paffage Semanthes the Sicyonian painter borrowed his defign in the facrifice of Iphigenia, and reprefents his Agamemnon, as Homer does his Priam Æfchy-
lus has likewife imitated this place, and draws his Niobe
exactly after the manner of Homer.   Euftathius.

Sure thought there muſt be, in a ſoul ſo brave,
So ſe ſenſe of duty, ſom deſire to ſave

 She ſpoke, and vaniſh'd.   Priam bids prepare 225
His gentle mules, and harneſs to the car;
There, for the gifts, a poliſh'd caſket lay:
His pious ſons the king's command obey.
Then paſt the monarch to his bridal room,
Where cedar-beams the lofty roofs perfume, 230
And where the treaſures of his empire lay;
Then call'd the queen, and thus began to ſay.

 Unhappy conſort of a king diſtreſt;
Partake the troubles of thy huſband's breaſt:
I ſaw deſcend the meſſenger of Jove, 235
Who bids me try Achilles' mind to move;
Forſake theſe ramparts, and with gifts obtain
The corps of Hector, at yon' navy ſlain.
Tell me thy thought   my heart impels to go
Thro' hoſtile camps, and bears me to the foe. 240

 The hoary monarch thus   Her piercing cries
Sad Hecuba renews, and then replies.
Ah! whither wanders thy diſtemper'd mind?
And where the prudence now that aw'd mankind?
Thro' Phrygia once, and foreign regions known, 245
Now all confus'd, diſtracted, overthrown!
Singly to paſs thro' hoſts of foes! to face
(Oh heart of ſteel!) the murd rer of thy race!
To view that deathful eye, and wander o'er
Thoſe hands, yet red with Hector's noble gore! 250

Alas! my lord! he knows not how to fpare,
And what his mercy, thy flain fons declare;
So brave! fo many fall'n! to calm his rage
Vain were thy dignity, and vain thy age.
No——pent in this fad palace, let us give   255
To grief, the wretched days we have to live.
Still, ftill for Hector let our forrows flow,
Born to his own, and to his parents woe!
Doom'd from the hour his lucklefs life begun,
To dogs, to vultures, and to Peleus' fon!   260
Oh! in his deareft blood might I allay
My rage, and thefe barbarities repay!
For ah! could Hector merit thus? whofe breath
Expir'd not meanly, in unactive death:
He pour'd his lateft blood in manly fight,   265
And fell a hero in his country's right.

   Seek not to ftay me, nor my foul affright
With words of omen, like a bird of night;
(Reply'd unmov'd the venerable man)
'Tis heav'n commands me, and you urge in vain.   270

⸖. 265. *He pour'd his lateft blood in manly fight,*
         And fell a hero————] This whole dif-
courfe of Hecuba is exceedingly natural, fhe aggravates
the features of Achilles, and fofiens thofe of Hector. her
anger blinds her fo much, that fhe can fee nothing great
in Achilles, and her fondnefs fo much, that fhe can difcern no defects in Hector.   Thus fhe draws Achilles in
the fierceft colours, like a Barbarian, and calls him ὠμηϛὴϛ.
but at the fame time forgets that Hector ever fled from
Achilles, and in the original directly tells us that *he knew*
not how to fear, or how to fly. Euftathius.

Had any mortal voice th' injunction laid,

Nor augur, prieſt, or ſeer had been obey'd

A preſent Goddeſs brought the high command,

I ſaw, I heard her, and the word ſhall ſtand

I go, ye Gods! obedient to your call: 275

If in yon' camp your pow'rs have doom'd my fall,

Content——By the ſame hand let me expire !

Add to the ſlaughter'd ſon the wretched ſire !

One cold embrace at leaſt may be allow'd,

And my laſt tears flow mingled with his blood !   280

   From forth his open'd ſtores, this ſaid, he drew

Twelve coſtly carpets of refulgent hue,

As many veſts, as many mantles told,

And twelve fair veils and garments ſtiff with gold

Two tripods next, and twice two chargers ſhine,   285

With ten pure talents from the richeſt mine,

And laſt a large well labour'd bowl had place,

(The pledge of treaties once with friendly Thrace)

Seem'd all too mean the ſtores he could employ,

For one laſt look to buy him back to Troy !   290

   Lo ! the ſad father, frantic with his pain,

Around him furious drives his menial train.

<hr/>

ỳ 291. *Lo! the ſad father*, etc] This behaviour of
Priam is very natural to a perſon in his circumſtances.
the loſs of his favourite ſon makes ſo deep an impreſ-
ſion upon his ſpirits, that he is incapable of conſolation ;
he is diſpleaſed with every body , he is angry he knows
not why; the diſorder and hurry of his ſpirits make
him break out into paſſionate expreſſions, and thoſe expreſſions are contained in ſhort periods, very natural to

In vain each flave with duteous care attends,
Each office hurts him, and each face offends.
What make ye here ? officious crouds ! (he cries) 295
Hence ! nor obtrude your anguifh on my eyes.
Have ye no griefs at home, to fix ye there ;
Am I the only object of defpair ?

men in anger, who give not themfelves leifure to exprefs their fentiments at full length · it is from the fame paffion that Priam, in the fecond fpeech, treats all his fons with the utmoft indignity, calls them gluttons, dancers, and flatterers. Euftathius very juftly remarks, that he had Paris particularly in his eye; but his anger makes him transfer that character to the reft of his children, not being calm enough to make a diftinction between the innocent and guilty.

That paffage where he runs into the praifes of Hector, is particularly natural: his concern and fondnefs make him as extravagant in the commendation of him, as in the difparagement of his other fons. they are lefs than mortals, he more than man. Rapin has cenfured this anger of Priim as a breach of the *manners*, and fays he might have fhewn himfelf a father, otherwife than by this ufage of his children. But whoever confiders his circumftances, will judge after another manner Priam, after having been the moft wealthy, moft powerful and formidable monarch of Afia, becomes all at once the moft miferable of men, he lofes in lefs than eight days the beft of his army, and a great number of virtuous fons, he lofes the braveft of them all, his glory and his defence, the gallant Hector. This laft blow finks him quite, and changes him fo much, that he is no longer the fame · he becomes impatient, frantic, unreafonable ' the terrible effect of ill fortune ' whoever has the leaft infight into nature, muft admire fo fine a picture of the force of adverfity on an unhappy old man.

Am I become my people's common show,
Set up by Jove your spectacle of woe?   300
No, you must feel him too; yourselves must fall;
The same stern God to ruin gives you all:
Nor is great Hector lost by me alone;
Your sole defence, your guardian pow'r is gone!
I see your blood the fields of Phrygia drown,   305
I see the ruins of your smoking town!
Oh send me, Gods! ere that sad day shall come,
A willing ghost to Pluto's dreary dome!

He said, and feebly drives his friends away:
The sorrowing friends his frantic rage obey.   310
Next on his sons his erring fury falls,
Polites, Paris, Agathon, he calls,
His threats Deiphobus and Dius hear,
Hippothous, Pammon, Helenus the seer,
And gen'rous Antiphon · for yet these nine   315
Surviv'd, sad relics of his num'rous line.

Inglorious sons of an unhappy sire!
Why did not all in Hector's cause expire?
Wretch that I am! my bravest offspring slain,
You, the disgrace of Priam's house, remain!   320
Mestor the brave, renown'd in ranks of war,
With Troilus, dreadful on his rushing car,

ϒ 313 *Deiphobus and Dius*] It has been a dispute
whether Δῖος or Ἀχαιὸς, in ϒ. 251. was a proper name;
but Pherecydes (says Eustathius) determines it, and as-
sures us that Dios was a spurious son of Priam.

And laſt great Hector, more than man divine,
For ſure he ſeem'd not of terreſtrial line!
All thoſe relentleſs Mars untimely ſlew,   325
And left me theſe, a ſoft and ſervile crew,
Whoſe days the feaſt and wanton dance employ,
Gluttons and flatt'rers, the contempt of Troy!
Why teach ye not my rapid wheels to run,
And ſpeed my journey to redeem my ſon?   330
   The ſons their father's wretched age revere,
Forgive his anger, and produce the car
High on the ſeat the cabinet they bind:
The new-made car with ſolid beauty ſhin'd;
Box was the yoke, emboſt with coſtly pains,   335
And hung with ringlets to receive the reins;
Nine cubits long the traces ſwept the ground;
Theſe to the chariot's poliſh'd pole they bound,
Then fix'd a ring the running reins to guide,
And cloſe beneath the gather'd ends were ty'd.   340
Next with the gifts (the price of Hector ſlain)
The ſad attendants load the groaning wain:
Laſt to the yoke the well-match'd mules they bring,
(The gift of Myſia to the Trojan king.)
But the fair horſes, long his darling care,   345
Himſelf receiv'd, and harneſs'd to his car:

  ℣ 342 *The ſad attendants load the groaning wain.*]
It is neceſſary to obſerve to the reader, to avoid confuſion, that two cars are here prepared, the one drawn
by mules, to carry the preſents, and to bring back the
body of Hector, the other drawn by horſes, in which
the herald and Priam rode. Euſtathius.

Gr ev'd as he was, he not this tafk deny'd;
The hoary herald help'd him at his fide.
While careful thefe the gentle courfers join'd,
Sad Hecuba approach'd with anxious mind;   350
A golden bowl that foam'd with fragrant wine,
(Libation deftin'd to the pow'r divine)
Held in her right, before the fteeds fhe ftands,
And thus configns it to the monarch's hands.

 Take this and pour to Jove; that fafe from harms, 355
His grace reftore thee to our roof, and arms.
Since victor of thy fears, and flighting mine,
Heav'n, or thy foul, infpire this bold defign:
Pray to that God, who high on Ida's brow
Surveys thy defolated realms below,   360
His winged meffenger to fend from high,
And lead thy way with heav'nly augury ·
Let the ftrong fov'reign of the plumy race
Tow'r on the right of yon' æthereal fpace.
That fign beheld, and ftrengthen'd from above,   365
Boldly purfue the journey mark'd by Jove;
But if the God his augury denies,
Supprefs thy impulfe, nor reject advice.

 'Tis juft (faid Priam) to the fire above
To raife our hands, for who fo good as Jove ?   370
He fpoke, and bad th' attendant handmaid bring
The pureft water of the living fpring ·
(Her ready hands the ewer and bafon held)
Then took the golden cup his queen had fill'd;

On the mid pavement pours the rofy wine,   375
Uplifts his eyes, and calls the pow'r divine.

   Oh firft, and greateft! heav'n's imperial lord!
On lofty Ida's holy hill ador'd!
To ftern Achilles now direct my ways,
And teach him mercy when a father prays.   380
If fuch thy will, difpatch from yonder fky
Thy facred bird, celeftial augury!
Let the ftrong fov'reign of the plumy race
Tow'r on the right of yon' æthereal fpace:
So fhall thy fuppliant, ftrengthen'd from above,   385
Fearlefs purfue the journey mark'd by Jove.

   Jove heard his pray'r, and from the throne on high
Difpatch'd his bird, celeftial augury!
The fwif wing'd chafer of the feather'd game,
And known to Gods by Perenos' lofty name   390
Wide, as appears fome palace-gate difplay'd,
So broad, his pinions ftretch'd their ample fhade,
As ftooping dexter with refounding wings
Th imperial bird defcends in any rings.

    ℣ 377. Oh firft, and greateft! etc] Euftathius ob-
ferves, that there is not one inftance in the whole Ilias
of any prayer that was juftly preferred, that failed of
fuccefs This proceeding of Homer's is very judicious,
and anfwers exactly to the true end of poetry, which is
to pleafe and inftruct Ths Priam prays that Achilles
may ceafe his wrath, and compaffionate his miferies;
and Jupiter grants his requeft the unfortunate king
obtains compaffion, and in his moft inveterate enemy
finds a friend.

A dawn of joy in ev'ry face appears:　　　　395
The mourning matron dries her tim'rous tears.
Swift on the car th' impatient monarch sprung;
The brazen portal in his paſſage rung.
The mules preceding draw the loaded wain,
Charg'd with the gifts: Idæus holds the rein:　　400
The king himſelf his gentle ſteeds controuls,
And thro' ſurrounding friends the chariot rolls.
On his ſlow wheels the following people wait,
Mourn at each ſtep, and give him up to fate;
With hands uplifted, eye him as he paſt,　　　405
And gaze upon him as they gaz'd their laſt.
Now forward fares the father on his way,
Thro' the lone fields, and back to Ilion they.
Great Jove beheld him as he croſt the plain,
And felt the woes of miſerable man,　　　　410
Then thus to Hermes.　Thou whoſe conſtant cares
Still ſuccour mortals, and attend their pray'rs;
Behold an object to thy charge conſign'd,
If ever pity touch'd thee for mankind.
Go, guard the ſire; th' obſerving foe prevent,　　415
And ſafe conduct him to Achilles' tent.

　　The God obeys, his golden pinions binds,
And mounts incumbent on the wings of winds,

℣ 417 _The deſcription of Mercury._] A man muſt have
no taſte for poetry that does not admire this ſublime
deſcription · Virgil has tranſlated it almoſt _verbatim_ in
the 4th book of the Æneis, ℣. 240.

——_Ille patris magni parere parabat_
Imperio, et primum pedibus talaria nectit

That high thro' fields of air his flight suftain,
O'er the wide earth, and o'er the boundlefs main: 420
Then grafps the wand that caufes fleep to fly,
Or in foft flumbers feals the wakeful eye;
Thus arm'd, fwift Hermes fteers his airy way,
And ftoops on Hellefpont's refounding fea.
A beauteous youth, majeftic and divine,   425
He feem'd; fair offspring of fome princely line!

Aurea, quæ fublimem alis, five æquora fupra,
Seu terram rapido pariter cùm flamine portant.
Tum virgam capit, hac animas ille evocat orco
Pallentes, alias fub triftia tartara mittit;
Dat fomnos, adimitque, et lumina morte refignat.

It is hard to determine which is more excellent, the
copy, or the original: Mercury appears in both pictures
with equal majefty; and the Roman drefs becomes him
as well as the Grecian. Virgil has added the latter part
of the fifth, and the whole fixth line, to Homer, which
makes it ftill more full and majeftical.

Give me leave to produce a paffage out of Milton of
near affinity with the lines above, which is not inferior
to Homer or Virgil: it is the defcription of the defcent
of an angel.

——Down thither, prone in flight
He fpeeds, and thro' the vaft æthereal fky
Sails between worlds and worlds; with fteady wing:
Now on the polar winds · then with quick force
Winnows the buxom air——
Of beaming funny rays a golden tiar
Circled his head, nor lefs his locks behind
Illuftrious, on his fhoulders fledg'd with wings,
Lay waving round,——etc.

Now twilight veil'd the glaring face of day,
And clad the dusky fields in sober gray;
What time the herald and the hoary king
Their chariots stopping, at the silver spring   430
That circling Ilus' ancient marble flows,
Allow'd their mules and steeds a short repose.
Thro' the dim shade the herald first espies
A man's approach, and thus to Priam cries.
I mark some foe's advance: O king! beware;   435
This hard adventure claims thy utmost care:
For much I fear, destruction hovers nigh:
Our state asks counsel, is it best to fly?
Or, old and helpless, at his feet to fall,
(Two wretched suppliants) and for mercy call?   440

ᵢ. 427. *Now twilight veil'd the glaring face of day.*]
The poet by such intimations as these recalls to our
minds the exact time which Priam takes up in his journey to Achilles· he set out in the evening; and by the
time that he had reached the tomb of Ilus, it was grown
somewhat dark, which shews that this tomb stood at
some distance from the city: here Mercury meets him,
and when it was quite dark, guides him into the presence
of Achilles By these methods we may discover how
exactly the poet preserves the unities of time and place,
and he allots space sufficient for the actions which he
describes, and yet does not croud more incidents into
any interval of time than may be executed in as much
at he allows thus it being improbable that so stubborn
a man as Achilles should relent in a few moments, the
poet allows a whole night for this affair, so that Priam
has leisure enough to go and return, and time enough
remaining to persuade Achilles

Th' afflicted monarch shiver'd with despair;
Pale grew his face, and upright stood his hair;
Sunk was his heart; his colour went and came;
A sudden trembling shook his aged frame:
When Hermes greeting, touch'd his royal hand,   445
And gentle, thus accosts with kind demand.

Say whither, father! when each mortal fight
Is seal'd in sleep, thou wander'st thro' the night?

$\dot{y}$. 447. *etc. The speech of Mercury to Priam*] I shall
not trouble the reader with the dreams of Euſtathius,
who tells us that this fiction of Mercury, is partly true
and partly falſe: It is true that his father is old; for Jupiter is king of the whole univerſe, was from eternity,
and created both men and gods: in like manner, when
Mercury ſays he is the ſeventh child of his father, Euſtathius affirms that he meant that there were ſix planets
beſides Mercury. Sure it requires great pains and thought
to be ſo learnedly abſurd: the ſuppoſition which he
makes afterwards is far more natural. Priam, ſays he,
might by chance meet with one of the Myrmidons, who
might conduct him unobſerved through the camp into
the preſence of Achilles: and as the execution of any
wiſe deſign is aſcribed to Pallas, ſo may this clandeſtine
enterprize be ſaid to be managed by the guidance of
Mercury.

But perhaps this whole paſſage may be better explained
by having recourſe to the Pagan theology: it was an
opinion that obtained in thoſe early days, that Jupiter
frequently ſent ſome friendly meſſengers to protect the
innocent, ſo that Homer might intend to give his readers
a lecture of morality, by telling us that this unhappy
king was under the protection of the gods.

Madam Dacier carries it farther. Homer (ſay ſhe)
inſtructed by tradition, knew that God ſends his angels
to the ſuccour of the afflicted   The ſcripture is full of

Why roam thy mules and steeds the plains along,
Thro' Grecian foes, so num'rous and so strong!   450
What could'st thou hope, should these thy treasures view,
These, who with endless hate thy race pursue?
For what defence, alas! could'st thou provide?
Thy self not young, a weak old man thy guide.
Yet suffer not thy soul to sink with dread;   455
From me no harm shall touch thy rev'rend head;
From Greece I'll guard thee too; for in those lines
The living image of my father shines.

Thy words, that speak benevolence of mind
Are true, my son' (the god-like sire rejoin'd)   460
Great are my hazards; but the Gods survey
My steps, and send thee, guardian of my way.

examples of this truth.   The story of Tobit has a wonderful relation with this of Homer. Tobit sent his son to Rages, a city of Media, to receive a considerable sum; Tobias did not know the way; he found at his door a young man clothed with a majestic glory, which attracted admiration, it was an angel under the form of a man. This angel being asked who he was, answered (as Mercury does here) by a fiction, he said that he was of the children of Israel, that his name was Azarias, and that he was son of Ananias   This angel conducted Tobias in safety, he gave him instructions, and when he was to receive the recompence which the father and son offered him, he declared that he was the angel of the Lord, took his flight towards heaven, and disappeared. Here is a great conformity in the ideas and in the style; and the example of our author so long before Tobit, proves, that this opinion of God's sending his angels to the aid of man was very common, and much spread amongst the Pagans in those former times.   Dacier.

Hail, and be bleft ! for fcarce of mortal kind
Appear thy form, thy feature, and thy mind.

   Nor true are all thy words, nor erring wide ;   465
(The facred meffenger of heav'n reply'd)
But fay, convey'ft thou thro' the lonely plains
What yet moft precious of thy ftore remains,
To lodge in fafety with fome friendly hand?
Prepar'd perchance to leave thy native land.   470
Or fly'ft thou now? what hopes can Troy retain?
Thy matchlefs fon, her guard and glory, flain !

   The king alarm'd. Say what, and whence thou art,
Who fearch the forrows of a parent's heart,
And know fo well how god-like Hector dy'd?   475
Thus Priam fpoke, and Hermes thus reply'd.

   You tempt me, father, and with pity touch :
On this fad fubject you enquire too much.
Oft' have thefe eyes that god-like Hector view'd
In glorious fight with Grecian blood embru'd :   480
I faw him, when like Jove, his flames he toft
On thoufand fhips, and wither'd half a hoft :
I faw, but help'd not : ftern Achilles' ire
Forbad affiftance, and enjoy'd the fire.

For him I ferve, of Myrmidonian race ;   485
One fhip convey'd us from our native place ;
Polyctor is my fire, an honour'd name,
Old like thyfelf, and not unknown to fame ;
Of fev'n his fons by whom the loft was caft
To ferve our prince, it fell on me, the laft.   490

To watch this quarter my adventure falls,
For with the morn the Greeks attack your walls;
Sleepless they sit, impatient to engage,
And scarce their rulers check their martial rage.

If then thou art of sterr Pelides' train,   495
(The mournful monarch thus rejoin'd again)
Ah tell me truly, where, oh! where are laid
My son's dear relics? what befalls him dead?
Have dogs dismember'd on the naked plains,
Or yet unmangled rest his cold remains?   500

O favour'd of the skies! (thus answer'd then
The pow'r that mediates between Gods and men)
Nor dogs nor vultures have thy Hector rent,
But whole he lies, neglected in the tent:
This the twelfth ev'ning since he rested there,   505
Untouch'd by worms, untainted by the air.
Still as Aurora's ruddy beam is spread,
Round his friend's tomb Achilles drags the dead:
Yet undisfigur'd, or in limb or face,
All fresh he lies, with ev'ry living grace,   510
Majestical in death! no stains are found
O'er all the corse, and clos'd is ev'ry wound;
(Tho' many a wound they gave) some heav'nly care,
Some hand divine, preserves him ever fair:
Or all the host of heav'n, to whom he led   515
A life so grateful, still regard him dead.

Thus spoke to Priam the cœlestial guide,
And joyful thus the royal sire reply'd.

Bleſt is the man who pays the Gods above
The conſtant tribute of reſpect and love!   520
Thoſe who inhabit the Olympian bow'r
My ſon forgot not, in exalted pow'r;
And heav'n, that ev'ry virtue bears in mind,
Ev'n to the aſhes of the juſt, is kind.
But thou, oh gen'rous youth! this goblet take,   525
A pledge of gratitude for Hector's ſake;
And while the fav'ring Gods our ſteps ſurvey,
Safe to Pelides' tent conduct my way.

  To whom the latent God.   O king forbear
To tempt my youth, for apt is youth to err: 530
But can I, abſent from my prince's ſight,
Take gifts in ſecret, that muſt ſhun the light?

  ℣. 519. *Bleſt is the man*, etc.] Homer now begins,
after a beautiful and long fable, to give the moral of it,
and diſplay his poetical juſtice in rewards and puniſh-
ments · thus Hector fought in a bad cauſe, and therefore ſuffers in the defence of it; but becauſe he was a
good man, and obedient to the gods in other reſpects,
his very remains become the care of heaven.

  I think it neceſſary to take notice to the reader, that
nothing is more admirable than the conduct of Homer
throughout his whole poem, in reſpect to morality. He
juſtifies the character of Horace,

  ——*Quid pulchrum, quid turpe, quid utile, quid non,*
Plenius et melius Chryſippo et Crantore dicit.

  If the reader does not obſerve the morality of the
Ilias, he loſes half, and the nobler part of its beauty:
he reads it as a common romance, and miſtakes the
chief aim of it, which is to inſtruct
  ℣. 531. *But can I, abſent*, etc] In the original of

What from our mafter's int'reft thus we draw,
Is but a licens'd theft that 'fcapes the law.
Refpecting him, my foul abjures th' offence;   535
And as the crime, I dread the confequence.
Thee, far as Argos, pleas'd I could convey:
Guard of thy life, and partner of thy way.
On thee attend, thy fafety to maintain,
O'er pathlefs forefts, or the roring main.   540

    He faid, then took the chariot at a bound,
And fnatch'd the reins, and whirl'd the lafh around:
Before th' infpiring God that prg'd them on,
The courfers fly, with fpirit not their own.
And now they reach'd the naval walls, and found   545
The guards repafting, while the bowls go round;
On thefe the virtue of his wand he tries,
And pours deep flumber on their watchful eyes:
Then heav'd the maffy gates, remov'd the bars,
And o'er the trenches led the rolling cars,   550
Unfeen, thro' all the hoftile camp they went,
And now approach'd Pelides' lofty tent.

---

this place (which I have paraphrafed a little) the word
Σ⌐λειην is remarkable. Priam offers Mercury (whom
he looks upon as a foldier of Achilles) a prefent, which
he refufes becaufe his prince is ignorant of it. this prefent he calls a direct *theft* or *robbery*, which may fhew
us how ftrict the notions of juftice were in the days of
Homer, when if a prince's fervant received any prefent
without the knowlege of his mafter, he was efteemed a
thief and a robber.   Euftathius.

Of fir the roof was rais'd, and cover'd o'er
With reeds collected from the marſhy ſhore;
And, fenc'd with paliſades, a hall of ſtate,   555
(The work of ſoldiers) where the hero ſate.

ẏ. 553. *Of fir the roof was rais'd.*⌉ I have in the
courſe of theſe obſervations deſcribed the method of encamping uſed by the Grecians: the reader has here a
full and exact deſcription of the tent of Achilles: this
royal pavilion was built with long paliſadoes made of
fir; the top of it covered with reeds, and the inſide was
divided into ſeveral apartments: thus Achilles had his
αὐλὴ μεγάλη, or large hall, and behind it were lodging
rooms. So in the ninth book Phœnix has a bed prepared for him in one apartment, Patroclus has another
for himſelf and his captive Iphis, and Achilles has a third
for himſelf and his miſtreſs Diomeda.

But we muſt not imagine that the other Myrmidons
had tents of the like dimenſions: they were, as Euſtathius obſerves, inferior to this royal one of Achilles:
which indeed is no better than an hovel, yet agrees very
well with the duties of a ſoldier, and the ſimplicity of
thoſe early times.

I am of opinion that ſuch fixed tents were not uſed
by the Grecians in their common marches, but only during the time of ſieges, when their long ſtay in one
place made it neceſſary to build ſuch tents as are here
deſcribed, at other times they lay like Diomed in the
tenth book, in the open air, their ſpears ſtanding upright, to be ready upon any alarm, and with the hides
of beaſts ſpread on the ground, inſtead of a bed.

It is worthy obſervation, that Homer even upon ſo
trivial an occaſion as the deſcribing the tent of Achilles,
takes an opportunity to ſhew the ſuperior ſtrength of
his hero; and tells us that three men could ſcarce open
the door of his pavilion, but Achilles could open it a-
lone.

Large was the door, whose well-compacted strength
A solid pine-tree barr'd, of wond'rous length,
Scarce three strong Greeks could lift its mighty weight,
But great Achilles singly clos'd the gate,   560
This Hermes (such the pow'r of Gods) set wide;
Then swift alighted the celestial guide,
And thus, reveal'd—Hear, prince! and understand
Thou ow'st thy guidance to no mortal hand:
Hermes I am, descended from above,   565
The king of arts, the messenger of Jove.
Farewell. to shun Achilles' sight I fly;
Uncommon are such favours of the sky,
Nor stand confest to frail mortality.
Now fearless enter, and prefer thy pray'rs;   570
Adjure him by his father's silver hairs,

℣. 569 *Nor stand confest to frail mortality.*] Eustathius thinks it was from this maxim, that the princes
of the east assumed that air of majesty which separates
them from the sight of their subjects, but I should rather believe that Homer copied this after the originals,
from some kings of his time it not being unlikely that
this policy is very ancient. Dacier.

℣. 571 *Adjure him by his father,* etc] Eustathius
observes that Priam does not intirely follow the instructions of Mercury, but only calls to his remembrance his
aged father Peleus · and this was judiciously done by
Priam: for what motive to compassion could arise from
the mention of Thetis, who was a goddess, and incapable of misfortune? Or how could Neoptolemus be any
inducement to make Achilles pity Priam, when at the
same time he flourished in the greatest prosperity? therefore Priam only mentions his father Peleus, who, like
him, stood upon the very brink of the grave, and was

His fon, his mother! urge him to beftow
Whatever pity that ftern heart can know.

Thus having faid, he vanifh'd from his eyes,
And in a moment fhot into the fkies: 575
The king, confirm'd from heav'n, alighted there,
And left his aged herald on the car.
With folemn pace thro' various rooms he went,
And found Achilles in his inner tent:
There fate the hero; Alcimus the brave,   580
And great Automedon, attendance gave:
Thefe ferv'd his perfon at the royal feaft,
Around, at awful diftance, ftood the reft.

Unfeen by thefe, the king his entry made;
And proftrate now before Achilles laid,   585
Sudden, (a venerable fight!) appears;
Embrac'd his knees, and bath'd his hands in tears;

liable to the fame misfortunes he fuffered. Thefe are
the remarks of Euftathius; but how then fhall we juftify
Mercury, who gave him fuch improper inftructions with
relation to Thetis? All that can be faid in defence of
the poet is, that Thetis, though a goddefs, has through
the whole courfe of the Ilias been defcribed as a partner
in all the afflictions of Achilles, and confequently might
be made ufe of as an inducement to raife the compaffion
of Achilles. Priam might have faid, I conjure thee by
the love thou beareft to thy mother, take pity on me!
for if fhe who is a goddefs would grieve for the lofs of
her beloved fon, how greatly muft the lofs of Hector
afflict the unfortunate Hecuba and Priam?

ỳ. 586. *Sudden, (a venerable fight!) appears*] I
fancy this interview between Priam and Achilles would
furnifh an admirable fubject for a painter, in the furprize

Thofe direful hands his kiffes prefs'd, embru'd
Ev'n with the beft, the deareft of his blood!

As when a wretch, (who confcious of his crime,   590
Purfu'd for murder, flies his native clime)
Juft gains fome frontier, breathlefs, pale! amaz'd!
All gaze, all wonder: thus Achilles gaz'd:
Thus ftood th' attendants ftupid with furprize;
All mute, yet feem'd to queftion with their eyes: 595
Each look'd on other, none the filence broke,
'Till thus at laft the kingly fuppliant fpoke.

Ah think, thou favour'd of the pow'rs divine!
Think of thy father's age, and pity mine!

of Achilles, and the other fpectators, the attitude of
Priam, and the forrows in the countenance of this unfortunate king

That circumftance of Priam's kiffing the hands of
Achilles is inimitably fine; he kiffed, fays Homer, the
hands of Achilles, thofe terrible, murderous hands that
had robbed him of fo many fons   by thefe two words
the poet recalls to our mind all the noble actions performed by Achilles in the whole Ilias; and at the fame
time ftrikes us with the utmoft compaffion for this unhappy king, who is reduced fo low, as to be obliged to
kifs thofe hands that had flain his fubjects, and ruined
his kingdom and family.

ɣ 598 The fpeech of Priam to Achilles.] The curiofity of the reader muft needs be awakened to know
how Achilles would behave to this unfortunate king; it
requires all the art of the poet to fuftain the violent
character of Achilles, and yet at the fame time to foften
him into compaffion.   To this end the poet ufes no
preamble, but breaks directly into that circumftance
which is moft likely to mollify him, and the two firft
words he utters are, μνῆσαι Πατρός, fee thy father, O A-

In me, that father's rev'rend image trace,   600
Those silver hairs, that venerable face:
His trembling limbs, his helpless person, see!
In all my equal, but in misery!
Yet now, perhaps, some turn of human fate
Expels him helpless from his peaceful state;   605
Think, from some pow'rful foe thou see'st him fly,
And beg protection with a feeble cry.
Yet still one comfort in his soul may rise;
He hears his son still lives to glad his eyes;

chilles, *in me*' Nothing could be more happily imagined than this entrance into his speech, Achilles has every
where been described as bearing a great affection to his
father, and by two words the poet recalls all the tenderness that love and duty can suggest to an affectionate
son

    Priam tells Achilles, that Hector fell in the defence
of his country: I am far from thinking that this was
inserted accidentally. it could not fail of having a very
good effect upon Achilles, not only as one brave man
naturally loves another, but as it implies that Hector had
no particular enmity against Achilles, but that though he
fought against him, it was in defence of his country.

    The reader will observe that Priam repeats the be-
ginning of his speech, and recalls his father to his memory in the conclusion of it. This is done with great
judgment, the poet takes care to enforce his petition
with the strongest motive, and leaves it fresh upon his
memory, and possibly Priam might perceive that the
mention of his father had made a deeper impression upon Achilles than any other part of his petition, therefore while the mind of Achilles dwells upon it, he again
sets him before his imagination by this repetition, and
softens him into compassion

And hearing still may hope, a better day   610
May send him thee, to chase that foe away.
No comfort to my griefs, no hopes remain,
The best, the bravest of my sons are slain!
Yet what a race; ere Greece to Ilion came,
The pledge of many a lov'd, and loving dame: 615
Nineteen one mother bore—Dead, all are dead †
How oft', alas' has wretched Priam bled?
Still one was left, their loss to recompense;
His father's hope, his country's last defence.
Him too thy rage has slain! beneath thy steel   620
Unhappy in his country's cause he fell!

For him, thro' hostile camps I bent my way,
For him thus prostrate at thy feet I lay;
Large gifts proportion'd to thy wrath I bear;
Oh hear the wretched, and the Gods revere!   625

Think of thy father, and this face behold!
See him in me, as helpless and as old!
Tho' not so wretched. there he yields to me,
The first of men in sov'reign misery.
Thus forc'd to kneel, thus grov'ling to embrace   630
The scourge and ruin of my realm and race:
Suppliant my children's murd'rer to implore,
And kiss those hands yet reeking with their gore!

These words soft pity in the chief inspire,
Touch'd with the dear remembrance of his sire.   635

℣ 634 *These words soft pity*, etc.] We are now
come almost to the end of the poem, and consequently
to the end of the anger of Achilles. and Homer has de-

Then with his hand (as prostrate still he lay)
The old man's cheek he gently turn'd away.
Now each by turns indulg'd the gush of woe;
And now the mingled tides together flow:
This low on earth, that gently bending o'er,   640
A father one, and one a son deplore:
But great Achilles diff'rent passions rend,
And now his sire he mourns, and now his friend.
Th' infectious softness thro' the heroes ran;
One universal solemn show'r began;   } 645
They bore as heroes, but they felt as man.

Satiate at length with unavailing woes,
From the high throne divine, Achilles rose;
The rev'rend monarch by the hand he rais'd;
On his white beard and form majestic gaz'd,   650
Not unrelenting · then serene began
With words to soothe the miserable man.

Alas! what weight of anguish hast thou known?
Unhappy prince! thus guardless and alone

scribed the abatement of it with excellent judgment.
We may here observe how necessary the conduct of
Homer was, in sending Thetis to prepare her son to use
Priam with civility. it would have been ill suited with
the violent temper of Achilles to have used Priam with
tenderness without such pre-admonition, nay, the un-
expected sight of his enemy might probably have carried
him into violence and rage: but Homer has avoided
these absurdities; for Achilles being already prepared
for a reconciliation, the misery of this venerable prince
naturally melts him into compassion.

℣. 653. *Achilles's speech to Priam.*] There is not a

To pass thro' foes, and thus undaunted face   655
The man whose fury has destroy'd thy race?
Heav'n sure has arm'd thee with a heart of steel,
A strength proportion'd to the woes you feel
Rise then. let reason mitigate our care:
To mourn, avails not: man is born to bear.   660
Such is, alas! the Gods severe decree:
They, only they are blest, and only free.
Two urns by Jove's high throne have ever stood,
The source of evil one, and one of good;

more beautiful passage in the whole Ilias than this before
us: Homer to shew that Achilles was not a mere soldier,
here draws him as a person of excellent sense and sound
reason: Plato himself (who condemns this passage)
could not speak more like a true philosopher: and it
was a piece of great judgment thus to describe him;
for the reader would have retained but a very indifferent
opinion of the hero of a poem, that had no qualification
but mere strength: it also shews the art of the poet
thus to defer this part of his character to the very conclusion of the poem: by these means he fixes an idea of
his greatness upon our minds, and makes his hero go
off the stage with applause

Neither does he here ascribe more wisdom to Achilles
than he might really be master of; for as Eustathius
observes, he had Chiron and Phœnix for his tutors, and
a goddess for his mother.

Ỷ. 663. *Two urns by Jove's high throne*, etc.] This
is an admirable allegory, and very beautifully imagined
by the poet. Plato has accused it as an impiety to say
that God gives evil: but it seems borrowed from the
eastern way of speaking, and bears a great resemblance
to several expressions in scripture: thus in the Psalms,
In the hand of the Lord there is a cup, and he poureth out

From thence the cup of mortal man he fills,   665
Bleſſings to theſe, to thoſe diſtributes ills;
To moſt, he mingles both: the wretch decreed
To taſte the bad, unmix'd, is curſt indeed;
Purſu'd by wrongs, by meagre famine driv'n,
He wanders, outcaſt both of earth and heav'n.   670
The happieſt taſte not happineſs ſincere,
But find the cordial draught is daſh'd with care.
Who more than Peleus ſhone in wealth and pow'r?
What ſtars concurring bleſt his natal hour?
A realm, a Goddeſs, to his wiſhes giv'n,   675
Grac'd by the Gods with all the gifts of heav'n!
One evil yet o'ertakes his lateſt day,
No race ſucceeding to imperial ſway:

*of the ſame, as for the dregs thereof, all the ungodly of
the earth ſhall drink them.*

It was the cuſtom of the Jews to give condemned
perſons juſt before execution, οινον ἐσμυρνισμένον, wine
mixed with myrrh, to make them leſs ſenſible of pain:
thus Prov. xxxi. 6. *Give ſtrong drink to him that is
ready to periſh.* This cuſtom was ſo frequent among
the Jews, that the cup which was given him before execution, came to denote death itſelf, as in that paſſage,
Father, let this cup paſs from me.

Some have ſuppoſed that there were three urns, one
of good, and two of evil, thus Pindar,

> Εἰ γὰρ ἐσθλὸν, πήματα σύνδυο
> Δαίονται βροτοῖς ἀθάνατοι.

But, as Euſtathius obſerves, the word ἕτερος ſhews that
there were but two, for that word is never uſed when
more than two are intended.

An only fon! and he (alas!) ordain'd
To fall untimely in a foreign land!   680
See him, in Troy, the pious care decline
Of his weak age, to live the curfe of thine!
Thou too, old man, haft happier days beheld;
In riches once, in children once excell'd,
Extended Phrygia own'd thy ample reign,   685
And all fair Lefbos' blifsful feats contain,
And all wide Hellefpont's unmeafur'd main.
But fince the God his hand has pleas'd to turn,
And fill thy meafure from his bitter urn,
What fees the fun, but haplefs heroes falls?   690
War, and the blood of man, furround thy walls!
What muft be, muft be   Bear thy lot, nor fhed
Thefe unavailing forrows o'er the dead ;
Thou canft not call him from the Stygian fhor,
But thou, alas! may'ft live to fuffer more!   695

   To whom the king.   O favour'd of the fkies!
Here let me grow to earth! fince Hector lies
On the bare beech, depriv'd of obfequies.

v 685. *Extended Phryg.a.* etc] Homer here gives
us a piece of geography, and fhews the full extent of
Priam's kingdom.   Lefbos bounded it on the fouth,
Phrygia on the eaft, and the Hellefpont on the north.
This kingdom, according to Strabo in the 13th book,
was divided into nine dynafties, who all depended upon
Priam as their king: fo that what Homer here relates
of Priam's power is literally true, and confirmed by hiftory.   Euftathius.

O give me Hector ! to my eyes restore
His corse, and take the gifts: I ask no more. 700
Thou, as thou may'st, these boundless stores enjoy;
Safe may'st thou sail, and turn thy wrath from Troy;
So shall thy pity and forbearance give
A weak old man to see the light and live.

Move me no more (Achilles thus replies, 705
While kindling anger sparkled in his eyes)

ỷ. 706. *While kindling anger sparkled in his eyes.*] I
believe every reader must be surprized, as I confess I
was, to see Achilles fly out into so sudden a passion,
without any apparent reason for it. It can scarce be
imagined that the name of Hector (as Eustathius thinks)
could throw him into so much violence, when he had
heard it mentioned with patience and calmnes by Priam
in this very conference. especially if we remember that
Achilles had actually determined to restore the body of
Hector to Priam. I was therefore very well pleased to
find that the words in the original would bear another
interpretation, and such a one as naturally solves the
difficulty. The meaning of the passage I fancy may be
this. Priam preceiving that his address had mollified
the heart of Achilles, takes this opportunity to persuade
him to give over the war, and return home; especially
since his anger was sufficiently satisfied by the fall of
Hector. Immediately Achilles takes fire at this proposal,
and answers " Is it not enough that I have determined
" to restore thy son? ask no more, lest I retract that
" resolution." In this view we see a natural reason for
the sudden passion of Achilles.

What may perhaps strengthen this conjecture is the
word πρῶτον, and then the sense will run thus, since I
have found so much favour in thy sight, as first to permit me to live, O wouldest thou still inlarge my happi-
nefs, and return home to thy own country! *etc.*

Nor feek by tears my fteady foul to bend;
To yield thy Hector I myfelf intend:
For know, from Jove my Goddefs-mother came,
(Old Ocean's daughter, filver-footed dame)   710

This opinion may be farther eftablifhed from what
follows in the latter end of this interview, where Achilles
afks Priam, how many days he would requeft for the interment of Hector? Achilles had refufed to give over
the war, but yet confents to intermit it a few days, and
then the fenfe will be this. " I will not confent to re-
" turn home, but afk a time for a ceffation, and it fhall
" be granted " And what moft ftrongly fpeaks for
this interpretation is the anfwer of Priam, I afk, fays
he, eleven days to bury my fon, and then let the war
commence again, fince *it muft be fo*, ἴπερ αἰάγκη, fince
you neceffitate me to it, or fince you will not be perfuaded to leave thefe fhores.

⯒ 700 *While kindling anger fparkled in his eyes*]
The reader may be pleafed to obferve that this is the laft
fally of the refentment of Achilles; and the poet judicioufly defcribes him moderating it by his own reflection · fo that his reafon now prevails over his anger,
and the defign of the poem is fully executed.

⯒ 709. 710. *For know, from Jove my Goddefs mother
came*] The injuftice of La Motte's criticifm, (who
blames Homer for reprefenting Achilles fo mercenary,
as to inquire into the price offered for Hector's body
before he would reftore it) will appear plainly from this
paffage, where he makes Achilles exprefly fay, it is not
for any other reafon that he delivers the body, but that
heaven had directly commanded it. The words are
very full.

-------- ----- Διῖεν δί μοι ἀγγελος ῆλθε
Μήτηρ ἥ μ' ἔτεκεν, θυγάτηρ ἁλίοιο γέροντος,
Και δε τε γε ἴσκω Πιαμε φρεσιν, ὐδί με λήθεις,
Ὅτ'ι Θεῶν τις ἤγε θοάς ἐπι νῆας Αχαιῶν

Nor com'ft thou but by heav'n; nor com'ft alone,
Some God impels with courage not thy own:
No human hand the weighty gates unbarr'd,
Nor could the boldeft of our youth have dar'd
To pafs our out-works, or elude the guard. 715
Ceafe; left negleftful of high Jove's command
I fhow thee, king ' thou tread'ft on hoftile land;
Releafe my knees, thy fuppliant arts give o'er,
And fhake the purpofe of my foul no more.

The fire obey'd him, trembling and o'er-aw'd. 720
Achilles, like a lion, rufh'd abroad:
Automedon and Alcimus attend,
(Whom moft he honour'd, fince he loft his friend;)
Thefe to unyoke the mules and horfes went,
And led the hoary herald to the tent; 725
Next heap'd on high the num'rous prefents bear
(Great Hector's ranfom) from the polifh'd car.
Two fplendid mantles, and a carpet fpread,
They leave, to cover, and inwrap the dead.
Then call the handmaids with affiftant toil 730
To wafh the body and anoint with oil;
Apart from Priam, left th' unhappy fire
Provok'd to paffion, once more rouze to ire
The ftern Pelides; and nor facred age
Nor Jove's command, fhould check the rifing rage. 755
This done, the garments o'er the corfe they fpread;
Achilles lifts it to the fun'ral bed:
Then, while the body on the car they laid,
He groans, and calls on lov'd Patroclus' fhade.

If, in that gloom which never light must know,   740
The deeds of mortals touch the ghosts below:
O friend! forgive me, that I thus fulfill
(Restoring Hector) heav'n's unquestion'd will.
The gifts the father gave, be ever thine,
To grace thy manes, and adorn thy shrine.   745

He said, and ent'ring, took his seat of state,
Where full before him rev'rend Priam sate:
To whom, compos'd, the God-like chief begun.
Lo! to thy pray'r restor'd, thy breathless son;
Extended on the fun'ral couch he lies;   750
And soon as morning paints the eastern skies,
The sight is granted to thy longing eyes.
But now the peaceful hours of sacred night
Demand refection, and to rest invite:
Nor thou, O father! thus consum'd with woe,   755
The common cares that nourish life, forego.
Not thus did Niobe, of form divine,
A parent once, whose sorrows equall'd thine:

℣ 757. *Not thus did Niobe,* etc.] Achilles, to comfort Priam, tells him a known history, which was very
proper to work this effect.   Niobe had lost all her children, Priam had some remaining.   Niobe's had been
nine days extended on the earth, drowned in their
blood, in the sight of their people, without any one
presenting himself to interr them: Hector has likewise
been twelve days, but in the midst of his enemies, therefore it is no wonder that no one has paid him the last
duties.   The gods at last interred Niobe's children, and
the gods likewise are concerned to procure honourable
funerals for Hector.   Eustathius.

Six

Six youthful fons, as many blooming maids,
In one fad day beheld the Stygian fhades ;   760
Thefe by Apollo's filver bow were flain,
Thofe, Cynthia's arrows ftretch'd upon the plain.
So was her pride chaftiz'd by wrath divine,
Who match'd her own with bright Latona's line ;
But two the Goddefs, twelve the queen enjov'd ;   765
Thofe boafted twelve th' avenging two deftroy'd.
Steep'd in their blood, and in the duft outfpread,
Nine days neglected lay expos'd the dead ;
None by to weep them, to inhume them none ;
(For Jove had turn'd the nation all to ftone)   770
The Gods themfelves at length relenting, gave
Th' unhappy race the honours of a grave.
Herfelf a rock, (for fuch was heav'n's high will)
Thro' defarts wild now pours a weeping rill ;
Where round the bed whence Achelous fprings,   775
The wat'ry fairies dance in mazy rings,
There high on Sipylus his fhaggy brow,
She ftands her own fad monument of woe ;
The rock for ever lafts, the tears for ever flow

 Such griefs, O king ! have other parents known ; 780
Remember theirs, and mitigate thy own.
The care of heav'n thy Hector has appear'd,
Nor fhall he lie unwept, and uninterr'd,
Soon may thy aged cheeks in tears be drown'd,
And all the eyes of Ilion ftream around.   785

 He faid, and rifing, chofe the victim ewe
With filver fleece, which his attendants flew.

The limbs they fever from the reeking hide,
With skill prepare them, and in parts divide:
Each on the coals the fep'rate morfels lays,   790
And hafty, fnatches from the rifing blaze.
With bread the glitt'ring canifters they load,
Which round the board Automedon beftow'd:
The chief himfelf to each his portion plac'd,
And each indulging fhar'd in fweet repaft.   795
When now the rage of hunger was repreft,
The wond'ring hero eyes his royal gueft:
No lefs the royal gueft the hero eyes,
His god-like afpeét and majeftic fize;
Here, youthful grace and noble fire engage,   800
And there, the mild benevolence of age.

$\mathring{y}$. 798. *The royal gueft the hero eyes*, etc.] The poet
omits no opportunity of praifing his hero Achilles, and
it is obfervable that he now commends him for his more
amiable qualities : he foftens the terrible idea we have
conceived of him, as a warrior, with feveral virtues of
humanity; and the angry, vindiétive foldier is become
calm and compaffionate. In this place he makes his
very enemy admire his perfonage, and be aftonifhed at
his manly beauty. So that though courage be his moft
diftinguifhing charaéter, yet Achilles is admirable both
for the endowments of mind and body.

Ἐπικειόμενν The fenfe of this word differs in this
place from that it ufually bears; it does not imply
τραχυτεία ὑὁρ fixήν, any reproachful afperity of language,
but ἱσάγκσιν ψευδὗς φόβυ, the raifing of a falfe fear in the
old man, that he might not be concerned at his being
lodged in the outermoft part of the tent; and by this
method he gives Priam an opportunity of going away
in the morning without obfervation. Euftathius.

Thus gazing long, the filence neither broke,
(A folemn fcene ') at length the father fpoke.

   Permit me now, belov'd of Jove! to fteep
My careful temples in the dew of fleep: 805
For fince the day that number'd with the dead
My haplefs fon, the duft has been my bed,
Soft fleep a ftranger to my weeping eyes,
My only food, my forrows and my fighs '
Till now, encourag'd by the grace you give,   810
I fhare thy banquet, and confent to live.

   With that, Achilles bad prepare the bed,
With purple foft, and fhaggy carpets fpread;
Forth, by the flaming lights, they bend their way,
And place the couches, and the cov'rings lay.   815
Then he: now father fleep, but fleep not here.
Confult thy fafety, and forgive my fear,
Left any Argive (at this hour awake,
To afk our counfel, or our orders take)
Approaching fudden to our open'd tent,   820
Perchance behold thee, and our grace prevent.

   ẏ. 819. *To afk our counfel, or our orders take.*] The
poet here fhews the importance of Achilles in the army;
though Agamemnon be the general, yet all the chief com-
manders apply to him for advice: and thus he promifes
Priam a ceffation of arms for feveral days, purely by his
own authority. The method that Achilles took to confirm the truth of the ceffation, agrees with the cuftom
which we ufe at this day, he gave him his hand upon it.

     ----------χεῖρα γέροντος
Ἑλλαβι δεξιτερην.   Euftathius.

Should such report thy honour'd perfon here,
The king of men the ranfom might defer;
But fay with fpeed, if ought of thy defire
Remains unafk'd; what time the rites require 825
T' interr thy Hector? For, fo long we ftay
Our flaught'ring arm, and bid the hofts obey.

If then thy will permit (the monarch faid)
To finifh all due honours to the dead,
This, of thy grace accord · to thee are known 830
The fears of Ilion, clos'd within her town,
And at what diftance from our walls afpire
The hills of Ide, and forefts for the fire.
Nine days to vent our forrows I requeft,
The tenth fhall fee the fun'ral and the feaft: 835
The next, to raife his monument be giv'n;
The twelfth we war, if war be doom'd by heav'n!

This thy requeft (reply'd the chief) enjoy:
Till then, our arms fufpend the fall of Troy.

Then gave his hand at parting, to prevent 840
The old man's fears, and turn'd within the tent;
Where fair Brifeis bright in blooming charms
Expects her hero with defiring arms.
But in the porch the king and herald reft,
Sad dreams of care yet wand'ring in their breaft. 845
Now gods and men the gifts of fleep partake;
Induftrious Hermes only was awake,
The king's return revolving in his mind,
To pafs the ramparts, and the watch to blind.

The pow'r defcending hover'd o'er his head: 850
And fleep'ft thou, father! (thus the vifion faid)
Now doft thou fleep, when Hector is reftor'd?
Nor fear the Grecian foes, or Grecian lord?
Thy prefence here fhou'd ftern Atrides fee,
Thy ftill-furviving fons may fue for thee,   855
May offer all thy treafures yet contain,
To fpare thy age; and offer all in vain.

    Wak'd with the word, the trembling fire arofe,
And rais'd his friend · the God before him goes,
He joins the mules, directs them with his hand,   860
And moves in filence thro' the hoftile land.
When now to Xanthus' yellow ftream they drove,
(Xanthus, immortal progeny of Jove)
The winged deity forfook their view,
And in a moment to Olympus flew.   865
Now fhed Aurora round her faffron ray,
Sprung thro' the gates of light, and gave the day:
Charg'd with their mournful load, to Ilion go
The fage and king, majeftically flow.
Caffandra firft beholds, from Ilion's fpire,   870
The fad proceffion of her hoary fire,
Then, as the penfive pomp advanc'd more near,
Her breathlefs brother ftretch'd upon the bier:
A fhow'r of tears o'erflows her beauteous eyes,
Alarming thus all Ilion with her cries.   875

    Turn here your fteps, and here your eyes employ,
Ye wretched daughters, and ye fons of Troy!

If e'er ye rush'd in crouds, with vast delight
To hail your hero glorious from the fight;
Now meet him dead, and let your sorrows flow !   880
Your common triumph, and your common woe.

  In thronging crouds they issue to the plains,
Nor man, nor woman, in the walls remains,
In ev'ry face the self-same grief is shown,
And Troy sends forth one universal groan.   885
At Scæa's gates they meet the mourning wain,
Hang on the wheels, and grovel round the slain.
The wife and mother, frantic with despair,
Kiss his pale cheek, and rend their scatter'd hair:
Thus wildly wailing at the gates they lay;   890
And there had sigh'd and sorrow'd out the day;
But god-like Priam from the chariot rose;
Forbear (he cry'd) this violence of woes,
First to the palace let the car proceed,
Then pour your boundless sorrows o'er the dead 895

  The waves of people at his word divide,
Slow rolls the chariot thro' the following tide;
Ev'n to the palace the sad pomp they wait:
They weep, and place him on the bed of state.
A melancholy choir attend around,   900
With plaintive sighs, and music's solemn sound:

℣. 900. *A melancholy choir*, etc] This was a custom
generally received and which passed from the Hebrews
to the Greeks, Romans, and Asiatics. There were
weepers by profession, of both sexes, who sung doleful
tunes round the dead Ecclesiasticus chap xii v 5
When a rich man go into the use of his eternity, there

Alternately they sing, alternate flow,
Th' obedient tears, melodious in their woe.
While deeper sorrows groan from each full heart,
And nature speaks at ev'ry pause of art.   905

   First to the corse the weeping consort flew;
Around his neck her milk-white arms she threw,
And oh my Hector! Oh my Lord! she cries,
Snatch'd in thy bloom from these desiring eyes!

---

shall encompass him weepers. It appears from St. Matthew xi. 17. that children were likewise employed in this office. Dacier.

   ỳ. 906, *etc. The lamentations over Hector.*] The poet judiciously makes Priam to be silent in this general lamentation; he has already borne a sufficient share in these sorrows, in the tent of Achilles, and said what grief can dictate to a father and a king upon such a melancholy subject. But he introduces three women as chief mourners, and speaks only in general of the lamentation of the men of Troy, an excess of sorrow being unmanly; whereas these women might with decency indulge themselves in all the lamentation that fondness and grief could suggest. The wife, the mother of Hector, and Helen, are the three persons introduced; and though they all mourn upon the same occasion, yet their lamentations are so different, that not a sentence that is spoken by the one, could be made use of by the other: Andromache speaks like a tender wife, Hecuba like a fond mother, and Helen mourns with sorrow rising from self-accusation: Andromache commends his bravery, Hecuba his manly beauty, and Helen his gentleness and humanity.

   Homer is very concise in describing the funeral of Hector, which was but a necessary piece of conduct, after he had been so full in that of Patroclus.

Thou to the difmal realms for ever gone!   910
And I abandon'd, defolate, alone!
An only fon, once comfort of our pains,
Sad product now of haplefs love remains!
Never to manly age that fon fhall rife,
Or with encreafing graces glad my eyes: 915
For Ilion now (her great defender flain)
Shall fink a fmoaking ruin on the plain,
Who now protects her wives with guardian care?
Who faves her infants from the rage of war?
Now hoftile fleets muft waft thofe infants o'er,   920
(Thofe wives muft wait 'em) to a foreign fhore!
Thou too, my fon! to barb'rous climes fhalt go,
The fad companion of thy mother's woe;
Driv'n hence a flave before the victor's fword;
Condemn'd to toil for fome inhuman lord.   925
Or elfe fome Greek whofe father preft the plain,
Or fon, or brother, by great Hector flain,
In Hector's blood his vengeance fhall enjoy,
And hurl thee headlong from the tow'rs of Troy.
For thy ftern father never fpar'd a foe;   930
Thence all thefe tears, and all this fcene of woe!
Thence, many evils his fad parents bore,
His parents many, but his confort more.
Why gav'ft thou not to me thy dying hand?
And why receiv'd not I thy laft command?   935

V. 934 *Why gav'ft thou not to me thy dying hand?*
And why receiv'd not I thy laft command?

I have taken thefe two lines from Mr Congreve;
whofe tranflation of this part was one of his firft effays

Some word thou would'ſt have ſpoke, which ſadly dear,
My ſoul might keep, or utter with a tear ;
Which never, never could be loſt in air,
Fix'd in my heart, and oft repeated there !

Thus to her weeping maids ſhe makes her moan ; 940
Her weeping handmaids echo groan for groan.

The mournful mother next ſuſtains her part.
O thou, the beſt, the deareſt to my heart !
Of all my race thou moſt by heav'n approv'd,
And by th' immortals ev'n in death belov'd !   945
While all my other ſons in barb'rous bands
Achilles bound, and ſold to foreign lands,
This felt no chains, but went a glorious ghoſt
Free, and a hero to the Stygian coaſt,
Sentenc'd, 'tis true, by his inhuman doom,   950
Thy noble corſe was dragg'd around the tomb,
(The tomb of him thy warlike arm had ſlain)
Ungen'rous inſult, impotent and vain !
Yet glow'ſt thou freſh with ev'ry living grace,
No mark of pain, or violence of face ;   955
Roſy and fair ! as Phœbus' ſilver bow
Diſmiſs'd thee gently to the ſhades below.

Thus ſpoke the dame, and melted into tears.
Sad Helen next in pomp of grief appears :

in poetry. He has very juſtly rendered the ſenſe of
Πυκινὸν ἔπος, dictum prudens, which is meant of the words
of a dying man, or one in ſome dangerous exigence ; at
which times what is ſpoken is uſually ſomething of the utmoſt importance, and delivered with the utmoſt care which
is the true ſignification of the epithet Πυκινον in this place.

Faſt from the ſhining ſluices of her eyes   960
Fall the round cryſtal drops, while thus ſhe cries.

Ah deareſt friend! in whom the Gods had join'd
The mildeſt manners with the braveſt mind;
Now twice ten years (unhappy years) are o'er
Since Paris brought me to the Trojan ſhore;   965
(Oh had I periſh'd, ere that form divine
Sedúc'd this ſoft, this eaſy heart of mine ')
Yet was it ne'er my fate, from thee to find
A deed ungentle, or a word unkind:
When others curſt the auth'reſs of their woe,   970
Thy pity check'd my ſorrows in their flow:
If ſome proud brother ey'd me with diſdain,
Or ſcornful ſiſter with her ſweeping train,
Thy gentle accents ſoften'd all my pain.

For thee I mourn, and mourn my ſelf in thee,   975
The wretched ſource of all this miſery!
The fate I caus'd, for ever I bemoan;
Sad Helen has no friend now thou art gone!
Thro' Troy's wide ſtreets abandon'd ſhall I roam!
In Troy deſerted, as abhorr'd at home '   980

So ſpoke the fair, with ſorrow-ſtreaming eye:
Diſtreſsful beauty melts each ſtander-by;
On all around th' infectious ſorrow grows;
But Priam check'd the torrent as it roſe.

Perform, ye Trojans ' what the rites require,   985
And fell the foreſts for a fun'ral pyre;
Twelve days, nor foes, nor ſecret ambuſh dread;
Achilles grants theſe honours to the dead.

He fpoke; and at his word, the Trojan train
Their mules and oxen harnefs to the wain,   990
Pour thro' the gates, and fell'd from Ida's crown,
Roll back the gather'd forefts to the town.
Thefe toils continue nine fucceeding days,
And high in air a fylvan ftructure raife.
But when the tenth fair morn began to fhine,   995
Forth to the pile was born the man divine,
And plac'd aloft: while all, with ftreaming eyes,
Beheld the flames and rolling fmokes arife.
Soon as Aurora, daughter of the dawn,
With rofy luftre ftreak'd the dewy lawn;   1000
Again the mournful crouds furround the pyre,
And quench with wine the yet-remaining fire,
The fnowy bones his friends and brothers place
(With tears collected) in a golden vafe;
The golden vafe in purple palls they roll'd,   1005
Of fofteft texture, and inwrought with gold.
Laft o'er the urn the facred earth they fpread,
And rais'd the tomb, memorial of the dead.
(Strong guards and fpies, till all the rites were done,
Watch'd from the rifing to the fetting fun)   1010
All Troy then moves to Priam's court again,
A folemn, filent, melancholy train:
Affembled there, from pious toil they reft,
And fadly fhar'd the laft fepulchral feaft.
Such honours Ilion to her hero paid,   1015
And peaceful flept the mighty Hector's fhade.

The End of the fourth Volume.

WE have now paſt through the Iliad, and ſeen the anger of Achilles, and the terrible effects of it, at an end: as that only was the ſubject of the poem, and the nature of epic poetry would not permit our author to proceed to the event of the war, it may perhaps be acceptable to the common reader to give a ſhort account of what happened to Troy and the chief actors in this poem, after the concluſion of it.

I need not mention that Troy was taken ſoon after the death of Hector, by the ſtratagem of the wooden horſe, the particulars of which are deſcribed by Virgil in the ſecond book of the Æneis.

Achilles fell before Troy, by the hand of Paris, by the ſhot of an arrow in his heel, as Hector had propheſied at his death, *lib.* 22.

The unfortunate Priam was killed by Pyrrhus the ſon of Achilles.

Ajax, after the death of Achilles, had a conteſt with Ulyſſes for the armour of Vulcan, but being defeated in his aim, he ſlew himſelf through indignation.

Helen, after the death of Paris, married Deiphobus his brother, and at the taking of Troy betrayed him, in order to reconcile herſelf to Menelaus her firſt huſband, who received her again into favour.

Agamemnon at his return was barbarouſly murthered by Ægyſthus at the inſtigation of Clytæmneſtra his wife, who in his abſence had diſhonoured his bed with Ægyſthus.

Diomed after the fall of Troy was expelled his own country, and ſcarce eſcaped with life from his adulterous wife Ægiale, but at laſt was received by Daunus in Apulia, and ſhared his kingdom: it is uncertain how he died.

Neſtor lived in peace with his children, in Pylos his native country

Ulyſſes alſo, after innumerable troubles by ſea and land, at laſt returned in ſafety to Ithaca, which is the ſubject of Homer's Odyſſes.

I must end these notes by discharging my duty to two of my friends, which is the more an indispensable piece of justice, as the one of them is since dead: the merit of their kindness to me will appear infinitely the greater, as the task they undertook was in its own nature, of much more labour, than either pleasure or reputation. The larger part of the extracts from Eustathius, together with several excellent observations, were sent me by Mr. Broome: and the whole essay upon Homer was written upon such memoirs as I had collected, by the late Dr. Parnell, archdeacon of Clogher in Ireland: how very much that gentleman's friendship prevailed over his genius, in detaining a writer of his spirit in the drudgery of removing the rubbish of past pedants, will soon appear to the world, when they shall see those beautiful pieces of poetry, the publication of which he left to my charge, almost with his dying breath.

For what remains, I beg to be excused from the ceremonies of taking leave at the end of my work, and from embarassing myself, or others, with any defences or apologies about it. But instead of endeavouring to raise a vain monument to myself, of the merits or difficulties of it, (which must be left to the world, to truth, and to posterity) let me leave behind me a memorial of my friendship, with one of the most valuable men, as well as finest writers, of my age and country: one who has tried, and knows by his own experience, how hard an undertaking it is to do justice to Homer: and one, who (I am sure) sincerely rejoices with me at the period of my labours. To him therefore, having brought this long work to a conclusion, I desire to *dedicate* it, and to have the honour and satisfaction of placing together, in this manner, the names of Mr. CONGREVE, and of

March 25.   A. POPE
1720.

Τῶν Θεῶν δὲ ἐυνοίᾳ --------- το μὴ ἐπὶ πλιον με πρὸκ ὰαι ἰν
Ποιητικῇ καὶ ἄλλοις ἐπιτηδεύμασι, ἐν οἷς ἴσως ἂν κατισχεῖν, εἰ
ᾐσθόμην ἐμαυτὸν ἐυόδως προϊόντα   M. AUREL. ANTON *de*
seipso, l. I. §. 14.

AN INDEX

OF

PERSONS AND THINGS.

A

book ver.

ACAMAS   2 966
he kills Proma
chus   14 559
ACHILLES prays his
mother to revenge
his injuries on the
Greeks   1 460
his speech to the
Greeks   1 79
his quarrel with Aga-
memnon   1 155,
297, 386
entertains Agamem-
non's ambassadors 9 267
answers Ulysses   9 406
answers Phoenix   9 713
answers Ajax   9 762
his double fate   9 532
seeing Machaon
wounded sends Patro-
clus to him   11 730
inquires of Patroclus
the cause of his
grief   16 9
sends Patroclus to the

book ver.

battel, and gives him
orders   16 68
arms his Myrmidons 16 190
and animates them 16 329
his bowl   16 273
offers a libation with
prayers to Jove   16 282
not heard of the death
of Patroclus   17 462
his horses lament the
death of Patroclus 17 486
he grieves for the
death of Patroclus 18 25,
367
tells Thetis his grief 18 99
a description of his
shield   18 551
is concerned lest Patro-
clus's body should
putrify   19 28
calls an assembly   19 44
makes a speech to the
assembly   19 57
refuses to take any food
before the battel   19 197
moans exceedingly for

	book	ver
the death of Patro-		
clus	19	335
he is armed	19	398
Agamemnon's prefents		
are delivered to A-		
chilles	19	243
he and Agamemnon		
recorciled	19	57
his anfwer to Aga-		
memnon	19	143
diffuades Aeneas from		
contendingwith him	20	214
contemns Æneas for		
flying from him	20	393
he kills Iphition	20	439
Demoleon	20	457
Hippodamas	20	463
Polycore	20	471
and many others	20	525
adverfes the fpirit of		
Patroclus	23	25
kills many Trojans in		
tre river Xanthus	21	25
denies Lycaon his life	21	112
he purfues Hector	22	182
kills him	22	453
declares the rites to be		
obferved by his		
Myrmidons	23	8
cuts off his hair, devot-		
ed to the river		
Sperchius	23	171
he prays to the winds	23	237
inftitutes funeral		
games	23	319
gives a cup to Neftor	23	704
is deprived of fleep	24	9
receives the petition of		
Priam	24	652

	book	ver.
lays Hector's body on		
Priam's chariot	24	717
ADRESTUS	2	1007
taken by Menelaus	6	45
ÆNEAS	2	952
feeks Pandarus	5	214
together affault Dio-		
med	5	298
he kills Crethon and		
Orfilochus	5	760
he encounters with		
Achilles	20	193
anfwers Achilles	20	240
tells his lineage	20	252
the fight of Æneas		
and Achilles	20	307
Aetolians	2	694,
		779
AGAMEMNON	3	220
reftores Chryfeis to		
her father	1	406
takes Brifeis from A-		
chilles	1	423
tells his dream in		
council	2	69
his fpeech, advifing a		
return to Greece	2	139
his prayer to Jupiter	2	489
orders Machaon to be		
called to affift Me-		
nelaus wounded	4	230
exhorts his foldiers	4	266
	5	650
blames the indolent	4	273
fpeaks to Idomeneus	4	292
goes to the two Ajaxes	4	311
goes to Neftor	4	334
blames Meneftheus	4	390
blames Diomed	4	422

book ver.

his words to wounded
  Menelaus   4 186
kills Deicoon   5 660
treats the generals 7 385
his speech to the ge-
  nerals   9 23
swears he has not car-
  nally known Bri-
  seis   9 172
acknowleges his
  fault, and makes
  large offers to satisfy
  Achilles   9 148
sends ambassadors to
  Achilles   9 119
AGAMEMNON and
  MENELAUS in
  great perplexity 10 3
they deliberate toge-
  ther   10 41
he goes to Nestor 10 81
he arms   11 21
fights bravely 11 127
kills a great number 11 281
is wounded   11 325
goes out of the battel 11 360
advises flight   14 71
for which Ulysses
  blames him 14 88
is reconciled to Achil-
  les   19
he swears he has not
  enjoyed Briseis 19 267
his speech concerning
  the goddess Dif-
  cord   19 81
AGENOR deliberates
  if he shall meet
  Achilles   21 649
meets him, and is

saved by Apollo 21 695
The Ægis of Jupiter 2 5 6
    5 911
    15 350
    21 467
Agapenor   2 741
AJAX Oileus's son 2 631
  contends with U-
  lysses in the foot-
  race   23 880
  quarrels with Ido-
  meneus   23 555
AJAX TELAMON
  fights with Hector 7 250
  his speech to Achilles 9 740
  his retreat nobly de-
  scribed   11 672
The two AJAXES fight
  together   13 1023
AJAX TELAMON
  challenges Hector 13 620
  his fight over the
  dead body of Al-
  cathous   13 628
  he wounds Hector 14 471
  kills Archilocus 14 540
  exhorts his men 15 591,
    666, 890
  defends the ships 15 814
  is hard pressed 16 130
  he speaks to Mene-
  laus   17 282
  kills Hippothous 17 338
  he is in fear 17 705
  advises Menelaus to
  send Antilochus to
  inform Achilles of
  Patroclus's death 17 737
  contends with Ulys-
  ses in wrestling 23 820

book ver.

fights with Diomed 23 956
Amphimachus 2 755,
1060
Amphius 2 1007
Antenor advises to re-
store Helen 7 419
ANDROMACHE and
HECTOR 6 490
Andromache ignorant
of Hector's death,
runs to the tumult 22 562
her grief for his
death 22 592
her lamentation 24 906
ANTILOCHUS kills
Echepolus 4 522
kills Mydon 5 709
kills Menalippus 15 692
informs Achilles of
Patroclus's death 18 21
he chears up his hor-
ses in the race 23 522
yields the contested
prize to Mene-
laus 23 676
Antiphus 2 827,
1052
APOLLO sends a plague
among the Greeks 1 61
encourages the Tro-
jans 4 585
reprimands Diomed 5 533
raises the phantom of
Æneas to deceive
his enemies 5 546
excites Mars 5 553
drives Patroclus from
the walls of Troy 16 863
and overthrows him 16 954
informs Hector of the

book ver.

death of Euphorbus 17 84
encourages Æneas 17 378
and Hector 17 658
incites Aeneas to en-
counter Achilles 20 410
forbids Hector to en-
gage Achilles 20 431
saves Hector from
Achilles 20 513
refuses to fight with
Neptune 21 536
takes Agenor from
Achilles 21 710
discovers the deceit to
Achilles 22 15
complains to the Gods
of the cruelties done
to Hector's body 24 44
Archilocus 2 996
Ascalaphus and Jal-
menus the sons of
Mars 2 612
Ascanius 2 1050
Asius 2 1015
he is angry with Ju-
piter 12 184
Aspledon and Orcho-
menians 2 610
Asteropaeus meets A-
chilles and is killed 21 157
Astyanax 22 643
Athenians 2 655
Automedon and Al-
cimedon rule the
horses of Achilles 17 488,
548

B

Bellerophon 6 194
The bowl of Achilles 16 273
Briseis 2 841

book ver.

she is restored to A-
chilles   19 254
grieves for Patroclus 19 303
Buprasians   2 747

C.

Calchas the prophet   1   91
he is blamed by Aga-
memnon   1 131
Castor and Pollux   3 302
Cebrion brother and
charioteer to Hector 16 895
Chromis   2 1046
Chryses desires his
daughter who
was captive   1   15
his prayers to Apollo 1   53
Coon   13 590
The Cestus of Venus 14 245
Cretans   2 785

D

Dardanus   20 255
The dead are buried   7 495
Deiphobus is stricken
by Merion, but not
wounded   13 213
kills Hypsenor   13 509
he asks Æneas to af-
sist him in attack-
ing Idomeneus   13 575
kills Ascalaphus   13 655
DIOMED   2 683
blames Sthenelus   4 666
is wounded by Pan-
darus   5 130
invokes Minerva   5 146
kills Pandarus   5 352
wounds Venus   5 417
is in fear of Hector   5 732
wounds Mars   5 1050

book ver.

exhorts Ulysses to
succour Nestor   8 117
he relieves Nestor   8 159
his speech to Aga-
memnon   9 43
going a spy to the ene-
my's camp, chuses
Ulysses for his
companion   10 283
prays to Minerva   10 335
Diomed and Ulysses
surprize Dolon,
whom they take
and examine   10 455
Diomed kills Dolon   10 524
kills the Thracians
while sleeping   10 560
returns with Ulysses
to the fleet   10 624
he strikes Hector   11 452
advises the wounded
to go into the army
to encourage others 14 121
Dione comforts Venus 5 471
Dius   2 1043
Dolon, a spy, taken   10 447
is killed   10 524
Dulichians   2 763

E.

Elephenor   2 654
Ennomus the augur   2 1049
Epistrophus   3 1043
Erichthonius   20 260
Eumelus's mares   2 926
Euphemus   2 1026
Euphorbus wounds
Patroclus   16 978
advises Menelaus to
yield to him   17 14

book ver

is killed by Menelaus 17 50
Euryalus   2 682
Eurypylus   2 893
  wounded, is cured by
  Patroclus   11 982

G.

Ganymedes   20 278
Glaucus   2 1069
  accuses Hector of
  flight   17 153
Glaucus and Diomed
  in the battel meet
  and discourse toge-
  ther   6 150
  interchange armour 6 286
  his prayers to Apollo 16 633
  exhorts the Trojans
  to defend the corse
  of Sarpedon   16 654
Gods, an assembly of
  them   4 2
Gods engage, some on
  one side and some
  on the other   20 91
The fight of the Gods 21 450
Grecian sacrifices   1 599
                      2 502
  they retreat from Troy 2 173
  prepare for war   2 470
  go to battel   3 522
  their forces march 4 484
  their flight   8 97
  their watch   9 110
  the Grecians are
  willing to accept
  Hector's challenge 7 196
  build a wall round
  the fleet   7 520
  buy wine   7 566

book ver.

an assembly of their
  generals   15 339
their ships are burnt 16 140·
Guneus   2 906

H

HECTOR sends out his
  forces to battel   2 988
tells Paris's challenge
  to the Greeks   3 123
retreats out of the
  battel into Troy   6 296
exhorts the Trojans
  to supplicate Mi-
  nerva   6 338
goes to the house of
  Paris   6 389
to his wife Andro-
  mache   6 463
his discourse with her 6 510
challenges the Greeks
  to single combate   7 79
exhorts his men   8 210
encourages his horses 8 226
sends Dolon as a spy 10 376
his glory   11 83
he exhorts his forces,
  and rushes to battel 11 368
derides Polydamas's
  advice   12 267
forces open a gate of
  the Grecian wall   12 537
exhorts his men   13 205
seeks for aid   13 967
rallies his forces, and
  attacks the enemy 13 991
answers Ajax   13 1041
kills Amphimacus   13 247
wounded, retreats   14 503
is encouraged by A-

	book	ver.
pollo	15	288
goes again to battel	15	296
kills Lycophron	15	500
exhorts Menalippus	15	654
kills Peripoetes	15	770
takes a ship	15	854
is put to flight	16	440
	16	797
encounters with Patro-		
clus	16	885
and kills him	16	987
excites his men	17	260
his speech to his war-		
like friends	17	205
he gives way to Ajax	17	140
answers Glaucus	17	187
puts on Achilles's ar-		
mour	17	219
he pursues Achilles's		
horses with the af-		
fiftance of Aeneas	17	550
again endeavours to		
take the body of		
Patroclus	18	187
refolves to combate		
with Achilles	20	415
affaults Achilles	20	485
his wound	23	470
he deliberates with		
himfelf	22	138
he fights with Achil-		
les	22	317
his death	22	453
his funeral	24	989
Hecuba defires he		
would not fight		
Achilles	22	110
fhe renews her defires		
he would not fight		

	book	ver.
Achilles	22	552
fhe mourns his death	24	942
Helen goes to fee the		
combate between		
Paris and Mene-		
laus	3	123
the Trojans admire		
her beauty	3	204
chides Paris	3	552
fpeaks to Hector	6	432
laments over Hec-		
tor's body	24	962
Helenus advifes Hec-		
tor and Aeneas	7	48
	6	95
Hippothous	2	1021
I		
Idaeus carries Paris's		
challenge to the		
Greeks	7	460
Idomeneus	2	791
	3	295
kills Othryoneus	13	457
Afius	13	483
Alcathous	13	537
Iphidamas, his death		
finely defcribed 11 283, *etc.*		
Iris orders the Trojans		
to arms	2	956
tells Helen of the fin-		
gle combate of Pa-		
ris and Menelaus	3	165
is fent to Pallas and		
Juno with Jove's		
orders	1	488
admonifhes Achilles to		
fuccour his friends		
fighting for the		
body of Patroclus	18	20

book ver.

summons the winds to raise the fire of Patroclus's pile   23   342

Ithacans   2   769

Juno sends Minerva to hinder the Greeks from retreating   2   191

her quarrel with Jupiter   4   35

she and Minerva prepare for fight   5   883

ask leave of Jupiter to go to battel   5   942

her speech to Neptune   8   242

dresses herself to deceive Jupiter   14   191

desires of Venus her girdle to deceive Jupiter   14   215

goes to the God of Sleep to put Jupiter into a sleep   14   266

by large promises obtains her requests   14   305

goes to Jupiter   14   331

denies it was at her request that Neptune assisted the Greeks   15   41

goes to the rest of the Gods   15   84

tells the order of Jupiter to Apollo and Iris   15   162

she advises with the Gods concerning Aeneas's fighting with Achilles   20   146

book ver.

sends Vulcan to oppose Xanthus   21   386

overcomes Diana   21   564

JUPITER promises Thetis to be revenged on the Greeks   1   672

inspires Agamemnon with a dream   2   9

forbids the Gods to assist either part   8   7

his golden chain   8   25

descends on Ida   8   57

sends Iris to order Juno and Minerva to retreat from the battel   8   488

sends Iris amongst the Greeks   11   4

sends Iris to forbid Hector some time from personally engaging   11   241

inspires Sarpedon to assault the Greek wall   12   348

is caused by Juno to sleep   14   305

awaking from sleep he is angry with Juno   15   5

orders Juno to send Iris and Apollo to him   15   59

sends Iris to order Neptune to desist from fighting   15   180

sends Apollo to encourage Hector   15   258

encourages Hector him-

	book	ver.
felf	15	722
is grieved for Sarpedon's death	16	530
orders Apollo to take care of Sarpedon's funeral	16	811
he examines Juno concerning the exciting Achilles to engage in battel	18	417
he gives the Gods leave to affift which party they pleafe	22	29
he pities Hector	17	227
fends Minerva to comfort Achilles	19	364
fends Thetis to Achilles, ordering him to deliver Hector's body to Priam	24	137
fends Iris to advife Priam to go to Achilles	24	178
orders Mercury to conduct Priam to Achilles	24	411

L

Lacedaemonians	3	704
Locrians	2	630
Lycaon overcome by Achilles	21	41
begs his life in vain	21	111

M.

Machaon	2	889
cures Menelaus	4	250
Magnefians	2	916
Mars is wounded by Diomed	5	1050
on which account he		

	book	ver.
expoftulates with Jupiter	5	1059
for which he is reprehended by Jupiter	5	1092
hearing of the death of his fon is enraged	15	126
Meges	2	761
Meleager, the ftory of him	9	653
Menelaus	2	710
undertakes to fight with Paris	3	137
is treacheroufly wounded by Pandarus	4	135
takes Adreftus	6	45
would undertake to fight with Hector, but is hindered by Agamemnon	7	127
he and Ajax affift Ulyffes	11	582
wounds Helenus	13	733
kills Pifander	13	753
exhorts Antilochus	15	680
he is defpifed by Euphorbus	17	18
kills Euphorbus	17	50
yields to Hector	17	101
exhorts the generals	17	294
is encouraged by Minerva	17	616
he fends Antilochus to tell Achilles of the death of Patroclus	17	775
is angry with Antilochus	23	651

book ver

Menestheus 2 665
sends Thoos to the
Ajaxes for aid 12 411
Mercury accompanies
Priam 24 447
and conducts him to
Achilles 24 541
admonishes Priam in
his sleep 24 780
Merion 2 792
wounds Deiphobus 13 668
kills Harpalion 13 813
Mestles 2 1054
MINERVA goes to
Pandarus to induce
him to break the
truce 4 119
strengthens Diomed 5 109
forces Mars from the
battel 5 45
derides Venus 5 509
prepares herself for
the war 5 883, 908
asks leave of Jupiter
to go to the war 5 942
speaks to Diomed 5 998
encourages Diomed to
assault Mars 5 1020
her speech to Jupiter 8 39
restrains Mars's an-
ger 15 140
knocks down Mars
with a mighty
stone 21 469
vanquishes Venus and
her lover 21 498
in the shape of Dei-
phobus persuades
Hector to meet A-

book ver.

chilles 22 291
Mycenians 2 686
Myrmidons 2 834
go to the fight 16 312
N
Nastes 2 1062
Neptune, his and Ju-
piter's discourse
concerning the
Grecian wall 7 530
his discourse with
Idomeneus 13 289
brings help to the
Greeks 12 17
encourages the two
Ajaxes 13 73
and the Greeks 13 131
is angry with Jupiter 15 206
advises about the
preservation of
Aeneas 20 341
preserves Aeneas
from Achilles's
fury 20 367
comforts Ulysses 21 333
urges Apollo to fight 21 450
Nereids, the catalogue
and names of them 18 42,
etc.
NESTOR endeavours
to reconcile Achil-
les and Agamem-
non 1 330
Nestor praised by Aga-
memnon 2 440
his speech to the sol-
diers 2 402
NESTOR 2 718
his speech to Aga-

	book	ver
memnon	4	370
exhorts the foldiers	6	84
his fpeech for bury- ing the dead, and building a wall	7	392
blames the Greeks for not daring to encounter Hector	7	145
is in great danger	8	101
flies with Diomed	8	190
his advice for guards and refrefhment	9	86
for pacifying Achil les	9	141
approves Diomed's fpeech to Agamemnon	9	73
goes by night to U- lyffes	10	157
encourages Diomed	10	180
advifes to fend fpies into the enemy's camp	10	241
recites what he did in his youth	11	817
goes on an uproar to know the caufe	14	1
prays to Jupiter	15	428
exhorts the Greeks to oppofe the enemy	15	796
advifes his fon con- cerning the race	23	369
Niobe, her fable	24	757
Nireus, the moft hand- fome Greek	2	817

O

	book	ver
Orcus his helmet	5	1037
Odius	2	1043

P

	book	ver
Pandarus	2	1001

	book	ver.
treacherously wounds Menelaus	4	135
is killed by Diomed	5	352
Paris boafts at the be- ginning of the fight	3	26
cowardly flies	3	44
blamed of Hector	3	55
undertakes a fingle combate with Me- nelaus	3	101
is armed	3	409
and fights with Me- nelaus	3	417
is taken from the combate by Venus	3	467
blamed by Helen	3	533
refcued from fight, is put to bed with Helen	3	555
refufes to reftore He- len	7	418
wounds Diomed	11	482
Machaon	11	619
Eurypylus	11	709
kills Euchenor	13	626
Patroclus returns to Achilles	15	462
entreats Achilles to let him go to aid the Greeks	16	31
armed	16	162
exhorts the Myrmi- dons	16	314
he and his men kill many of the Tro- jans	16	448
	16	483
	16	847
exhorts the two A-		

	book	ver.
jaxes	16	681
kills Cebrion	16	895
is ſtruck by Apollo	16	954
a fierce conteſt about the body of Patroclus	17	314, 472, 613
appears to Achilles in a dream	23	78
his funeral pile	23	198
his ſepulchre	23	305
his funeral games	23	323
Phidippus	2	817
Phocians	2	620
Phoenix intreats Achilles to be reconciled with Agamemnon	9	562
ſits as one of the judges of the race	24	435
Phorcis	2	1050
Podalirius	2	889
Podarces	2	860
Polydamas adviſes to force the Greek lines	12	67
interprets a prodigy, and gives his advice	12	245
blames Hector	13	907
kills Prothenor	14	525
Polypoetes	2	904
and Leontius	12	141
Prayers and injuſtice, their influence on the Gods	9	624
PRIAM enquires of Helen about the Grecians which they ſaw	3	220
is called by an herald to agree to a treaty	3	319
returns into the city	3	386
ſpeaks to the Trojans	7	444
commands the ſoldiers to open the gate	21	620
intreats Hector not to meet Achilles	22	51
bemoans the death of Hector	23	515
tells his wife the commands of Jupiter	24	233
takes the gifts to carry to Achilles	24	341
rebukes his ſons,	24	311
his council to Hecuba	24	355
he prays to Jupiter	24	377
he meets Achilles	24	579
deſires to ſleep	24	
he carries the body of Hector into the city	24	882
Prodigies	11	70
	12	233
of a dragon which devoured a neſt of birds and the dam	2	372
Proteſilaus	2	853
Prothous	2	916
Pylaemenes	2	1034
is ſlain	5	705
Pylians	2	715
Pyraechmes	2	1028
R.		
Rhefus	10	505
is ſlain by Diomed	10	576
Rhodians	2	795
S.		
Sarpedon	2	1069

book ver.

wounded by Tlepole-
mus, defires the
affiftance of Hec-
tor   5 842
exhorts Glaucus to
fight   12 371
breaks down a battle-
ment of the wall   12 483
Soldiers, the good and
bad defcribed   13 359
Sleep, (the God of
Sleep,) at the in-
ftance of Juno
puts Jupiter into
a fleep   14 266
incites Neptune   14 411
Sthenelus   2 683
anfwers Agamem-
non fharply   4 456

T

Talthybius   1 421
Teucer from behind
the fhield of Ajax,
kills many Tro-
jans   8 310
is wounded by Hector 8 387
kills Imbrius   13 227
and Clitus   15 522
his bow is broke by a
divine power   15 544
Thalpius   2 755
Thamyris his ftory   2 721
Themis prefents the
nectar bowl to Ju-
no   15 96
Therfites his loquacity 2 255
Thetis, her words to
Achilles   1 540
her petition to Jove

book ver.

for her fon   1 652
fhe in great grief
fpeaks to the Ne-
reids   18 69
enquires of Achilles 18 95
promifes Achilles ar-
mour made by Vul-
can   18 172
goes to Vulcan   18 431
befeeches Vulcan to
make Achilles's
armour   18 529
carries the armour
made by Vulcan to
Achilles   19 13
Thoas   2 775
kills Pirus   4 610
Titarefius a river   2 910
Tlepolemus   2 793
fights with Sarpe-
don   5 776
Trojans and Grecians
march to battel   3 1
they fign a treaty   3 338
Trojans and Greeks
in battel   4 508
many of the Trojans
killed   6 5
the Trojans watch   8 686
Trojans march, at-
tack the Greek
trenches   12 95
  12 295
Trojans fly   14 596
Trojans make a great
flaughter   15 372
The Trojans fight
bravely at the
Grecian fleet   15 842

	book	ver.
they fly before the Greeks	17	676
An affembly of the Trojans	18	289

V

VENUS conveys Paris from the fight	3	467
befpeaks Helen	3	481
is angry with Helen	3	513
carries Helen to Paris	3	533
conveys Æneas out of the battel	5	385
is wounded by Diomed	5	417
complains of her being wounded to Dione	5	465
is laughed at by Minerva	5	499
with Apollo keeps the body of Hector from putrifying	23	226

ULYSSES | 2 | 765 |
	3	254
delivers Chryfeis to her father	1	579
contends with Ajax in the courfe	23	828
prevents the Greeks from retreating	2	225
provokes Therfites	2	305
exhorts the foldiers to battel	2	347
anfwers Agamemnon	4	402
his fpeech to Achilles to reconcile him and Agamemnon	9	562

	book	ver.
exhorts Diomed to battel	11	408
is furrounded by the enemy	11	510
is wounded by Socus	11	547
kills Socus	11	561
advifes to give the foldiers refrefhment before the battel	19	153
advifes Achilles to refrefh himfelf	19	215
Vulcan admonifhes Juno	1	746
remembers the benefits he has received of Thetis	18	465
enquires of Thetis the caufe of her coming	18	496
makes a fuit of armour for Achilles	18	537
dries up the river, Xanthus	21	400

X.

Xanthus, Achilles's horfe, forefhews the deftruction of Achilles	19	452
Xanthus, the river, fpeaks to Achilles	21	232
rifes againft Achilles	21	258
invokes Simois againft Achilles	21	364
fupplicates Vulcan and Juno	21	423

A

POETICAL INDEX

TO

HOMER's ILIAD.

The firſt number marks the book, the ſecond the verſe.

FABLE

THE great moral of the Iliad, that concord among governors, is the preſervation of ſtates, and diſcord the ruin of them, purſued through the whole fable The anger of Achilles breaks this union in the opening of the poem, *l* 1. He withdraws from the body of the Greeks, which firſt interrupts the ſucceſs of the common cauſe, *ibid* The army mutiny, 2 The Trojans break the truce, 4 A great number of the Greeks ſlain, 7 391 Forced to build fortifications to guard their fleet, *ibid* In great diſtreſs from the enemy, whoſe victory is only ſtopt by the night, 8 Ready to quit their deſign, and return with infamy, 9. Send to Achilles to perſuade him to a re union, in vain, *ibid* The diſtreſs continues, the generals and all the beſt warriors are wounded, 11 The fortification overthrown, and the fleet ſet on fire, 15 Achilles himſelf ſhares in the misfortunes he brought upon the allies, by the loſs of his friend Patroclus, 16. Hereupon the hero is reconciled to the general, the victory over Troy is compleat, and Hector ſlain by Achilles, 19, 20, 21, 22, *etc*

EPISODES OF FABLES *which are interwoven into the poem, but foreign to its deſign.*

The fable of the conſpiracy of the Gods againſt Jupiter,

FABLE

1 516 Of Vulcan's fall from heaven on the island of Lemnos, 1 761 The imprisonment of Mars by Otus and Ephialtes, 5 475 The story of Thamyris, 2 721 The embassy of Tydeus to Thebes, 4 430 The tale of Bellerophon, 6 195 Of Lycurgus and the Bacchanals, 6 161 The war of the Pylians and Arcadians, 6 165. The story of Phoenix, 9 572 Of Meleager and the wars of the Curetes and Aetolians, 9 653. The wars of Pyle and Elis, 11 818 The birth of Hercules, and labour of Alcmena, 19 103. The expulsion of Ate from heaven, 19 93 Vulcan's abode with Thetis, and his employment there, 18 363. The family and history of Troy, 20 255 The transformation of Niobe, 24 757 Building of the walls of Troy by Neptune, 21. 518

Allegorical FABLES.

Moral] Prudence restraining Passion, represented in the machine of Minerva descending to calm Achilles, 1 261 Love all firing, and extinguishing Honour, in Venus bringing Paris from the combate

to the arms of Helen, 3 460, etc. True Courage overcoming Passion, in Diomed's conquest of Mars and Venus, by the assistance of Pallas, 5. 507, etc *through that whole book* Prayers the daughters of Jupiter, following Injustice, and persecuting her at the throne of heaven, 9 625 The Cestus, or girdle of Venus, 14 247 The allegory of Sleep, 14 265 The allegory of Discord cast out of heaven to earth, 19 93 The allegory of the two Urns of Pleasure and Pain, 24 663

Physical or Philosophical]The combate of the elements till the water subsided, in the fable of the wars of Juno or the Air, and Neptune or the Sea, with Jupiter or the Aether, till Thetis put an end to them, 1 516 Fire derived from heaven to earth, imaged by the fall of Vulcan on Lemnos, 1 761 The gravitation of the Planets upon the Sun, in the allegory of the golden chain of Jupiter, 8 25 The influence of the Aether upon the Air, in the allegory of the congress of Jupiter and Juno, 14 395 The Air supplied by the vapours of the Ocean and Earth, in the

FABLE.

story of Juno nourished by Oceanus and Tethys, 14. 231 The allegory of the Winds, 23 242. The quality of Salt preserving dead bodies from corruption, in Thetis or the Sea preserving the body of Patroclus, 19 40

For the rest of the Allegories see the System of the Gods as acting in their allegorical characters, under the article CHARACTERS.

Allegorical or fictitious persons in HOMER.

The lying dream sent to Agamemnon by Jupiter, 2 7 Fame the messenger of Jove, 2 121 Furies, punishers of the wicked, 3 351 Hebe, or Youth, attending the banquets of the Gods, 4 3 Flight and Terror attendants upon Mars, 4. 500 Discord described, 4 502 Bellona Goddess of war, 5 726 The Hours, keepers of the gates of heaven, 5. 929. Nymphs of the mountains, 6 532 Night, a Goddess, 6 342 Iris, or the Rainbow, 8 486 Prayers the daughters of Jupiter, 9 615 Eris or Discord, 11 5 Ilythiae, Goddesses presiding in

FABLE.

womens labour, 11 349. Terror the son of Mars, 13. 386 Sleep, 14 265 Night, 14 293 Death and Sleep, two twins, 16 831 Nereids, or nymphs of the sea, a catalogue of them, 18 45. Ate, or the Goddess of Discord, 19 93 Scamander the river-God, 21 231. Fire and Water made persons in the battel of Scamander and Vulcan, 21 387 The East and West Winds, ibid Iris, or the Rainbow, and the Winds, 23 242.

The MARVELLOUS or supernatural FICTIONS in HOMER.

Omen of the birds and serpent, representing the event of the Trojan war, 2 370. The miraculous rivers Titaresius and Styx, 2 910. The giant Typhon under the burning mountain Typhaeus, 2 952 Battel of the cranes and pygmies, 3. 6. Prodigy of a comet, 4. 101. Diomed's helmet ejecting fire, 5 6. Horses of coelestial breed, 5 327 Vast stone heaved by Diomed, 5 370. And Hector, 12 537 And Minerva, 20. 470 The miraculous chariot, and arms of Pallas, 5. 885,

FABLE.

967, etc The Gorgon, helmet, and Ægis of Jupiter, ibid. The gates of heaven, ibid. The leap of immortal horses, 5 960. Shout of Stentor, 5 978. Roaring of Mars, 5, 1054. Helmet of Orcus, which rendered the wearer invisible, 5 1036 The blood of the Gods, 5. 422 The immediate healing of their wounds, 5 1116. The chimaera, 6 210 Destruction by Neptune of the Grecian rampart, 12 15. Wall pushed down by Apollo, 15 415 The golden chain of Jupiter, 8 25 Horses and chariot of Jupiter, 8 50 His balances, weighing the fates of men, 8 88 —12 271 Jupiter's assisting the Trojans by thunders and lightnings, and visible declarations of his favour, 8 93, 165, etc —17. 670. Prodigy of an eagle and fawn, 8 297 Horses of the Gods, stables and chariots, pompously described, 8. 535, etc Hector's lance of ten cubits, 8 615 Omen of an heron 10 320 The descent of Eris, 11 5 A shower of blood, 11. 70. —16 560. Omen of an eagle and serpent, 12 230. The progress of Neptune through the seas, 13 42.

FABLE.

The chain of War and Discord stretched over the armies, 13 451 The loud voice of Neptune, 14 173 Solemn oath of the Gods, 14. 307 —15. 41. Minerva spreads a light over the army, 15 808 Jupiter involves the combatants in thick darkness, 16 422, 695. Horses begot by the wind on a harpye, 16 183 A shower of blood, 16 560 Miraculous transportation and interment of Sarpedon by Apollo, Sleep and Death, 16. 810, etc Prophecy at the hour of death, 16 1026 — 22 450 Achilles unarmed puts the whole Trojan army to flight on his appearance, 18 240, etc Moving tripods and living statues of Vulcan, 18 440 488. The horse of Achilles speaks by a prodigy, 19 450. The battel of the Gods, 20 63, etc Horses of a miraculous extraction, the transformation of Boreas, 20 164 The wonderful battel of the Xanthus, 21 230, etc Hector's body preserved by Apollo and Venus, 23 216 The ghost of Patroclus, 23. 77 The two urns of Jupiter, 24 663. The vast quoit of Aetion, 23 975. The transformation of Niobe

FABLE.

and her people into stones, 24. 757.

Under this head of the marvellous may also be included all the immediate

FABLE.

machines, and appearances of the Gods in the poem, and their transformations, the miraculous birth of heroes, the passions in human and visible forms, and the rest.

CHARACTERS or MANNERS.

Characters of the Gods *of* Homer, *as acting in the* physical *or* moral *capacities of those deities.*

JUPITER

Acting and governing all, as the supreme Being.] See the article Theology in the next Index

JUNO

As the element of Air] Her congress with Jupiter, or the Æther, and production of vegetables, 14 390 *etc.* Her loud shout, the air being the cause of sound, 5 978 Nourished by Oceanus and Tethys, 14. 231,

As Goddess of Empire and Honour] Stops the Greeks from flying ignominiously, 2 191. and in many other places Incites and commands Achilles to revenge the death of his friend, 18 203, *etc.* Inspires into Helen a contempt of Paris, and sends Iris to

call her to behold the combate with Menelaus, 3 185,

APOLLO.

As the Sun.] Causes the plague in the heat of summer, 1. 16 Raises a phantom of clouds and vapours, 5 545. Discovers in the morning the slaughter made the night before, 10 606. Recovers Hector from fainting, and opens his eyes, 15. 280. Dazzles the eyes of the Grecks, and shakes his Aegis in their faces, 15 362 Restores vigour to Glaucus, 16. 647 Preserves the body of Sarpedon from corruption, 16 830. And that of Hector, 23 230 Raises a cloud to conceal Aeneas, 20. 515
As Destiny] Saves Aeneas

CHARACTERS.

from death, 5 441. And Hector, 20 513 Saves Agenor, 21. 706 Deserts Hector when his hour is come, 22 277.

As Wisdom] He and Minerva inspire Helenus to keep off the general engagement by a single combate, 7 25. Advises Hector to shun encountering Achilles, 20 431.

MARS

As mere martial courage without conduct.] Goes to the fight against the orders of Jupiter, 5 716 Again provoked to rebel against Jupiter by his passion, 15 126 Is vanquished by Minerva, or Conduct, 21. 480.

MINERVA

As martial courage with Wisdom] Joins with Juno in restraining the Greeks from fight, and inspires Ulysses to do it, 2. 210 Animates the army, 2 525 Described as leading a hero safe through a battel, 4 632. Assists Diomed to overcome Mars and Venus, 5 407, 1042. Overcomes them herself, 21 480 Restrains Mars from rebellion against Jupiter, 5 45 —— 15 140 Submits to Jupiter, 8. 40. Advises U-

CHARACTERS

lysses to retire in time from the night expedition, 10. 593 Assists him throughout that expedition, 10. 350, *etc* Discovers the ambush laid against the Pylians by night, and causes them to sally, 11 851 Assists Achilles to conquer Hector, 22 277, *etc*

As Wisdom separately considered] Suppresses Achilles's passion, 1 261 Suppresses her own anger against Jupiter, 4 31. Brings to pass Jupiter's will in contriving the breach of the truce, 4 95 Teaches Diomed to discern Gods from men, and to conquer Venus, 5 155, *etc* Called the best beloved of Jupiter, 8. 48. Obtains leave of Jupiter, that while the other Gods do not assist the Greeks, she may direct them with her counsels, 8 45 Is again checked by the command of Jupiter, and submits, 8 560, 580 Is said to assist, or save any hero, in general through the poem, when any act of prudence preserves him.

VENUS.

As the passion of love] Brings Paris from the fight to the embraces of Helen; and inflames the lovers, 3. 460,

CHARACTERS

530, *etc.* Is overcome by Minerva, or Wisdom, 5. 407. And again, 21 500 Her Cestus or girdle, and the effects of it, 14. 247

NEPTUNE

As the Sea] Overturns the Grecian wall with his waves, 12. 15 Assists the Greeks at their fleet, which was drawn up at the sea side, 13 67, *etc.* Retreats at the order of Jupiter, 15. 245. Shakes the whole field of battel and sea-shore with earthquakes, 20. 77.

VULCAN.

Or the Element of Fire] Falls from heaven to earth, 1. 761. Received in Lemnos, a place of subterraneous fires, *ibid* His operations of various kinds, 18 440, 468, 540. Dries up the river Xanthus, 21. 460 Assisted by the winds, 21. 390.

Characters of the HEROES.

N. B. *The Speeches, which depended upon, and flow from these several characters, are distinguished by an S.*

ACHILLES.

Furious, passionate, disdainful, and reproachful, *lib.* 1, v.

CHARACTERS.

155 S. 195. S. 295 S —9 405. S 746 S —24 765. Revengeful and implacable in the highest degree, 9. 755, 765.—16 68. S 121 °S. —18 120, 125 S — 19. 211. S —22 333 S 437 S — Cruel, 16 122 — 19 395. —21. 112.—22 437 S. 495. S —23. 30.—24. 51 —

Superior to all men in valour, 20 60, 437, *etc* —21 22, throughout

Constant and violent in friendship, 9 730 —18 30, 371 —23. 54, 272 —24 5. —16 9 S 208 S —18. 100 S 380 S —19 335. S —22 482 S —Achilles scarce ever speaks without mention of his friend Patroclus

ÆNEAS.

Pious to the Gods, 5 216 S. —20. 131, 290, 345 — Sensible and moral, 20 242, 293, *etc* S

Valiant, not rash, 20 130, 240 S —

Tender to his friend, 13 590

See his character in the notes on l 5 v. 212 and on l 13 v. 578.

AGAMEMNON.

Imperious and passionate, 1.

CHARACTERS.
34, 729. S——
Sometimes cruel, 6 80 —2
140 S,
Artful and defigning, 2 68,
95.——
Valiant, and an excellent General, 4. 256, 265, etc —11
throughout
Eminent for brotherly affection, 4. 183, etc. S ——7
120 ——

See his character in the notes
on l 11 v. 1.

AJAX.
Of fuperior ftrength and fize,
and fearlefs on that account,
13 410.——7 227 S 274
S —15 666
Indefatigable and patient, 11
683, etc ——13 877 ——15
throughout ——14 535 ——
fhort in his fpeeches, 7 227
——9 742 —15 666, etc

See his character in the notes
on l 7 v, 226

DIOMED.
Daring and intrepid, 5 through-
out, and 8 163, 180 S —9
65, 820 —10 260 ——
Proud and boafting, 6 152
——11 500.
Vain of his birth, 14 125
Generous, 6 265 ——
Is guided by Pallas or Wif-
dom, and chufes Ulyffes to

CHARACTERS
direct him, 5 throughout
—10 287, 335

See his character in the notes
on l 5 v 1

HECTOR
A true lover of his country,
8 621 S —12 284 ——15.
582 S.
Valiant in the higheft degree,
3 89 —7. 80 —12. 270
S —18 333 S.——etc
Excellent in conduct, 8 610.
S —11 663 ——
Pious, 6 140, 339, 605.——
Tender to his parents, 6 315.
——to his wife, 6 456
——to his child, 6 606
——to his friends, 20 485
—24 962.—— '50
                    '5
See his character in the notes
on l. 3 v 53.

IDOMENEUS.
An old foldier, 13 455, 618 ——
A lover of his foldiers, 13
280 ——
Talkative upon fubjects of
war, 13 340, 355, etc.— —4.
305 S ——
Vain of his family, 13 565,
etc.
Stately and infulting, 13 472,
etc

See his character in the notes
on l 13. v 279

CHARACTERS.

MENELAUS.

Valiant, 3 35 —13 733 —
17 throughout
Tender of the people, 10
32 —
Gentle in his nature, 10 138
—23 685 —
But fired by a sense of his
wrongs, 2 711 —3 45
—7 109 S —13 780 S
—17 640

See his character in the notes
on l 3 v 278

NESTOR

Wise and experienced in council 1 331, 340 —2 441 —
Skilful in the art of war, 2
432, 670 —4 338, etc S
—7 392 S —
Brave, 7 165 —11 817 —
15 796 S
Eloquent, 1 332, etc
Vigilant, 10 88, 186, 624,—
Pious, 15 427
Talkative through old age, 4
370,—7 145 —11 800.
—23 373, 718 —and in
general through the book

See his character in the notes
on l. 1 v 339 —91 2
402, etc.

PRIAM.

A tender father to Hector, 22
51 S —24 275

CHARACTERS.

——to Paris, 3 381.
——to Helen, 3 212 S.
An easy prince of too yielding
a temper, 7 443.
Gentle and compassionate, 3.
211, 382.
Pious, 4 70 —24 520 S.
See his character in the notes
on l. 3 v 211.

PARIS

Effeminate in dress and person,
3 27, 55, 80, 409
Amorous, 3 550
Ingenious in arts, music, 3.
80 Building, 6 390
Patient of reproof, 3 86
Naturally valiant, 6 669 —
13 985

See his character in the notes
on l 3 v. 26, 37, 86.

PATROCLUS

Compassionate of the suffer-
ings of his countrymen, 11.
947 —16 5, 31 S
Rash, but valiant, 16 709
Of a gentle nature, 19 320
—17 755

SARPEDON

Valiant, out of principle and
honour, 5 575 S —12 371.
S
Eloquent, ibid,

CHARACTERS.

Careful only of the common cause in his death, 16. 605. S

See his character in the notes on l 16 v 512.

ULYSSES.

Prudent, 3 261 —10 287 —19 218 —

Eloquent, 3. 283.—9 295. S *etc*

Valiant in the field with caution, 4 566 —11 515, *etc.*

Bold in the council with prudence, 14 90

See his character in the notes on l 2 v. 402. et sparsim

Characters of other HEROES

Agenor, valiant and considerate, 21 648

Antenor, a prudent counsellor, 7 418

Ajax Oileus, famous for swiftness, 2 631 —14. 618

Antilochus, bold-spirited, but

CHARACTERS.

reasonable, and artful, 4. 522 —23 505, 618, 666 S. —23 920, 930

Euphorbus, beautiful and valiant, 16. 973 —17. 11, 57 —

Glaucus, pious to his friend, 16 660 —17. 165 180.

Helenus, a prophet and hero, 6 92.

Meriones, dauntless and faithful, 13 325, *etc*

Machaon, an excellent physician, 2 890 —11 630.

Phoenix, his friendship and tenderness for Achilles, 9. 605

Polydamas, prudent and eloquent *See his speeches,* 12. 70, 245.—13 907 —18. 300 —

Teucer, famous for archery, 8 320 —15 510, *etc*

Thoas, famous for eloquence, 15 322

For other less distinguished characters, see the article, Descriptions of the passions.

SPEECHES or ORATIONS.

A TABLE *of the most considerable in the* ILIAD.

*In the exhortatory or delibera-
tive kind.*

The oration of Neſtor to Agamemnon and Achilles, per-
ſuading a reconciliation, 1.
340 The orations of Ne-
ſtor, Ulyſſes, and Agamemnon, to perſuade the army
to ſtay, 2 350, 402, 452.
Of Sarpedon to Hector, 5.
575. Of Neſtor to encou-
rage the Greeks to accept
the challenge of Hector, 7.
145 Of Hector to the Tro-
jans, 8 621 Of Neſtor
to ſend to Achilles, 9 127,
Of Ulyſſes, Phoenix, and A-
jax, to move Achilles to a
reconciliation, 9 295, 561,
742. Achilles's reply to each,
ibid. Sarpedon to Glaucus,
12 271 Of Neptune to
the Greeks, to defend the
fleet, 13 131. Of Ajax to
the Greeks, 15 666. Ne-
ſtor to the ſame, 15 796.
Of Ajax again, 15 890 Scamander to the river Simois,
21. 360 Juno to Vulcan,
21 387 Achilles to Patro-
clus, 16 70, *etc.*

In the vituperative kind.

The ſpeech of Therſites, 2
275. That of Ulyſſes an-
ſwering him, 2 306. Of
Hector to Paris, 3 55 Of
Agamemnon to Diomed, 4.
422 Of Hector to Paris,
6 406 Of Diomed to A-
gamemnon, 9 43 Of U-
lyſſes to the ſame, 14 90
Sarpedon to Hector, 5 575
Glaucus to Hector, 17. 153.

In the narrative.

Achilles to Thetis, 1. 476.
Pandarus to Æneas, 5 230.
Glaucus to Diomed, 6 190.
Phoenix to Achilles, 9 561,
652 Agamemnon to the
Greeks, 19 90 Æneas to
Achilles, 20 240 Of Ne-
ſtor, 7 163 —11 800.
—and the ſpeeches of Ne-
ſtor in general

In the pathetic.

Agamemnon on Menelaus
wounded, 4 186
Andromache to Hector, and his
anſwer, 6 510 570.

SPEECHES

Patroclus and Achilles, 16 10, etc.

Jupiter on fight of Hector, 17 231

Lamentation of Briseis for Patroclus, 19 303

——of Achilles for Patroclus, 19 335

——of Priam to Hector, 22 51 530

——of Hecuba to the same, 22 115 and again, 24 243, 943

——of Andromache at Hector's death, 22 608

——of Andromache at his funeral, 24 908

——of Helena, 24 961

Lycaon to Achilles, 21 85

Thetis to the Nereids, 17 70.

The ghost of Patroclus to Achilles 23 83

Priam to Achilles, 24 600.

SPEECHES

In the irony, or sarcasm.

The speech of Pallas on Venus being wounded, 5 509

Ulysses over Socus, 11 566

Idomeneus over Othryoneus, 13 472

Four sarcastic speeches over the dead, 14 529, 550, 561, 587 Juno to Mars concerning Ascalaphus, 15 120 Æneas to Meriones, 16 745. Patroclus on Cebriones, 16 903 Hector on Patroclus, 16 1063 Achilles to Otryntides, 20 450 ——to Lycaon, 21 135 —— to Hector, 22 415

Speeches to horses

Hector to his horses, 8 215 Achilles to his horses, 19 440. Jove to the horses of Achilles, 17 504 Antilochus, 23 483. Menelaus, 23 522

DESCRIPTIONS of IMAGES.

A Collection of the most remarkable throughout the Poem.

Descriptions of PLACES

Of the apartment of Juno, 14 191 Of a burning mountain, 2 950.

City in flames, 17 825 Court of justice, 18 577. Ends of the earth and sea, the residence of Saturn and Iapetus, 8 597 Fountains of Scamander, 22 195

DESCRIPTIONS.

Field, plowed, 18 617
Foreft, when timber is felled, 11 120 —13 144
Heaven, the feat and pleafures of the Gods, 1 690, 772 —4 3 The gates of heaven, 5 928 —8 478 The Gods affembled, 20 9
Ida, its forefts, temple, and profpect, 8 57 —14 320
Landfcapes of a fine country, 2 840, 1036, 1040 Of pafture-gronnds and fheep, 18 677
Mount of Hercules near Troy, 20 174
Palace of Neptune, 13 35.
Palace of Priam defcribed, 6. 304 Of Paris, 6 59
River Axius defcribed, 2. 1030
River Titarefius and Peneus, 2 910.
Sea, and iflands rifing out of it, 2 770
Tempe defcribed, 2 918.
Tent of Achilles defcribed, 24 553
Troy, the country about it, and roads, 22 191 —13 20 —14 260
Tomb of Ilus, 11 477 Of Batcia, 2 934 Of Sarpedon, 16 820
Vulcan, his palace, forge, etc. 18 431, etc.
A vineyard, 18 651
Wall of the Grecians, 7 523
Winds, their court and man-

DESCRIPTIONS.

fion defcribed, 23 241.

Defcriptions of PERSONS.

Achilles's dreadful appearance, 29 59 —22 31, etc. 393.—
Apollo's perfon, enfigns, and defcent to earth, 1. 61.
Apollo's appearance in the war, 15 348
Ajax, his fullen retreat defcribed, 11 675, etc to 696.
Brothers, two killed together, 10 531.
A coward, defcribed in Therfites, beaten, 2. 326 A coward defcribed throughout, 13 359.—again in Theftor, 16 488. A coward furprized, 10 443.
Diana cuffed and buffeted, 21. 570
Gods, Homer's great ideas of them, in the defcriptions of their armour, 5 907. Motion, 13 30 —15. 90.—5. 960 Battels, 15 252 — 20 63, etc —21 450, etc.
Hours at the gates of heaven, 5 929
Hector's horrible appearance in battel, 8 417 —12 553. —13 1010 —15 730 Hector's dead body dragged at the chariot of Achilles, 22. 500
Jupiter in his glory, 1 15, 172 —8 550 —in his chariot, 8 50, 542, etc.—in

DESCRIPTIONS

his terrors, 17. 670.

Juno, dreft, 14 200

Lycaon, his youth and un-
happy death, 21 40, etc

Mars and Bellona before Hector in battel, 5 726.——
Mars in arms, 7. 252.——
13 385 - 15 726.——his
monftrous fize, 21 473.

Mercury defcribed, 24. 417

Neptune, his chariot and progrefs, 13 28, etc

Niobe, turned into a rock, 24
73

Old man, a venerable one, 1
330 Old connfellors of
Troy converfing, 3. 197,
etc. A miferable old man,
in Priam, 22 80; etc

Priam paffing through his
people, in forrow, to go to
redeem Hector, 24. 402
Priam weeping at the feet of
Achilles, 24 636

Pallas, her defcent from heaven, 4 99. Her armour,
fpear, and veil, 5 905 ——
8 466

Teucer, behind Ajax's fhield,
8 321

Youth, a beautiful one, killed,
4 542 — 17 55, etc —
20 537 Interceding for
mercy in Adraftus, 21 75

A young and old man flain in
war, their pictures, 22 100

DESCRIPTIONS.

Defcriptions of THINGS

Of an affembly gathering to
gether, 2 110

Battel. [See the article Military Defcriptions]

Burning up of a field, 21.
400 A bow, 4 137.——
Blood trickling from a wound,
4. 170, etc

Brightnefs of a helmet, 5 5.

Burial of the dead, 7. 494

A breach made in an attack,
12 485 ——

Boiling water in a cauldron,
18 405 —21 4-5

Beacon, 19. 405 —

Beafts facrificed, 23. 41.

A bird fhot through, 23. 1033.

Chariot of Jupiter, 8 50,
542 Of Neptune, 13 41.
Chariot defcribed at large,
24 335.——5 889, etc 'A
chariot-race, 23 353, etc.
Chariots overturned, 16
445. Chariots crufhing the
bodies, 20 577.

A child frighted at a helmet,
6 595

Golden chain of Jupiter, 8.
25

A conflagration, 21 387,
400

Cookery defcribed, 9 277 —

Ceftus, the game defcribed, 23
765, etc

Deformity, 2 263 ——

Dancing, 18 681, etc.

DESCRIPTIONS

Discus, the game described, 23. 927, etc.

Diving, 24 105

Driving a chariot, 11. 383, 655 ——

Dreadful appearance of the Myrmidons, 16 192.—of Achilles, 18 254.

Darkness, 17. 422

Death, 16 1033 ——22 485. ——The descriptions of different sorts of deaths in Homer, are innumerable, and scattered throughout the battles

Ægis, or shield of Jupiter, 2 526 ——5 909.——15. 350 ——21 465.

An entrenchment, 7 520 ——

Eagle stung by a serpent 12 233 Eagle soaring, 24 390

Furnace and forge described, 18 540

Fishes scorched, 21 413.

Flowers of various kinds, 14 396 ——

Famine, 19 160, etc.

Fall of a warrior headlong into the deep sands, 5 715.

Fatigue in the day of battel, 2. 458 ——16. 132.——17. 445

Fainting, 5 856.——11 460. ——14 487, 509 ——

Fires by night, described, 8. 685, etc

Recovery from fainting, 15 271

Fortification attacked, 12 170,

DESCRIPTIONS.

etc 201, 304, 407.

Funeral of a warrior, 23 156 ——funeral pile described, 23. 200

Gates of a fortification broken, 12 545

Goblet described, 11. 774

Girdle of Venus, 14 245

Horses, the famous ones of Eumelus, 2 924 Of Hector, 8 226 Of Achilles, 16 181 Of Tros, 5 327 Of Erichtonius, 20. 262

Horse pampered and prancing, 6 652 Horse killed by a dart, 8 105 Horses afraid of leaping a ditch, 11 57 Horses of Achilles mourning for Patroclus, 17. 490.

A feat of horsemanship, 15. 822

Helmet of Jupiter 5 918. Helmets nodding their plumes, 13 945

Hospitable life of a good man, 6 16.

Harvest, 18 637

Herds of oxen, 18 665

Inundation, 12 13 ——15 465. Of Scamander against Achilles, 21 258, etc 350, etc ——

Lightnings and thunder, 7. 571 ——8 93, etc 161, etc.

Light coming over a plain, 15 810 ——17 430 ——

Light streaming from a bea-

DESCRIPTIONS

con by night, 19 405.

Majesty of a prince, 2 564
—3 221

Majestic march of Sarpedon,
12 356 Of Juno, 14 26

Melancholy, 6 245

Moon and stars described, 8
687.

Marriage-pomp, 18 570 —

Monument over the dead, 17
492

Noise, a loud one, 5 1054
—13 1055 — 14 172,
457 —16 767

Night past in inquietude by
the soldiers, and their several postures of taking rest,
10 82, 170

Old age, 3 150 The picture
of its miseries in state of
war, 22 80

Orphan, its misery 22 620 etc.

Procession described, 6 367.

Peaceful life, 9 520

Posture of a man receiving a
dart on his shield lifted up,
13 511 —10 325, etc

Panting described, 13 555,
720 —

Perfumes, 14 198

Plume of a helmet, 19 410
—13 947

Plowing, 12 617

Rainbow, 11 37,—24 100.
— 17 616.

Reaping, 18 637

Running away, 21 634.

Running round Troy, Hec-
tor and Achilles, 22. 250,

DESCRIPTIONS.

etc Seeming to run in a
dream, 22 257

Rough way described, 23 139.

A race described, 23 881, etc.

Shield of Achilles, described at
large, 18 550, etc Of
Hector, 6. 143 Of Ajax,
7 265

Scales of Jupiter, 22 271.

Smoke cleared, and light returning, 16 350

Sailing of a ship, 1 625.

Ship anchoring and coming
into port, 1 566

The stately stalk of a hero,
7 251 —15 815 ——

A sacrifice described, 1 600.
—7 360 —

Sleep, 2 .nit —14 265, etc.

A slaughter by night, 10 560.

Snow, 12 331 ——

Soldiers, when off from duty,
their amusements, 2 938.

Shooting with the bow, 4.
144 to 156 —23 1005.
—8 389

Spear of Achilles, 19 420.

A spear driven deep into the
earth, 21 188

A stone whirling on the ground
with vast force, 14 174

Stone, thrown by a hero, 5.
370 —7 320 —12 537.
—14 472 ——

Swiftness of horses, 20. 270.

Swooning, 16 955

Vintage, 18, 651

Wall, overwhelmed by wa-
ters, 7. 550.—12. 23.

DESCRIPTIONS.

Woodman's dinner, 11 120.
Woods felled down, 23 144.
——16 767
War, its miseries, 9. 709.
Watch by night, 10. 208.
Wrestling described, 23
821 —
Wound of Venus described, 5.
417. Diomed wounded, 5.
A wound healing, 5. 1111.
Water, troops plunging in,
21 9 A fight in the wa-
ter, 21 A tree falling in
the water, 16 269. Wa-
ter rolling down a hill in a
current, 21 290 Arms
floating upon the water, 21
351
Winds rising, 23 261

Descriptions of TIMES and
SEASONS.

Day break, 10 295 ——
Morning, 2. 60 — 7 515 —
8 183 — 9 833.—11. 1
—11 115 — 19 1.—
Sun-rising, 11. 871.
Noon, 19 938 —
Sun-setting, 1 716 — 7 556.
——8 605
Evening, 16 942 ——
Night, 2 init.— 10th book
throughout A starry night,
8 687
Spring, 14 3, 5
Summer, 18 637
Autumn, 18 651 —5. 1060
—22. 40.

DESCRIPTIONS.

Winter, 12 175, 331.

MILITARY Descriptions.

An army descending on the
shore, 2. 517. An army
marching, 2. 181, 940.
The day of battel, 2 458.
A vast army on the plain,
535, etc to 563 An ar-
my going forth to battel, 2
976 —13 59.——16 255
—19 377
A chariot of war, 5 890, etc
Confusion and noise of battel,
16 621 —
A single combate, with all the
ceremonial, 3 123, etc.
The combate between Paris
and Menelaus, 3 423
————of Hector and Ajax, 7.
250 to 335
————of Hector and Achil-
les, 22
Squadrons embattled, 4 322
—5 637 — 8 260 —
First onset of battel, 4 498
to 515
A circle inclosing the foe, 5
772
Stand of an army, 7 75
Joining in battel, 8 75,
etc —13 421 A rout,
11 193 —14 166 —16.
440, etc —21 710 A for-
tification attacked, 12 170,
201, 304 A breach made,
12 485 An obstinate close
fight, 12 510 —15 860.

DESCRIPTIONS.

An army in close order, 13.
177 to 185.——17. 406
An attack on the sea-side,
14 452 Levelling and
paffing a trench, 15. 408.
Attack of the fleet, 15 677,
etc. 786, 855, etc. A hero
arming at all points, Agamemnon, 11. 21. Patro-
clus, 16 162 Achilles,
19 390. Siege of a town,
18. 591, etc Surprize of
a convoy, ibid Skirmifh,
ibid. Battel of the Gods,
20 63 to 90. Two heroes
meeting in battel, 20. 191.
The rage, deftruction, and
carnage of battel, 20 574,

Defcriptions of the INTERNAL
PASSIONS, or of their vi-
fible EFFECTS.

Anxiety, in Agamemnon, 10
13, etc 100, etc.
Activity, in Achilles, 19. 416.
Admiration, 21 62 —24
800 ——
Affright, 16 968 —
Amazement, 24 590.
Ambition, 13 458.
Anger, 1 252
Awe, 1 430
Buffoonry in Therfites, 2 155,
etc
Contentment, 9 520
Conjugal love, in Hector and
Andromache, 6 510, etc

DESCRIPTIONS.

Courage, 13. 109, 366 —17.
250.
Cowardice, 13. 359.——16.
488 ——
Curiofity, in old men, 3. 194,
etc
Defpair, 22. 377.
Diffidence, 3 280.
Diftrefs, 8. 290.—9. 12, etc.
—10 96
Doubt, 14. 21, etc ——21.
651, etc.—22 138
Fear, 10. 443 —24. 441 ——
Fear in Priam, 21 615 For
his fon, 22 43, 51, etc.
Fear of a child, 6 596
Fidelity, in Lycophron, fervant
of Ajax, 15 502. Cale-
fius, fervant of Axylus, 6 10.
Grief in a fine woman, 1.
150 ——3 185 ——2.
450 ——
Grief of a fifter for her dead
brothers, 3 300, etc.
Grief in two parents in tendernefs for their child, 6.
504
Grief occafioned by love of
our country, in Patroclus,
16 ibit
Grief for a friend in Achilles
for Patroclus, 18 25, 100,
etc. —19 335 —22 482.—
24 5 —
Furious grief, 18 367
Frantic grief, 14. 291.
Grief of a father for his fon,
in Priam, 22 122, etc.—24.
200, 275, 291.

DESCRIPTIONS.

Grief of a wife for her huſband, 22 561. to the end, the epiſode of Andromache, and again, 24. 906

Grief out of gratitude, in Briſeis, 19 319 in Helen, 24

Haſte, expreſſed in Hector, 15 395, 402, etc

Hate, in Achilles to Hector, 22. 335, 433, etc.

Hardneſs of heart, 9 750 —

Inſolence, in Tlepolemus, 5. 783. in Epeus, 24 767

Joy, its viſible effects, 23 678

Love, in Helen and Paris, 3. 551, etc in Jupiter and Juno, 14 332, etc 357 —

Conjugal love, in Hector and Andromache, 6, etc

Love of a mother to her ſon, in Thetis to Achilles, 18 70 — 24 117

Brotherly love, in Agamemnon and Menelaus, 4 183.

Filial love, in Harpalion, 13. 805.

Lovers ſorrow at parting, in Achilles and Briſeis, 1 450. In Hector and Andromache, 6 640 Effects of beauty on old men, 3 203 —

Malice in Therſites, 2. 255. — Modeſty, 14 373.

DESCRIPTIONS.

Pride, in Othryoneus, 13 457.

Pity, of a people for their prince in miſery, 24. 402.

Repentance, in Helen, 3. 230, 493 — 6 432 to 450.—

Raſhneſs, in Aſius, 12. 125, etc

Reſentment, in Achilles, 1. 635 — 15. 72.—

Revenge, in Menelaus, 2. 710. In Achilles, for Patroclus, 18. 125, etc — 19. 211, 394 —

Revenge and glory, 16 123.

Reſolution, 19 466. In Hector, 22 47, 107.

Shame, in Helen, 3 185, etc. 521.— In Juno, 14. 373 —

Spite, in Juno, 15. 110 — In Menelaus, 17 640.

Tenderneſs, of parents for their child, in Hector and Andromache, 6 504, 598, 616 —

Wiſh, of Hector, to be immortal, 13 1046

—of Achilles, for a general Deſtruction, 16 122

—of Ajax, to die in the daylight, 17 730,

SIMILES.

From BEASTS

The ſtatelineſs of a bull, to the port of Agamemnon, 2 566 —Of a ram ſtalking before the flock, to Ulyſſes, 3 259. A wanton ſtallion breaking from the paſtures and mares, to Paris iſſuing from his apartment, 6 652 A hound following a lion, to Hector following the Grecians, 8 407 Dogs watching the folds, to the guards by night, 10 211 Hounds chaſing a hare through thick woods, to Diomed and Ulyſſes purſuing an enemy by night, 10 427 A hind flying from a lion, to the Trojans flying from Agamemnon, 11 153 Beaſts flying from a lion, to the ſame, 10 227. Hounds cheared by the hunter, to troops encouraged by the general, 11 378 A hunted boar, to Ajax, 11 516 A wounded deer encompaſſed with wolves to Ulyſſes ſurrounded by enemies, 11 595 An aſs ſurrounded by boys, to Ajax, 11 683 A fawn carried off by two lions,

to the body of Imbrius carryed by the Ajaxes, 13 165. A boar enraged, to Idomeneus meeting his enemy, 13 595 An ox rolling in the pangs of death, to a dying warrior, 13. 721 Beaſts retreating from hunters, to the Greeks retiring, 15 303 Oxen flying from lions, to the Greeks flying from Apollo and Hector, 15 366 A hound faſtening on a roe, to a hero flying on an enemy, 15 697 A wild beaſt wounded and retiring from a multitude, to Antilochus his retreat, 15 702 A hideous aſſembly of wolves, to the fierce figure of the Myrmidons, 16 194 Wolves invading the flocks, to the Greeks, 16 420 A bull torn by a lion to Sarpedon killed by Patroclus, 16 600. A bull ſacrificed, to Aretus, 17 588 Hounds following a boar, to the Trojans following Ajax, 17 811. Mules dragging a beam, to heroes carrying a dead body, 17 832 A panther hunted, to Agenor, 21 978 A hound purſuing a fawn, to Achilles purſuing Hector, 22. 243.

SIMILES.

From LIONS.

A lion rouzing at his prey, to Menelaus at fight of Paris, 3 37 A lion falling on the flocks, and wounded by a shepherd, to Diomed wounded, 5. 174 A lion among heifers, to the same, 5 208. Two young lions killed by hunters, to two young warriors, 5. 681 A lion destroying the sheep in their folds, to Ulysses slaughtering the Thracians asleep, 10 564 The four retreat of a lion, to that of Ajax, 11 675 A lion, or boar hunted, to a hero distressed, 12 47. A lion rushing on the flocks, to Sarpedon's march, 12. 357 A lion killing a bull, to Hector killing Periphas, 15 750 A lion slain, after he has made a great slaughter, applied to Patroclus, 16 909 Two lions fighting, to Hector and Patroclus, 16 915 A lion and boar at a spring, to the same, 16 993 A lion putting a whole village to flight, to Menelaus, 17. 70. Retreat of a lion, to that of Menelaus, 17 117 A lioness defending her young, to his defence of Patroclus, 17 115 Another retreat

SIMILES.

of a lion, to that of Menelaus, 17 741. The rage and grief of a lion for his young, to that of Achilles for Patroclus, 18. 371 A lion rushing on his foe, to Achilles, 20. 200.

From BIRDS.

A flight of cranes or swans, to a numerous army, 2 549 The noise of cranes, to the shouts of an army, 3 5 — An eagle preserving and fighting for her young, to Achilles protecting the Grecians, 9. 424 A falcon flying at a quarry, to Neptune's flight, 13 91 An eagle stooping at a swan, to Hector's attacking a ship, 15 836 Two vultures fighting, to Sarpedon and Patroclus, 16 522. A vulture driving geese, to Automedon, scattering the Trojans, 17 527 An eagle casting his eyes on the quarry, to Menelaus looking through the ranks for Antilochus, 17 761 Cranes afraid of falcons, to the Greeks afraid of Hector and Æneas, 17 845. A dove afraid of a falcon, to Diana afraid of Juno, 21 576 A falcon following a dove, to Achilles pursuing Hector, 22 183. An eagle at an hare,

SIMILES

to Achilles at Hector, 22.
391 The broad wings of
an eagle extended, to palace-
gates set open, 24 391.

From SERPENTS.

A traveller retreating from a
serpent, to Paris afraid of
Menelaus, 3 47 A snake
rolled up in his den, and
collecting his anger, to Hector expecting Achilles, 22.
130.

From INSECTS.

Bees swarming, to a numerous
army issuing out, 2 111
Swarms of flies, to the same,
2 552 Grashoppers chirp-
ing in the sun, to old men
talking, 3 201 Wasps
defending their nest, to the
multitude and violence of
soldiers defending a battle-
ment, 12 190 Wasps
provoked by children flying
at the traveller, to troops
violent in an attack, 16
314 A hornet angry, to
Menelaus incensed, 17 642
Locusts driven into a river,
to the Trojans in Scamander,
21 14.

From FIRES.

A forest in flames, to the lustre

SIMILES.

of armour, 2 534 The
spreading of a conflagration,
to the march of an army,
2. 948 Trees sinking in
a conflagration, to squadrons
falling in battel, 11 201.
The noise of fire in a wood,
to that of an army in confusion, 14 461 A con-
flagration, to Hector, 15.
728 The rumbling and
rage of a fire, to the confusion and roar of a routed army, 17 825 Fires on
the hills, and beacons to give
signals of distress, to the
blaze of Achilles's helmet,
18, 245 A fire running o-
ver fields and woods, to the
progress and devastations
made by Achilles, 20 569.
Fire boiling the waters, to
Vulcan operating on Scamander, 21 425 A fire raging
in a town, to Achilles in the
battel, 21 608 A town
on fire, 22. 518.

From ARTS

The staining of ivory, to the
blood running down the thigh
of Menelaus, 4 170 An
architect observing the rule
and line, to leaders preserving the line of battel, 4 474.
An artist managing four
horses, and leaping from one
to another, compared to A-

SIMILES

jax ftriding from fhip to fhip,
15. 822 A builder cement-
ing a wall, to a leader embodying his men, 16 256.
Curriers ftraining a hide, to
foldiers tugging for a dead
body, 17 450   Bringing
a current to water a garden,
to the purfuit of Scamander
after Achilles, 21 290 The
placing of rafters in a building, to the pofture of two
wrefthers, 23 825 The
motions of a fpinfter, the
fpindle and thread, to the
fwiftnefs of a racer, 23
889   The finking of a
plummet, to the paffage of
Iris, through the fea, 24.
107.

From TREES.

The fall of a poplar, to that
of Simoifius, 4 552   Of
a beautiful olive, to that of
Euphorbus, 17 57   Two
tall oaks on the mountains,
to two heroes, 12 145
The fall of an afh, to that
of Imbrius, 13 241. Of a
pine or oak ftretched on the
ground, to Afius dead, 13
493   An oak overturned
by a thunderbolt, to Hector
felled by a ftone, 14 408
An oak, pine or poplar falling, to Sarpedon, 16, 591
The fhort duration and quick

SIMILES.

fucceffion of leaves on trees,
to the generation of men, 6.
181.——21. 540

From the SEA.

Rolling billows, to an army
in motion, 2 175   The
murmurs of waves, to the
noife of a multitude, 2 249
Succeffion of waves, to the
moving of troops, 4 478.
A frefh gale to weary ma-
riners, like the coming of
Hector to his troops, 7 5
——The feas fettling them-
felves, to thick troops compofed in order and filence,
7 71   The fea agitated
by different winds, to the
army in doubt and confufion,
9 5   The waves rolling
neither way, till one wind
fways them, to Neftor's
doubt and fudden refolution,
14 21   A rock breaking
the billows, to the body of
the Greeks, refifting the
Trojans, 15 746. The
fea roaring at its reception
of a river into it, to the
meeting of armies at a charge,
17 310   A beacon to
mariners at fea, to the light
of Achilles's fhield, 19 405
A dolphin purfuing the leffer
fifh, to Achilles in Scamander,
21. 30

SIMILES.

From the SUN, MOON,
STARS.

The moon and stars in glory,
to the brightness and number of the Trojan fires. 8.
687 A star sometimes
shewing and sometimes hiding itself in clouds, to Hector seen by fits through the
battalions, 11 83 The
sun in glory, to Achilles,
19 436 The evening star,
to the point of his spear, 22
399 The dog-star rising,
to Diomed's dreadful ap-
pearance, 5 8.———to A-
chilles, 22 37. The red
rays of the dog-star, to A-
chilles's helmet, 19 411
The morning-star, its beauty,
to young Astyanax, 6 499

From TORRENTS,
STORMS, WINDS

Torrents rushing to the val-
lies, to armies meeting in
an engagement, 4 516
Torrents drowning the field,
to the rage of a hero, 5
116 A torrent stopping a
shepherd, to Hector stopping
Diomed, 5 731 The
violence of a torrent, to A-
jax, 11 615 A storm o-
verwhelming a ship at sea,
to the Trojans mounting a

SIMILES.

breach, 15 440 An au-
tumnal storm and a deluge,
to the ruin of a routed army,
16. 467 A storm roaring
in a wood, to armies shouting, 16 913 The wind
tossing the clouds, to Hector
driving the Greeks, 11 396.
Different winds driving the
dust, to different passions urg-
ing the combatants, 13 415.
A whirlwind on the waters,
to the hurry of an army in
motion, 13. 1000 Winds
roaring through woods, or
on the seas, to the noise of
an army, 14 457 A
tempest and shipwreck, compared to the rage of Hector
and terrors of the Greeks,
15. 752 The north wind
drying a garden, to Vulcan
drying the field after an inundation, 21 403

From heavenly appearances,
THUNDER *and* LIGHT-
NING, COMETS, CLOUDS,
etc

A mountain shaken by thunder, to the trampling of an
army, 2. 950 The blaze
of a comet, to the descent of
Pallas, 4 101 The dark-
ness of troops, to the gathering of clouds, 4 314 The
regular appearance of clouds
on the mountain tops, to a

SIMILES.

line of battel, 5 641 Pestilential vapours ascending, to Mars flying to heaven, 5 1058 The quick flashes of lightning, to the thick sighs of Agamemnon, 10 5 Thick flakes of snow, to showers of arrows, 12 175 Snow covering the earth, to heaps of stones hiding the fields, 12 331 The blaze of lightning, to the arms of Idomeneus, 13 318 Clouds dispersed and the prospect appearing, to the smokes being cleared from the ships, and the navy appearing, 16 354 A cloud shading the field as it rises, to the rout of the Trojans flying over the plain, 16 434 The figure of a rain bow, to the appearance of Pallas, 17 616 The lustre of snow, to that of armour, 19 380

From RURAL AFFAIRS

Waving of corn in the field, to the motion of plumes and spears, 2 172 A shepherd gathering his flocks, to a general ranging his army, 2 562 A thick mist on the mountains, to the dust raised by an army, 3 15 The bleating of flocks, to the noise of men, 4 492 Chaff flying from the barn-floor, to

SIMILES

the dust, 5 611, Corn falling in ranks, to men slain in battel, 10 90 The joy of a shepherd seeing his flock, to the joy of a general surveying his army, 13 620 The corn bounding from the threshing-floor, to an arrow bounding from armour, 13 739. Two bulls plowing, to two heroes labouring in a battel side by side, 13 879 Felling of timber, to the fall of heroes in battel, 16 767 Oxen trampling out the corn, to horses trampling on the slain, 20 580 The morning dew reviving the corn, to the exaltation of joy in a man's mind, 23 678

From LOW LIFE.

A mother defending her child from a wasp, to Minerva's sheltering Menelaus from an arrow, 4 162 An heifer standing over her young one, to Menelaus guarding the body of Patroclus, 17 5 Two countrymen disputing about the limits of their land, to two armies disputing a post, 12 511 A poor woman weighing wool, the scales hanging uncertain, to the doubtful fates of two armies, 12 512. Boys

SIMILES.

building and destroying houses of sand, to Apollo's overturning the Grecian wall, 15 416. A child weeping to his mother, to Patroclus's supplications to Achilles, 16, 11

SIMILES *exalting the characters of men by comparing them to* GODS.

Agamemnon compared to Jupiter, Mars, and Neptune, 2 564. Ajax to Mars, 7 252 Meriones to Mars rushing to the battel, 13 384 Hector to Mars destroying armies, 15. 726

SIMILES *disadvantagious to the* CHARACTERS

Paris running from Menelaus, to a traveller frighted by a snake 3 47 A gaudy fopp in soldier, to a woman dressed out, 2 1063 Teucer shulking behind Ajax's shield, to a child, 8 325 Thestor pulled from his chariot, to a fish drawn by an angler 16, 495 Ajax, to an ass, patient and stubborn, 11 683 Patroclus weeping, to an infant, 16 11 Cebriones tumbling, to a diver, 16 904

SIMILES.

MISCELLANEOUS SIMILES.

Soft piercing words, to snow, 3 285 The closing of a wound, to milk turning to curd, 5 1114. The fall of a hero, to a tower, 4. 528. Indefatigable courage, to an axe, 3 90 Agamemnon weeping, to a fountain, 9 19 Juno flying, to the mind passing over distant places, 15 86. Dancers, to a wheel turning round, 18 695. A warrior breaking the squadrons, to a mound dividing the course of a river, 17 839 Men seeming to run in a dream, to the course of Hector and Achilles, 22 257 A father mourning at the funeral of his son, to Achilles for Patroclus, 23 272 A fragment of a rock falling, to the furious descent of Hector, 13 191 A poppy bending the head, to Gorgythion dying, 8 371. The swift motion of the Gods, to the eye passing over a prospect, 5 960 The smoothness of their motion, to the flight of doves, 5. 771

VERSIFICATION.

Expreſſing in the ſound the things deſcribed.

Made *abrupt* (and without conjunctions) in expreſſing haſte, 7 282 ——15 402
Short, in earneſt and vehement entreaties, 21 420 —— 23 506
Full of Breaks, where diſappointment is imaged, 18 101, 144, ——22 378
—where rage and fury is expreſſed, 18 137
—where grief is ſcarce able to go on, 18. 101.—22. 616, 650
Broken and diſordered in deſcribing a ſtormy ſea, 13. 1005
Straining, imaged in the ſound, 15 544
Trembling, imaged in the ſound, 10 446.
Panting, 13 721.
Relaxation of all the limbs in death, 7 18, 22
A confuſed noiſe, 12, 410
A hard-fought ſpot of ground, 12 513, *etc*
Tumbling of a wall, 7 552.

Bounding of a ſtone from a rock, 13 198,
A ſudden ſtop, 13 199
Stiffneſs and ſlowneſs of old age, 13. 649, 653.—23. 423
A ſudden fall, 13 146.
The ruſtling and craſhing of trees falling, 23 147
The rattling and jumping of carts over rough and rocky way, 23 139, 140.
A ſudden ſhock of chariots ſtoped, 16 445
Leaping over a ditch, 16. 460
The quivering of feathers in the ſun, 19 415
Supplanted by a ſtream, 21. 268, 269
The flaſhing of waters, 21. 273
Bounding and heaving on the waters, 21 350
Out of breath, 21 419, *etc.*
Voice of different animals expiring, 23 41, 42, *etc.*

INDEX

OF

ARTS and SCIENCES.

The first number marks the book, the second the verse

ART MILITARY

PRaife of art military, 4. 631

Ambufh efteem'd a venturous manner of fighting *l* 1 ver. 299 *l* 13 ver 355

Ambufcade defcrib'd, 18 605

Attack, 12, 95, *etc ibid* 171. *ibid* 305, *etc*

Arming, the policy of giving the beft arms to the ftrongeft, 14 438

Befieging, 11 61 — 12, 170, 303, 534 — 8. 262 —— 22 5.

S ngle combat, 3 123, *etc.—* 7 80, *etc*

Courts of Juftice in the camp, 11 938

Councils of war, 7 415 —— 8 610,—9 130, *etc* — 10 146 —232 —357 — 18 290 —

Military exercife, 7 289, *etc*

Encamping, the manner of encampment of the *Trojans*, 10 496 Of the *Thracians* in three lines, their weapons on the ground before them, the chariots as a fence, outward, 10 544

Fort fication, walls with battlements, in the line, towers upon thofe walls, gates at proper diftances, and trenches inclofed with palifadoes, 7. 406, 523 The ftrong gates to a fortification, how compos'd, 12. 545

Marfhalling armies, 2. 667, *etc* Cantoning the troops of each nation under their own leaders, 2 433 Embodying in an orb, 4 312 Difpofing in order of battel, 4 342, *etc* Lines of battel in exact order, 5 641, *etc* Where to place the worft foldiers, 4 344

Another order of battel, 11
62. In an *Orb*, 17 411
Close fight, 15 860. In
the *Phalanx*, 13. 177 *etc*
15 744. In the *Testudo*,
22. 6
Armies drawn up in *two
wings*, with a *center*, 13.
396
The strength of the army placed in the centre, 13 401.
Marching an army in silence
and discipline, 3. 11 ——
4 487
Method of passing a trench
and palisadoes, 12 65, *etc*
Plunder and Pillage forbidden
till the conquest is compleat,
6. 85.
Retreat The manner of retreat prescrib'd, 5 746.
That of *Ajax*, 11 675 ——
17 837
Soldiers taught to row in the
gallies, serving both as soldiers and sailors, 2 876
Scouts, 10 43, 245. and at
large in the story of *Diomed*, *Ulysses*, and *Dolon*, in
that book.
Spies, 18. 605
Watch towers, to observe the
motions of the foe, 2 261,
——22 192
Watch, at set stations, 7 455
Nightly watch by fires, 8
632 At the fortifications
in regular bodies under distinct captains, 9 110, *etc*
Management of the army

by night, under fears of
surprize, 10. 63 *to* 126.
The manner of the war-
riors sleeping, 19. 170.
The posture of the guards,
10. 310 Better to trust the
guard to native troops than
to foreigners, 10. 490, *etc*.

AGRICULTURE *and* RURAL
ARTS.

Tillage The manner of
plowing, 10 410 ——18.
617. Plowing with oxen,
13 880. with mules, 19.
410 Usual to plow the
field three times over, 18.
628. Reaping, 11. 89, ——
18 637 Treading out
the corn by oxen instead of
threshing, 10 580 Fan-
ning the chaff, 5 611.——
13. 746
Pasturage, 18 667. Meadow
grounds with running wa-
ter, *ibid Vintage*, 18 651.
Bringing currents to water
gardens, 21 290
Fishing, by angling, 24 107.
——by diving, 16 905
Hunting, the boar, 17 814.
——11 526 Lion, 11.
378 —— 17 743, The
deer, 11 595 ——15 697.
The panther, 21. 680.
The hare, 10. 421.
Shooting, flying, 23 1030.

ARCHITECTURE.

Architecture, the gift of Minerva, 5 80
Architecture of a palace upon arches, with apartments round a court built entirely of marble, 6 304
——Paris skilful in architecture, brings together architects to erect his palace, 6 391,
Rafters, how placed, 23 817. ——
Building walls, 16 156
The rule and line, 15 477
Architecture of a tent, with a suit of apartments within one another, 24 555, etc

ASTRONOMY

In general, 18 560.
Orion and the Bear, 18, 563
The rising of the *dog-star*, 5 10
A comet describ'd, 4, 101,——
The rainbow, 11 36
Power of the stars in nativities, 22 610.

DIVINATION.

Divination by *augury*, 2 375, etc —8 297 —10 320 —12 230 —13 1039. —24, 361, etc.

Hector's opinion of augury, 12 277
By *omens*, thunder and lightnings, 7 571 —9 310 — 11 58 ——13 319
The rainbow, 11 38 —17, 616
Comets, 4 101 ——
Showers of blood, 11 70 — 560
By *Lots*, 7, 215
By *Dreams*, 1 81 —5, 191.
By *Oracles*, 16 54 ——16, 290 that of *Dodona*, and the manner of it, *etc.*

GYMNASTICS.

Dancing, 16 217 The different kinds for men and women, 18 687 —The circular, 18 573 — Mixed, 18 690 ——
Dancing practised by warriors, 16 746
——with swords, 18 688.
Diving, 16 905, 495.
Tumblers, 18, 698 ——
Horsemanship] Manage of the horse, 5 280 Precepts of horsemanship, and the art of racing, 23 391, *etc.*
Four horses rid by one man at once, 15 121 Three thousand breeding mares at once in the stables of *Ericthonius* 20 262
The *Cestus*, 13 753, *etc*
The *Quoit*, or *Discus*, 23, 972, *etc*

Wreftling, 23, 820. *etc.*

Racing, 23 880, *etc*

GEOGRAPHY

A TABLE *of thofe places, whofe fituation, products, people, or hiftory,* etc. *are particulariz'd by* HOMER

Ætolia, and its royal family, 2 780.

Arcadia, and the genius of the inhabitants, 2 735

Aulis, its rocky fituation, 2 590

Imbrus and *Tenedos*, iflands near *Troy*, 13 50 ——

Iftiaea, famous for vineyards, 2 645.

Ithaca, and the neighbouring iflands in profpect, 2. 769, *etc*

Lariffa, its fertility, 2 1019

Lectos, fituate on the top of mount *Ida*, 14 320

Lemnos, traded in wines, 7 559

Maeander, the river, 2 1056

Maeonia, under the mountains of *Tmolus*, 2 1052

Meffe, a town of *Sparta*, abounding in doves, 2 705

Mycaleffus, its plain 2 593

Anthedon, the laft town in *Bœotia*, 2 607

Arene, its plain, watered by the river *Minyas*, 11, 860

Arifba, on the river *Selleis*, 2 1014

Arne, celebrated for vines, 2. 606

Æfepus, a *Trojan* river of black water, 2. 1000.

Argos, its fea coaft defcribed, with the products of that part of the country, 9 198, *etc.*

Athens, and fome cuftoms of the Athenians with mention of the temple of *Minerva*, 2 657, 663

Alybe, famous anciently for filver mines, 2 1045

Axius, the river, defcribed, 2. 1030

Boagrius, the river and places adjacent, 2 638

Bœbe, the lake and parts adjacent, 2 865

Calydon, its rocky fituation, 2 777 ——9 653

Cephiffus, the river and places upon its banks, 2 622.

Cerinthus, fituate on the fea-fhore, 2 648

Cyllene, the *Arcadian* mountain, with the tomb of Æpytus, 2 731

Crete, its hundred cities, 2 790

Carians, a barbarous mixed people, 2 1059

Dodona, its fite, temple, grove, *etc* 16. 287 – 2. 909

Dorion, the place of Thamyris's death, the celebrated mufician, 2 721

Elis, its exact boundaries, 2. 747 and the islands opposite to that continent, 760 to 774

Ephyre, the ancient name of Corinth, 6. 193

Epidaurus, planted with vineyards, 2 679

Eteon, its hills, 2 591.

Haliartus, pasture grounds, 2 598.

Hell-spont, 2 1024

Helos, a maritime town, 2. 703

Henetia, famous for its breed of mules, 2. 1035.

Hermaon and Asine, seated on the bay, 2 690

Hippemo'gians, their long life and nutriment, 13 12

Hippoplacian woods, 6 539 — 22 611 ——

Hyla, its watry situation and the genius of the inhabitants, 5 872

Hyperia, its fountains, 2 895

Mount *Ida*, its fountains and forests, 14 321

Catalogue of the rivers that run from mount Ida, 12 17

Jardanus and Celadon, two rivers, 7 163

Mycenae, and its maritime towns, 2 686

Onchestus, and the grove of Neptune, 2 600

Orchomenos, one of the principal cities for wealth in Homer's time, 9 498.

Parthenius, the river and places adjacent, 2 1038.

Pedasus, seated on the river Satnio, 6 41.

Peneus, the river running through Tempe, and mount Pelion, described, 2 918.

Phthia, its situation, 1 264. famous for horses, 203.

Phylace and Phyrrhasus, a beautiful country with groves and flowery meadows, described, 2 850.

Rhodes, its wealth, its plantation by Tlepolemus, and division into three dynasties, 2 808, *etc*

Samothracia, the view from its mountains, 13 19

Scamander, its two springs, 22. Its confluence with Simois, 5 965

Scyros, the island 19 353

Sidon, famous for works of sculpture, 23 866 and embroidery, 6 360,

Sipylus, its mountains, rocks, and deserts, 24 775

Sperchius, a river of Thessaly, 23 176

Styx, the river described, 2. 915

Thebae, in Ægypt, anciently the richest city in the world with a hundred gates, described, 2 506

Thessaly, its ancient division, and inhabitants, 2 833

Thisbe, famous for doves, 2. 601.

Thrace, its hills and promontories, 14. 260, *etc*

Titarefius, the river, 2. 910.

Troy, its situation and remarkable places about it, 2. 982. ——11 217.

Typhœus, the burning mountain, 2 953.

Xanthus, the river of Troy, defcribed, its banks, and plants produced there, 21. 507, *etc.*

Xanthus, the river of Lycia, 2 v *ult.*

Zelia, fituate at the foot of mount Ida, 2. 998.

HISTORY.

Hiftory preferved by Homer] Of the heroes before the fiege of Troy, Centaurs, *etc* 1 347 to 358 Of Tlepolemus planting a colony in Rhodes, 2 808 Of the expulfion of the Centaurs from Greece, 2 902 Of the wars of the Phrygians and Amazons, 3 245 Of the war of Thebes, and embaffy of Tydeus, 4 430 Of Bellerophon, 6. 194 Of Erythalion and Lycurgus, 7 164 Of the Curetes and Ætolians, 9 653 Of the wars of the Pylians and Ætolians, 11 818 Of the race of Troy, 20 255, *etc To this head may be referred the numerous Genealogies in our author.*

VOL. IV. F f

MUSIC.

Mufic practifed by princes, the ufe of the harp in Achilles, 9. 247 in Paris, 3 80

The ufe of the pipe, 10, 15. ——18 609.

Vocal mufic accompanying the inftruments, 1. 775.

Chorus's at intervals, 24. 902.

Mufic ufed in the army, 10. 15.

————at funerals, 24 900. ———— in the vintage, 18 661.

Trumpets in war, 18. 260.

MECHANICS.

Archery, making a bow, and all its parts defcribed, 4. 136, *etc*

Chariot making, a chariot defcribed in all its parts, 6. 889, *etc* 24 335

Poplar proper for wheels, 4. 554

Sycamore fit for wheels, 21. 44

Clockwork, 18 441.

Enamelling, 18 635

Ship-building, 5 80 ——15. 475.

Pine, a proper wood for the maft of a fhip, 16 592

Smithery, iron work, etc The Forge defcribed, 18 435, 540 Bellows, 435, 482. 540. Hammer, tongs, anvil, 547.

Mixing of metals, ibid

Spinning, 23 890

Weaving, 3 580 —6 580.

Embroidery, 6 361 —

Armoury, and instruments of war

A compleat suit, that of Paris, 3 410, etc. of Agamemnon, 11-22,—etc

Scale armour, 15 629.—

Helmets, with four plumes, 5 919 —

————without any crests, 10. 303 —

————lined with wool, and ornamented with boars teeth, of a particular make, 10 311

————lined with furr, 10 397.-

Bows, how made, 4 187.—

Battle-ax, described, 13 766

Belts, crossing each other, to hang the sword and the shield, 14. 468

Corselets, ornamented with sculpture, 11. 33

————how lined, 4 165 -—

Mace, or club, 7. 170.—13. 816

Shields, so large as to cover from the neck to the ankles, 6 145 —How made and covered, 7. 267 described in every particular, 11 43, etc.

Kings, 13 899

Spears, with brass points, 8. 617

Ash fit to make them, 16. 143. —19 422.

How the wood was joined to the point, 18 618

Swords, how ornamented with ivory, gems, 19 400.

ORATORY.

See the article Speeches in the poetical index.

POLICY.

Kings] Derive their honour from God, 2 233.—1. 315 Their names to be honoured, 2 313 One sole monarch, 2. 243. Hereditary right of kings represented by the sceptre of Agamemnon given by Jove, 2 119. Kings not to be disobeyed on the one hand, nor to stretch too far their prerogative on the other, 1 365, etc Kings not absolute in council, 9 133. Kings made so, only for their excelling others in virtue and valour, 11 337. Vigilance continually necessary in princes, 2 27 — 10 102 Against monarchs delighting in war, 9 82, etc —14 55. The true valour, that which preserves, not destroys mankind, 6. 196 Kings may do wrong, and are obliged to reparation, 9. 144 Character of a great prince in war and peace, 3. 236

Councils] The danger of a subject's too bold advice, 1 103 The advantage of wise councils seconded by a wise prince, 9 101 The nfe of advice, 9. 137 The singular blessing to a nation and prince, in a good and wise counsellor, 13 918 The deliberations of the council to be free, the prince only to give a sanction to the best, 9 133

Laws] Derived from God, and legislators his delegates, 1. 315 Committed to the care of kings, as guardians of the laws of God, 9 129

Tribute paid to princes from towns, 9 206

Taxes upon subjects to assist foreign allies, 17 266

Ambassadors, a facred character, 1 435 — 9 261.

Volunteers, listed into service, 11. 904

See the article Art Military

PHYSIC.

The praise of a physician, 11 637

Chiron learned it from Æsculapius, 4 251

Machaon and Podalirius professors of it, 2. 890

Botany] Professed by skilful

women, Agamede famous for it, 11 877

Anatomy] Of the head, 16. 415, etc.

The eye, 14 577.

Under the ear, a wound there mortal, 13 841.

The juncture of the head and nerves, 14 544.

The juncture of the neck and chest, the collar-bone, and its infertion, the disjointing of which renders the arm ufeless, 8 393, etc

The spinal marrow expressed by the vein that runs along the chine, a wound there mortal, 13 691 —— 20. 559 ——

The elbow, its tendons and ligaments, 20 554

Blood, a great effusion of it, by cutting off the arm, the cause of immediate death, 5 105 ——

The heart and its fibres, 16. 590.

The force of the muscle of the heart, 13 554

A wound in the bladder by piercing the Ischiatic joint, mortal, 13 813

The infertion of the thighbone, and its ligaments described, 5 375

The wounds of the Abdomen mortal, and excessively painful, 13 718

The tendons of the ankle, 4. 597.

Chirurgery] Extraction of darts, 4 228.

Sucking the blood from the wound, 4 250

Infusion of balms into wounds, 4 250 — 5 1111

Washing the wound with warm water, and the use of lenitives, 11 965

Staunching the blood by the bitter root, 11 983

Ligatures of wool, 13 752

Use of baths for wounded men, 14 10

Sprinkling water to recover from fainting, 14 509

Pharmacy and Diaetetics

The use of wine forbidden, 6 330.

Cordial potion of Nestor, 11. 782, *etc*

Infection, seizing first on animals, then men, 1 70 Nine days the crisis of diseases, 1 71 Fevers and plagues from the dog-star, 5 1058 —19. 412 —22 41.

PAINTING, SCULPTURE, *etc*

See the whole shield of Achilles, and the notes on lib 18

The CHARACTERS Homer distinguishes the character in the figures of Gods superior to those of men, 18 602.

Characters of majesty.] The majesty of Jupiter, from whence Phidias copied his statue, 1 683 Of Mars and Neptune, 2 569.

The majesty of a prince, in the figure of Agamemnon, 2 564, *etc* Of a wise man, in Ulysses's aspect, 3. 285 Of an old man, in Nestor and Priam, 1 330 —24 600 Of a young hero, in Achilles, 19 390, *etc* All variously characterized by Homer

Characters of beauty] Alluring beauty in the goddess Venus, 14 250 Majestic beauty in Juno, 14 216. Beauty of a *woman* in Helen, 3. 205. Beauty of a *young man* in Paris, 3 26. Euphorbus, 17 53, *etc* Beauty of a *fine infant* in Astyanax, 6 497

Beauties of the parts of the body] Largeness and majesty of the eyes in Juno's Blackness, in those of Chryseis Blue, in Minerva's, *etc* Eye-brows, black, graceful, 1 683 The beauty of the cheeks, and the fairness of hair, in the epithets of Helen Whiteness of the arms in those of Juno Fingers rather red than pale, in the epithet of *rosy fingered* to Aurora. Whiteness of the feet in that

of silver-footed to Thetis,
etc Colour of the skin to
be painted, differently, according to the condition of
the perfonages, applied to
the whiteneſs of the thigh
of Menelaus, 4. 275.

Character of Deformity] The
oppoſites to beauty in the
ſeveral parts, conſidered in
the figure of Therſites, 2.
263, etc

For pictures of particular
things, ſee the article I-
mages in the POETI-
CAL INDEX.

Hiſtory, landſkip-painting, animals, etc. in the buckler of
Achilles, 18. at large
The deſign of a goblet in
ſculpture, 11 775.
Sculpture of a coiſelet, 11
33, etc. Of a bowl, 23.
Hoſes carved on monu-
ments, 17. 495
Enamelling, and Inlaying, in
the buckler of Achilles, 18
635, 655. and breaſt-plate
of Agamemnon, 11 35
Tapeſtry, or weaving hiſtories,
flowers, etc 3 171 ——6
580 ——22 569 —
Embroidery of garments, 6
360.

POETRY

See the intire INDEX

THEOLOGY.

A View of HOMER's
Theology

JUPITER, or the Supreme
Being.

Superior to all powers of heaven, 7. 244 ——8 10, etc.
Enjoying himſelf in the
contemplation of his glory
and power, 11 107. Self-
ſufficient, and above all ſecond cauſes, or inferior
deities, 1. 647 The other
deities reſort to him as their
ſovereign appeal, 5 1065.
——11 590 His will is
fate, 8 10 His ſole will
the cauſe of all human e-
vents, 1 8 His will takes
certain and inſtant effect,
1 685 his will immuta-
ble and always juſt, 1 730.
All-ſeeing, 8 65 ——2 4
——Supreme above all, and
ſole-ſufficient, 11 107 The
ſole governor and fate of
all things, 2 147.——16
845 Diſpoſer of all the
glories and ſucceſs of men,
17 198 Fore-ſeeing all
things, 17 228. The giver
of victory, 7 118 Diſ-

poſer of all human affairs, 9. 31 His leaſt regard, or thought, reſtores mankind, 15 274. or turns the fate of armies, 17 675. Diſpenſer of all the good and evil that befalls mankind, 24. 663. His favour ſuperior to all human means, 9 152 His counſels unſearchable, 1 705 Themis or juſtice is his meſſenger, 20 5 God proſpers thoſe who worſhip him, 1. 290 Conſtantly puniſhes the wicked, though late, 4. 194 The avenger of injuſtice, 4 202 Nothing ſo terrible as his wrath, 5 217 His divine juſtice ſometimes puniſhes whole nations by general calamities, 16 468. Children puniſhed for the ſins of their parents, 11 166 and 16 393.

The inferior DEITIES

Have different offices under God ſome preſide over elements, 18 46.—13 240 Some over cities and countries, 4 75 ——
Some over woods, ſprings, etc. 20 12.

They have a ſubordinate power over one another Inferior deities or angels ſubject to pain, impriſonment, 5. 475, 1090 Threatened by Jupiter to be caſt into Tartarus, 8 15. Are ſuppoſed to converſe in a language different from that of mortals, 2 985 —Subſiſt not by material food, 5 4 Compaſſionate mankind, 8 42 —14 412 Able to aſſiſt mortals at any diſtance, 16 633 Regard and take care of thoſe who ſerve them, even to their remains after death, 14. 510. No reſiſting heavenly powers, 5. 495 The meanneſs and vileneſs of all earthly creatures in compariſon of the divine natures, 5 535

Prayer recommended on all enterprizes, throughout the poem

Prayers intercede at the throne of heaven, 9 614

Opinions of the ancients concerning hell, the place of puniſhment for the wicked after death, 8 15 —19 271.

Opinions of the ancients concerning the ſtate of ſeparate ſpirits, 23 89, etc 120. etc

FINIS

Lightning Source UK Ltd.
Milton Keynes UK
UKHW020558231119
354009UK00007B/248/P